CW00515941

The Time between Space

Space

Charlie Laidlaw

Ringwood Publishing

Glasgow

First published in Great Britain in 2023 by
Ringwood Publishing
0/1 314 Meadowside Quay Walk, Glasgow G11 6AY

www.ringwoodpublishing.com
e-mail mail@ringwoodpublishing.com

An earlier version of this story was first published in 2019
by Accent Press as The Space Between Time.

Ringwood now own the rights to The Space Between Time
but are publishing this revised, updated and improved
version under the title The Time Between Space

ISBN 978-1-901514-75-9

British Library Cataloguing-in Publication Data
A catalogue record for this book is available from the
British Library

"Two things are infinite: the universe and human stupidity; and I'm not sure about the universe."

Albert Einstein

"Time present and time past
Are both perhaps present in time future
And time future contained in time past.
If all time is eternally present
All time is unredeemable."

T.S. Eliot

From

I hope you enjoy!

Kind regards

Charlie x

For Douglas,
the real astrophysicist in the family.

Part One: Thesis

$$\Omega_0 = 1?$$

Density Parameter of the Universe

It's not easy being a fruitcake, and I should know. But I have been asked to write the story of my life. Quite why, I'm not sure, or how much of it will be true. We are, I suppose, who we invent for ourselves. That said, I have decided, somewhat reluctantly, but after careful consideration and under the influence of strong medication, to begin here:

Yippee! Mummy is taking me to the cinema and has told me that it's a surprise. This doesn't really make sense, because if taking me to the cinema is a surprise, why has she told me?

But this is typical Mum; opening her mouth and saying something, then realising that she shouldn't have said it and wishing that she could un-say it. Even in my short life, I know she's confused a lot of people and offended many others. Nothing nasty, but if someone at the shops says what a nice day it is, Mum will often disagree, and I'm old enough to know that you're not supposed to disagree about the weather.

Even if it's been pouring with rain for hours, you're supposed to agree that it's just a passing shower. It's not intentional, she simply doesn't think, then realises she may have been rude, and sometimes goes back into the shop to apologise, or doesn't go back and then frets that she should have done. Mum spends a lot of time worrying, usually about things that aren't worth worrying about.

My Mum's called Caitlin, by the way, although most grown-ups call her Cat. It's a better name than Dog or

3

Mouse, I suppose, and Mum does look a bit feline with her big eyes and unblinking gaze.

But it is a surprise to be going to the cinema, because we almost never go to the cinema, and then only to see cartoons about dogs and cats – and big cats like lions. I keep telling her that I don't like cartoons but – another Mum habit – she's rarely listening or, if she is, then the information just wafts around her brain like smoke and quickly gets blown out her ears.

She told me recently that her brain is a bit of a butterfly, as if that neatly explained things, which it didn't. I'd been telling her something really interesting about frogspawn and she'd been nodding and smiling in mostly the right places when the phone rang. It was Dad, who Mum spends most of the time worrying about, and who's rarely here, but does try to phone from London or New York, or wherever he says he is.

When Dad phones, one of Mum's feet taps on the floor, faster and faster. We have wooden floors, so it's like living with a large woodpecker. For some reason, Mum rarely believes that he's where he says he is.

Mum put down the phone and stared at it with narrowed eyes, as if it had done something naughty, then said *bastard* very loudly. 'It's a term of endearment,' she told me, ignoring my sceptical expression. 'Now, what were you telling me about toads?'

That's also when she told me about the butterfly inside her head, which I also didn't believe, because butterflies are only colourful insects and even stupider than frogs – and Mum is cleverer than a frog – but it also made a kind of sense. One minute I can be talking to the Mum-butterfly, admiring its plumage; the next I am talking frogspawn to the empty flower on which it had been sitting.

The drive to the cinema from our semi-posh flat in Edinburgh shouldn't take long. When Dad drives to the cinema it only takes a few minutes. But it's different with

4

Mum. We drive in silence because she's stressed and, when agitated, doesn't say much and, because she's driving, also doesn't like to be distracted. It takes all her concentration to keep to our side of the road, change gear, not hit the car in front, and avoid pedestrians legitimately crossing at traffic lights. Consequently, she is driving very slowly.

She also utterly hates driving Dad's Bentley and always wears dark glasses when she absolutely has no option but to drive it. Her own car is in the garage being repaired for something-or-other. Mum doesn't like to be thought of as posh or a show-off, even though the Bentley is second-hand and a bit scratched.

She'd prefer not be noticed, and certainly not be stared at in a fancy car. She'd much rather be in the background, hiding in shadows, or baking cakes. She's rather good at baking cakes, but pretty useless at cooking anything else. She also drives like she walks: a sort of uncertain bustle – hence the scratches. She's either walking – or driving – at full speed, or ambling along like a snail, biting her lip. Other cars often sound their horns at her, which makes her even more nervous, and is sometimes the cause of more scratches.

Dad doesn't much like her driving the Bentley, which he's only recently bought and is his pride and joy. Out of the car, she teeters if she wears high heels and sometimes trips over in long dresses. She's not very co-ordinated, and how she passed her driving test is a matter of bewilderment to Dad.

Apart from being borderline neurotic – not sure which side of the border – she is quite incredibly beautiful. Not catwalk beautiful, because they put stuff from jars on their faces; but flawless beautiful, like a fairy queen in one of the cartoons I don't like. Tall, long dark hair, wide lips – Dad calls them *sensual*, whatever that means – and large oval, dark eyes. She also has a perfect figure, according to Dad, who is very proud to show her off in public and sometimes puts a hand on her bottom, to show everyone who her bottom

– and the rest of her – is married to.

It's her saving grace, her beauty. Her absolute redeeming feature, and the only reason – probably – why Dad married her. Even I can't think of any other reason. Strangely, she's quite unaware of how attractive she is, and sometimes wonders aloud why men keep staring at her, and then worries about that as well, and then checks herself in a mirror to make sure that there isn't bird poo on her head.

As far as I know, she's always been kind and unfailingly faithful to Dad, always saying nice things about him – at least in public – and smiling sweetly, making men blush and stammer and their wives look uncomfortable. She's always, always, been kind and loving to me and always kisses me goodnight and tells me that she loves me.

I adore her utterly, although she can also be a bit dim, even by my standards. Once, we had guests around for an early evening drink, which is why I wasn't in bed. Someone asked what her father did for a living, and she said that he was a banker. 'Oh, is he high up?' this man asked.

'Yes, he works on the fifth floor,' she replied to much laughter. Everyone thought she'd made a joke, but Mum doesn't do jokes. But maybe I'm being unkind. Maybe it was a joke.

I can't remember either her banker father or mother: they didn't approve of Dad and didn't go to the small registry office marriage. They never came to visit us, and Mum only rarely visited them, usually alone. I only have one picture of Mum's parents, taken on a holiday somewhere that could have been Blackpool or Barbados – but probably Blackpool. They're standing on a beach, wearing grey cardigans, and Mum and her little sister Fran are standing below them, in their shadow. The parents, my grandparents, loom over them, trying to look happy. The children are wearing swimsuits and are also trying to look happy, but with less effort.

It's an unsettling photograph, hinting at something that I can't discern but am too young to ask about. Was it thwarted ambition, still only working on the second floor, or something more? Mum doesn't much talk about her parents, and I suspect that they didn't get on, probably because of Dad. Shortly afterwards, they were both killed in a car accident, and Dad didn't bother going to the funeral.

All I know about them is that they loved reading, according to Mum. *Never without a book in their hands!* she would say brightly, as if it was the best thing she could say about them, and which is maybe what they were doing when their car collided with a mobile library.

We surprisingly arrive at the cinema in one piece, but it takes ages to find a parking space, and Mum is hopeless at parking. She's bad enough in her own small car and the Bentley is simply huge in comparison. We drive past several spaces large enough before Mum finds one big enough for a bus.

'It's like trying to park a fucking battleship,' she remarks as we reverse into the space for about the millionth time, with other cars honking and the Bentley no doubt picking up a few more scratches.

I don't say anything in reply because only last week on TV I'd seen a real battleship being parked, and it looked quite easy. I can feel nervous tension beaming from her; it's like sitting next to a neurotic radiator.

We hurry away from the Bentley, without Mum checking to see if we are parked legally, and she is finally able to take off her sunglasses. 'That's better,' she remarks, when we're far enough away from the car not to be associated with it. 'Driving is so stressful.'

Dad, on the other hand, flings the car around bends, one hand vaguely on the steering wheel, and seemingly not looking where we're going. It doesn't look stressful when Dad's driving. It's the opposite of stressful, whatever that is.

Mum takes my hand in hers, which is still shaking, and we cross the street to the cinema. Of course, we're now late, having spent hours parking the battleship, and she's now having to deal with another source of nervous tension. She hates being late. If she has to go to meetings, which she sometimes does, she invariably arrives hours early and then has to sit in her car. Mum's comfort zone could only accommodate a hamster.

We bustle into the cinema, Mum tripping slightly on a loose paving stone outside, and the cashier behind the cinema desk looks doubtfully from my mother to me and suggests in a low voice that, perhaps the film might not be suitable for someone so young. Mum then mouths something in return which I don't hear because I'm looking suspiciously at the cinema posters to see if we're going to see yet another cartoon about dogs and cats or talking penguins. I don't know why I don't like cartoons because everybody else my age seems to like them.

It's always exciting going into the auditorium; the squeals and yabbering of other kids, the slurps of soft drinks and the low crunch of popcorn; the dimmed lighting and tiered seating. This time I'm surprised because there is only a reverential hush, and then I realise that everybody else is an adult. I am about to see a grown-up film! Another yippee! The film is called *The Octagon Project*. I have no idea what an octagon is, and Mum doesn't know either, which doesn't surprise me.

Almost immediately the lights fade completely and for a few moments we're in complete darkness. I can barely control my excitement and am bouncing in my seat. The woman next to me gives me a dirty look.

The film starts with a man and woman sitting outside a Paris café, drinking coffee, and talking about a shipment of arms that are about to be delivered to a local mobster. I have no idea why someone would want a shipment of just arms, when they could have a shipment of arms *and* legs. I don't bother to ask Mum because she's biting her lip, which is another sign of inner turmoil. She's clutching tight to her handbag, as if frightened that the local mobster might

8

actually be in the cinema.

MAN: We want the money transferred to Zurich. Bearer bonds only.

ME [*thinking*]: Barer bonds. Sounds rude!

WOMAN: When?

MAN: In four days' time. The shipment will then be made available to you through the usual channels.

The man lights a cigarette and leans back in his seat. In the background is a glimpse of the Eiffel Tower – which is why I know they're in Paris. Now that they've finished talking nonsense, I wait for them to say something that I can actually understand.

MAN: There is also the small matter of the Octagon Project.

I lean forward in my seat. I'm about to discover what this rubbish film is actually about.

WOMAN: The project is an inter-government network of intelligence agencies, with a remit to prevent the illegal transfer of weapons without end-user certificates from one jurisdiction to another. You know this.

I lean back in my seat. I have learned absolutely nothing, and sigh loudly.

MAN: Our organisation is merely concerned that information might have leaked, and that some of our activities may therefore have been compromised.

I am beginning to feel my eyelids close. This is absolutely the worst film I have ever seen. I am also beginning to wish we had come to see a cartoon, even with improbable talking animals.

Then the scene changes. The man is walking into a hotel. He picks up his key at reception and takes the lift to the fifth floor – I see which button he presses. He opens the door to his bedroom, throws his room key onto the bed, opens a small cupboard at floor level, and takes out a very small bottle. He opens the bottle and pours the liquid into a glass. He takes the glass to his large bedroom window with a lovely view of the Eiffel Tower. I therefore know that he's still in Paris.

There is a knock at the door and the man turns, crosses the room, and opens the door.

I gasp. 'It's Daddy!'

A few people around us look round. One tut-tuts. Even through the cinema is mostly in darkness, I can see that Mum has conjured sunglasses onto her nose.

MAN: Haven't seen you in a while, Jim. How are you?

DADDY: Just fine and dandy, Gus.

Dad is speaking American, and his hair is slicked back. He's wearing a grey suit. He moves into the room and lights a cigarette. Mum tut-tuts.

MAN: You want a drink, buddy?

DADDY: Sure thing. Whisky, straight up.

The man crosses to the floor-level cupboard and lifts out another small bottle. When he turns round, Dad is holding a gun with a silencer. I know about silencers; I saw a film on TV.

DADDY: But first I want information.

MAN: I thought as much. And if I give you information, do you still intend to kill me?

'Mum, is Daddy going to kill that man?'

More murmurs of disapproval from around us.

'No, of course not, Emma,' says Mum in a very low voice. I don't know how she can possibly see the film in her sunglasses.

DADDY: That depends on the information.

MAN: I see. But I may not have the information you want. And I suspect you'll kill me anyway.

DADDY: Then let's start with the Octagon Project. Tell me what you know.

MAN: I don't know nothing.

DADDY: That's real disappointing, buddy.

MAN: Instead, I'll give you what I know. He indicates a briefcase on the bed. Daddy nods. The man goes to the bed and opens the briefcase. The camera angle allows us to see that he's taken out a gun and, quick as flash, he's turned and shot Dad twice in the chest. Dad slumps to the floor. His gun falls from his hand.

'HE'S KILLED DADDY!' I scream and burst into tears and an usherette appears and says that we'll have to leave. I'm still crying loudly as I lead Mum down the stairs to the exit. Walking downstairs in the dark while wearing sunglasses can't be easy.

Of course, I already knew that Dad was an actor. I'd been taken to see him at the Dundee rep, in a play that my parents thought might be suitable. (It wasn't). But I'd always thought that stage actors were different creatures to film actors. He'd played at several theatres around the country. I knew that too. But in a theatre, you know that the people on stage are play-acting. In film, it seems so real. So, it felt like Daddy had been killed. That's why it was such a shock.

When we were outside the cinema, I tell her that she should have said something. I am still sobbing.

'I thought it would be a surprise.'

'But not a very nice one.'

We now have the rigmarole of remembering where she's parked the car (in a bus stop), peeling the parking ticket from the Bentley's windscreen and getting the car from its parking space, watched angrily by several people waiting at the bus stop (for a bus, not a Bentley). This takes some time, before Mum realises that she's still wearing sunglasses and it's getting dark. With a sigh she takes them off.

'Not all surprises are nice, sweetie.'

'I just don't like *bad* surprises,' I say back to her. I'm feeling a bit angry now. She could have told me that Dad was going to be killed. I would have expected it, and not been shocked, and we could have seen the rest of the film. Or maybe not. Without Daddy in the rest of it, it probably wasn't worth watching.

'Is Daddy famous now?' I ask.

My sobs have subsided, but there is still a knot of anger

and panic in my stomach, which is also rumbling. Mum hadn't had time to buy me popcorn, which she mostly always does.

'Not yet, Emma.'

'Did the film people give him a lot of money?'

Mum taps the Bentley's steering wheel with one manicured finger. 'Enough to buy this fucking thing.'

She inches the battleship from its moorings, engages full steam ahead, and we bustle off home. I have seen the worst film in the history of films – well, a bit of it – seen my father killed, and nearly had several car accidents.

It hasn't been a good day.

$$\frac{\Omega_0(\theta - \sin\theta)}{t_f H_0 (\Omega_0 - 1)^{3/2}} = 2$$

Timescale for a closed universe

It wasn't an afternoon that I like to remember, and not just because of my shrieking tantrum. Once I'd calmed down, Mum told me I'd been very silly, because it was all make-believe on a cinema screen. I reminded her that she'd cried when Bambi's mum died, and that was a film *and* a cartoon. Mum said that it wasn't the same thing at all. But I wasn't being silly because I wasn't old enough to know the difference between pretence and reality.

Dad had looked pretty dead on the screen. The blood on his chest had looked real. If it had been a different dead person, I would have been OK. Children don't really know where make-believe ends and the real world begins and, partly because of who I am, it's remained hazy ever since. I also don't like to remember that film because it was the moment when I realised that our lives were about to change, and I didn't know if that would be a good thing.

Sounds strange, yes? Here's something stranger: I am a child of the sea, I sometimes think, and have done ever since we first moved to live beside it. I feel subject to its vagaries and tempers, with its foaming margins framed against a towering sky. I am familiar with its unchanging mood swings. That's how I like things; I find the familiar comforting. I find change threatening.

I am the daughter of someone who, not long after that ghastly cinema outing, became one of the most famous actors of his generation and, importantly for me, the granddaughter of a rather brilliant but obscure physics professor. But

13

despite their overachievements, I have inherited no aptitude for mathematics and my father positively hated the idea of his only offspring following in his thespian footsteps. He knew how cruel and badly paid the profession could be. But I still look up to my grandfather and think of his ludicrous moustache with affection.

Granddad once told me that there are more stars in the universe than grains of sand on Earth. Just think of all those sandpits, beaches, and deserts! That's an awful lot of stars. He then told me, his only grandchild, that I was his shining star, which was a nice thing to say and why I remember him talking about sand and stars. On clear nights, with stars twinkling, I often think about him.

I still believe in my grandfather and admire his stoic acceptance in the face of professional disdain, because I believe in the unique power of ideas, right or wrong, and that it's our thoughts that shape our existence. We are who we believe ourselves to be.

I gave up believing in my father long ago, because speaking other people's words and ideas seemed like a lame excuse for a job, even if he *was* paid millions, and had met the Queen on several occasions. She must have liked him because she awarded him an OBE for services to film, theatre and charity. *Charity*! Who the hell told the Queen *that*?

I stopped believing in him one Christmas Day a long time ago, when he simply didn't turn up. It wasn't his presents that I missed, or even his presence, but the warm, fuzzy feeling of being important to him. During that day of absence and loss I concluded that his wife and daughter couldn't much matter to him, otherwise he'd have made a bigger effort to get home. That Christmas Day, my father was simply somewhere else, probably in a bar, immaculately dressed, his hair slicked back, the object of male envy and the centre of every woman's attention for miles around.

In that respect, Dad was more tomcat than father, except that by then his territory, his fame, stretched around the globe.

I know this: by then he had a Golden Globe to prove it. He gushed pheromones from every pore, squirting attraction in every direction, and even women with a poor sense of smell could sniff him out.

I feel mostly Scottish but am a little bit Italian. It explains my name, Emma Maria Rossini; my dark complexion, black hair, the slightly long nose, and thin and lanky body. Obese I am not, and will never be, however much pasta I eat, and I eat lots. It also explains my temper, according to some people, although I don't agree with them, and my brown cow's eyes, as an almost-boyfriend once described them, thinking he was paying me a compliment, before realising that he had just become an *ex*-almost-boyfriend.

But mostly I am a child of the sea. That's what happens if you live for long enough by its margins: it becomes a part of you; its mood echoing your mood, until you know what it's thinking, and it knows everything about you. That's what it feels like when I contemplate its tensile strength and infinite capacity for change. On calm flat days in North Berwick, with small dinghies marooned on the glassy water, and loud children squealing in its shallows, it can make me anxious and cranky.

The sea, on those days, seems soulless and tired, bereft of spirit. But on wilder days, the beach deserted, or with only a hardy dog-walker venturing across the sand, with large waves thundering in, broaching and breaking, then greedily sucking back pebbles into the foam, I feel energised. This is what the sea enjoys, a roaring irresponsibility, and I share in its pleasure. We are all children of the sea, I sometimes think, or should be – even those who have never seen an ocean or tasted its saltiness. I can stand for hours and contemplate its far horizons, lost within myself, sharing its passion. In the Firth of Forth is the ebb and flow of my past and my existence, wrapped tight against the west wind. It is what I am, placid and calm, or loud and brash.

I still hear the sea, the shush of waves and the screech of

seabirds, in the Edinburgh flat where I now live. Children of the sea are like that; it's in our blood, coursing through our veins. It reminds us where we came from, where we were born, and tells us without compassion that it will still be around long after we have gone.

When I was small, the pulse of the sea's waves would find a rhythm with my own, or maybe it was the other way around; I felt melded to the sea, that we shared some great secret, temporarily forgotten, and that, inexplicably, we were one of a kind.

I sometimes wonder if I would feel the same if I'd been born in Italy rather than Scotland. Would a warm Italian sea speak to me in the same language as a cold Scottish one? Do the oceans of the world speak a universal language? Or do cold seas speak of ice, and warm seas of fire? When I lie in bed at night, I hear the measured breathing of the sea, marking time with my own breathing, timeless and eternal, lulling me to sleep.

My Italian bit is the fault of my grandfather, who is utterly bonkers. Not in a knife-wielding, dribbling sort of a way; just that he lives in a parallel universe of numbers and equations that only make sense to him. If you're a mathematical geek, you might have heard of him. If you're not, then you won't have. Of course, I utterly adore him.

Back before my father was properly famous, we lived in a quasi-mansion flat in a semi-posh part of Edinburgh. It had high ceilings and three bedrooms and stripped wooden floors. I couldn't understand why we didn't buy carpets, but the wooden floors – apart from splinters – were nice for sliding on. On a good day, I could run along the hallway in my socks and then slide across the living room to the fireplace. On the mantelpiece was a photograph of Mum and Dad on their wedding day. Mum is looking slinky in a tight-fitting white dress and, unusually for her, is smiling boldly into the camera and looking radiant. Dad has a protective arm around her shoulder and is looking faintly menacing. He is able to do that, so that it's hard to know exactly what he's thinking. There was also a smaller photograph of me on the day I was born. I look wrinkled, small, and very old.

I know it's a photograph that means a lot to Mum and Dad because it was the day of my arrival, but I sometimes wonder why they don't put a nicer photograph on the mantelpiece, one in which I'm not looking like a squashed alien. Visitors to our flat often look at it, and then seem lost for words. I wasn't a very pretty baby. In the photograph, Mum is looking tired – 'the longest bloody labour in the history of womankind', according to Mum, while Dad is looking relaxed. 'The bastard got bored and went to play golf,' according to Mum, a fact that Dad utterly disputes.

I am quite excited because Granny and Gramps are coming for supper and to stay the night. (Not the book-loving grandparents; by then, they'd met their mobile library). The nice Granny and the bonkers Gramps.

Mum is pottering. She likes to potter, or so my father says. He doesn't potter. He is either doing something, which usually involves a lot of noise, or he isn't doing very much, usually in front of the TV, with a large glass of wine perched by his elbow. I am sitting at the dining room table. In front of me is a big book with lots of numbers written in it.

My mother is in the kitchen next door and I can hear her humming a Beatles tune, which I only recognise because she hums it quite often, and I asked her what it was. I think it's almost the only song that she can hum, although she does also know the words. Mum only sings the words when she's drunk, holding an imaginary microphone in one hand. Her shadow slides like a ghost through the open door. She's emptying the dishwasher; I hear plates being stacked and cupboard doors being opened and closed.

I suck on my pencil and chew the end of it. It tastes metallic. I sigh and look at the numbers in the book, then at the blank sheet of paper onto which I have to fill in my homework. The numbers seem meaningless, lines and lines of them, with plus and minus signs in between, with an equals sign at the end of every line. After the equals signs are question marks. I have to fill in the question marks with answers. Maths is my least favourite subject, and also my worst subject. My legs don't quite reach the floor and I swing my legs backwards and forwards like a metronome. Outside, the sun is shining, sunlight chasing across a hillside; there's birdsong from the big tree outside our flat, swallows darting by the open window.

The phone is ringing and my mother answers.

'What do you mean you've been *detained*?' she demands angrily. She has stopped humming and one foot is tapping on the parquet floor. 'Well, it's not fucking good enough!' she adds for good measure. Mum says 'fuck' quite a lot, which I know isn't a very nice word, and which is why I'm not allowed to fucking say it.

Dad is away on business but had promised faithfully that he'd be home to see his parents. I therefore suspect that it must be him on the other end of the line, probably sounding apologetic. He is often away on business and often sounds apologetic on the telephone. I know this because I sometimes speak to him on the phone and then have to relay apologetic messages to Mum.

Once, Brad Pitt phoned to reassure Mum that Dad really *was* still in California. Mum hadn't believed Dad when he'd phoned earlier. 'Filming schedules often overrun,' said Brad. 'Only in the films that Paul's in,' said Mum, still not convinced about the truth of it, or if the person on the other end of the line really was Brad Pitt.

'Well, what am I supposed to tell your bloody parents?' she asks after a pause. Her voice has risen. 'They're only here for a couple of days. Honestly, Paul, why can't you ever just say *no*!' It's clear that my mother is now very angry; the foot-tapping has become louder, the taps faster; the woodpecker working its way to a frenzy.

18

She puts the phone down, but her shadow remains motionless, trailing in through the open kitchen door. Suddenly she appears, a dishcloth in her hands. 'Your father's in London,' she tells me.

'What about Granny and Gramps?' I ask.

'Another time, I suppose,' she says, coming to the back of my chair and placing a slightly shaking hand on my shoulder. Her cheeks are flushed, and her lips are pressed together. 'He's got to see some hot-shot producer … or so he says,' my mother adds. I don't really know what a "hot-shot producer" is, although my father sees quite a lot of them. 'Anyway,' my mother now adds more brightly, finally taking an interest in my homework, 'maybe Gramps can help you with this stuff.'

It would have been pointless asking Mum to help with my maths homework. She's even worse than me at numbers. They don't make any sense, so she says. If she ever has to add things up, she uses a calculator, and even finds difficulty with that. My mother smiles down at me and squeezes my shoulder.

'When are they coming?' I ask.

'Soon,' she replies.

My father, who isn't here again, is just as useless with numbers, and has to have accountants – plural – who do them for him. But Mum's right: if anybody can help with my homework it's Gramps.

A little later, and as always, Granddad takes the stone steps to our flat two at a time, the clatter of his feet setting up an echo. The lights in our stairwell are controlled by a time button on the ground floor and unless you are an Olympian athlete the lights will have gone off by the time you reach *Flat 3B, Rossini, Mr & Mrs*, according to the bit of paper stuck beside the outside buzzer.

Visitors therefore usually arrive at our front door like ghostly shadows, hanging onto the banister, feeling their way up like blind people. Granddad is one of the heroic few able to scale the stairwell before the lights click off. He is grinning broadly, and his arms are held out wide.

A battered brown briefcase is held in one hand; he embraces my mother and then me, his moustache tickling my cheek. He is tall and large and given to big gestures. Granddad is incapable of small gestures. My grandmother is probably also smiling, although it is hard to tell: not being an Olympian or my Granddad, she's climbing slowly and carefully through darkness, her feet searching out each step. When she finally kisses me, she smells of lavender.

Then Gramps bends down and kisses the stone lions that sit outside our doorway, one on either side. He has christened them Romulus and Remus and he kisses them on their noses. As on previous visits, we all laugh. Dad bought them in a fit of madness or drunken exuberance and they look idiotic in the shared stairwell outside our front door. They are a constant source of irritation to Mum, who hates them with a vengeance. But the neighbours don't seem to mind, although people do have to awkwardly manoeuvre around them to get to the next floor up.

If Dad is the fake actor, my grandfather is the real showman. Dad, trained in technique, can make the movement of one finger seem eloquent. Granddad can only communicate with both arms at once, loud voice, and exuberant moustache. For good measure he then kisses the lions on both cheeks, and we dutifully laugh once again.

Mum explains that Dad has been 'detained' and won't be home to see them. My grandfather's moustache seems to droop at this, and I can usually tell what he's thinking by how it looks. 'Well, he's a busy man,' he says, although I know he's disappointed.

'In either London or Los Angeles, I believe,' says Mum, in a tone of voice that suggests that he's probably somewhere in the known universe, but somewhere only known to Dad.

I know that Dad and Gramps don't see eye to eye. My grandfather is Italian, and still speaks with an Italian accent, with a drawn-out vowel at the end of every word. My father is Scottish, although he is able to speak in whatever accent is required. In his first break, the ghastly film when I screamed the place down, he spoke with a Brooklyn accent – not just an American accent, but a proper New York accent. The next year, in a Bond film, playing sidekick to a white-cat-stroking megalomaniac, he spoke with a menacing Germanic accent. In real life, depending on who he's speaking to, he either talks with a faint Scottish accent or no accent at all.

My father has changed his name, that's the nub of it – although the stuck-on bit of paper outside our block of flats still says *Rossini*. He has clipped off the last three letters from his surname to make him sound more British. Even at drama school, according to Mum, he had his career planned out. The Glasgow Metropole. The Bristol Old Vic. The West End. The Royal Shakespeare Company. Then TV and film. He has cultivated a stiff upper lip, the gift of mimicry, and an absolute belief in his own destiny.

But, if he was to play suave English gentlemen or dashing secret agents, he needed a British name. By airbrushing away three offending letters, he has removed what he thinks of as an obstacle, and I know that Gramps doesn't like to think that his son is ashamed of his family name.

Now that Dad is semi-famous, he loves being recognised in the street, signing autographs with a flourish or patting small children on the head. Restaurants always give him the best table, and then take his picture with the owner and stick it – autographed – on the wall to add celebrity endorsement. He loves the way that women's eyes follow his every move; he can see what they're coyly offering, given half the chance. He never turns down opportunities to open a supermarket or office block, once cutting the ribbon of a new children's hospice and speaking eloquently about the suffering of the young. As far as I'm aware he's never given a fuck (oops!) about supermarkets or sick kids, but maybe that's unkind.

He's currently starring in a TV drama called *War and*

Remembrance and is playing a British Army officer in love with Nicole Kidman. The film is about the Second World War, with Dad being injured on D-Day – shot again! – and is partly set in Edinburgh. I spent an afternoon on the set, in the gardens below the Castle. There were lots of lights and trucks and miles of cables, and cameras on little railways, with Dad and Nicole strolling hand in hand along a pathway and looking longingly at one another. It being the Second World War, Dad has to smoke a lot of cigarettes and comes home in the evenings smelling like a 'bloody ashtray.'

Mum keeps asking him suspicious questions about Nicole Kidman, just in case she really has fallen in love with him, or vice versa. Nicole did stay with us for a weekend and seemed very pleasant and not at all flirty with Dad, although Mum never left them alone for a moment. Having famous people stay with us is becoming normal for me, but not for Mum. She gets nervous and bustles at high speed, doing lots of housework, reading recipe books and cooking inedible food.

Now, when we have guests, we usually eat out. It's safer. But Mum doesn't seem to realise that Dad has also become someone quite famous, and that the Bentley outside our semi-quasi mansion flat is now new, not second-hand. Dad lives in terror of it being vandalised and is forever rushing to the window if he hears someone on the street outside. More usually, the Bentley resides in Edinburgh airport's car park.

Granddad helps me with my homework. He looks at my book of numbers and shows me how to add the sums up. Unlike my teacher, he doesn't think of me as slow or dim-witted. Instead, he tries to make me understand how important they are and how the world is shaped by numbers. His eloquence and dexterity with a pencil make it all seem easy but, despite his enthusiasm, I can't share his passion for equations. Written down, they seem dry and arid. I know they govern every law of physics, because he's told me, but I don't understand what physics is either.

22

Unlike Mum, I like cooking, and I've inherited that from Granny Mary. My mother cooks roast beef on Sundays, fish on Fridays, and boiled vegetables with pork or chicken in between – or tries to. My father, always in denial of his father's birthplace, never eats spaghetti – at least, I've never seen him eat it – and rarely visits the kitchen. If he does, he merely stands at Mum's shoulder and prods vegetables in a knowledgeable way, sometimes with a hand on her bottom, which she doesn't seem to mind, but strikes me as a bit gross.

All the things I've learned about cooking, I've learned from my grandmother, who loves cooking and being married to an Italian, has had to adopt the culinary skills of his country. On previous visits, she's taught me how to cook pasta – my father again being detained somewhere else – how to bake bread, and how to flavour risotto with wild mushrooms that we picked from ditches in the early morning. I may not know how to add up sums, but I do know which mushrooms to eat and which ones to feed to my worst enemies. The mushrooms that we picked smelled of the earth.

I watch her now, homework complete, as pots and pans bubble on the stove. I like watching her cook; I like watching boring things being washed, sliced and becoming food. I like the way that things like potatoes can become chips. It's a kind of alchemy, cooking, and my grandmother is happy to teach me.

Mum merely frowns at cookery books and mutters 'Oh my!' if guests are arriving – or, once, 'what the fuck *are* anchovies anyway?' Granddad is sprawled on the sofa in the living room. He is fast asleep and snoring loudly. Given his size and exuberance, he could never snore softly. My mother is pottering elsewhere.

'Mum says that Gramps has written a book,' I say.

Granny Mary turns from the stove to run a hand over her forehead. It is slick with steam. 'He has that, Emma. He's brought a copy of it for you. For each of you,' she smiles. 'He's even signed the inside cover.' Granny is from somewhere in the north of Scotland and speaks in a lilting voice. She met Gramps in Cambridge when he first came to Britain. She was working at the university doing something or other. I've never actually found out what.

'Is it a very big book?' I ask. I'm at an age when big books can be daunting. I want to read big books, but they have too many words, many of which I still didn't understand, and too few pictures.

'It is quite a big book,' she says. 'It's certainly got lots and lots of pages.'

'Is it a very clever book?' I ask, knowing that my grandfather is very clever. He's a professor at Edinburgh University, so he must be.

'Your grandfather thinks it is.' She laughs and wipes her hands on a towel. 'But he's not sure what other people will think. It's only just been published.'

'Is it a book with a story?' I persist. 'Does it have people in it and stuff?'

'No, Emma. Good gracious, no! It's a book about space and mathematics.'

Although disappointing, this makes perfect sense. I didn't think my grandfather would have written a book for real people to read, with nice pictures of rabbits and puppies, because professors at universities only write books for other professors. I don't mind rabbits and puppies in books. I just don't like them in cartoon films.

'So, it doesn't have a story.'

She comes and sits at the kitchen table. Through the open door, we can hear Mum moving furniture about. 'Well, I suppose that it does have a story. It's about us.'

'Why would Granddad want to write a book about *us*?'

She lays a hand on mine, not quite laughing. 'It's a history of the world, and about the universe in which we live. So, yes, it does have a story about us, right back to the beginning of time.' She smiles at me kindly. 'Alberto's grandfather was a train driver in Italy, did you know that? Back then, of course, there were only steam trains. God, they were horrible, messy things! You'd probably love them, of course. But it was them that gave your grandfather the idea for his book.' She sighs and rises from the table to peer into a bubbling saucepan. 'Alberto wouldn't have been that much older than you when he started to get his big idea.'

I think about this. 'Then it's taken him a fucking long time to write it,' I say eventually.

The dream that I have, over and over, is of walking in a green meadow. The sky is blue. At my feet are wildflowers. I'm not sure where I am. I can hear birdsong. At first, I am happy, feeling grass against my bare legs and the sun on my face. A thunderstorm has just passed, and the air still feels full of electricity. I then become uneasy. I don't know where I am, so I don't know how to get home. It's also hot and the heat is making me drowsy. All I want to do is lie down and close my eyes. But I can't do that because I know that I'm dreaming and that the meadow isn't real, the wet grass against my legs isn't real and that, if I lie down and go to sleep, I might not wake up.

$$\frac{3\Omega_0(\sinh\eta - \eta)}{2t_r H_0(1 - \Omega_0)^{3/2}} = 3$$

Timescale for an open universe

A year later, showered and spruced up in a blue suit and
open-neck shirt, Dad drives Granny Mary and me to Drem
station. Mum and Dad are driving up to Edinburgh later
and are going to meet us at Dad's favourite restaurant. It's a
special treat for Mum's birthday, although she isn't looking
very happy. Today, she has every reason not to be looking
happy, and not just because she's another year nearer to
being fossilised.

We've just been to North Berwick, a seaside town just
east of Edinburgh, to look at a rather dilapidated mansion
overlooking a golf course. A friend of a friend of Dad's had
mentioned it at a dinner party and things have rapidly got out
of hand. In the intervening days, Dad has spoken to lawyers,
estate agents, builders, architects, interior designers – but
not, apparently, to Mum, although moving house makes
absolute sense.

What with Dad's increasing celebrity, we couldn't go on
living in a semi-posh bit of Edinburgh forever; the stone lions
needed space, and Dad needed something to spend his money
on. He had immediately loved the run-down mansion. It had
belonged to a steel baron, apparently, and King somebody-
or-another once had tea there. Mum, of course, had thought
otherwise. 'Why do we need a huge bloody house?' she'd
demanded. 'We don't need all those bedrooms, and neither
of us plays tennis!' Even to me, it's clear that Dad has his
heart set on the place, and, against Dad's immovable force,

Mum doesn't stand a chance. Nobody has thought to ask *my* opinion.

Gran is there to make sure that I get safely into Edinburgh, while Mum and Dad go back to have another look at our 'fantastic future home' [Dad] or 'shithole from hell' [Mum]. I expect that Mum will go on swearing a great deal, huffing, and puffing, and Dad will continue not paying her the slightest bit of attention. When he has his heart set on something, he's like 'a fucking dog with a bone.'

Gran loves Dad's car as much as he does and, as we negotiate tight bends at high speed, sits upright in the front seat like a monarch. Mum, of course, still hates it: a vulgar bauble to attract attention to itself and, of course, its occupants. Mum still only travels in the Bentley with dark glasses firmly in place, eyes glued to the road ahead, and sometimes tightly closed if people point at the car and wave.

From the back seat, I look at him closely, wondering if I look like him and, if so, whether that's a good thing. I suppose that it must be a good thing, what with Dad being one of *The World's Top 20 Sexiest Men*, according to a magazine article he proudly showed us over breakfast.

'You're only number eighteen,' Mum had said, not raising her eyes from her own newspaper, and eating toast and marmalade. My father didn't mention it again, although I could tell he was delighted. His wife's opinions don't much matter, and such an accolade can only bring him one notch closer to his 007 ambitions, although I've never seen him drink vodka martini, shaken or stirred, or carry a firearm under his jacket.

The Bond movie in which he plays the Germanic baddie had not long been released and although the film hadn't received particularly good reviews, Paul Ross's performance, according to one newspaper, had been "eloquent, believable and outstanding". My Dad, it seemed, could be lovable, either as goodie or baddie.

'Number Eighteen' was grinning broadly as he pulled into the station and, with a flourish, opened Granny's door for her.

Drem station is a small halt on the east coast main line. Big trains can't be bothered stopping at Drem station. But there's a little train that runs on a branch line to North Berwick, and which stops at all the other little stations into Edinburgh. As we wait, an express train thunders through heading towards London. Sparks fly from the overhead power line, making the air fizz and crackle. Granny Mary has instinctively stepped back from the platform edge. Suddenly, the train sounds its horn, which gives us both a fright.

Granny Mary laughs nervously, looking shit-scared. This is another rude word I know, meaning poo, which I am allowed to say in front of Mum. I am *not* allowed to say 'shit' – despite Mum saying it quite often, as in her description of the house they're seeing in North Berwick.

'What's funny?' I ask.

'It just startled me, that's all.' Granny pauses, looking up and down the line to make sure that there are no more surprises speeding towards us. 'Actually, it's how your grandfather's book came about.' She takes a white handkerchief from her handbag and shakily dabs her forehead.

'It made you think about Granddad?'

She puts her handkerchief away and clicks her handbag shut. 'You see, many, many years ago, he was standing on a station platform in Italy and a train rushed past just like that one did.' She stops to point down the line, although the London express is no longer in sight. 'If it hadn't happened like that, he might never have written his book.' The book hasn't been much mentioned recently, and I know that other professors have said bad things about it. Granddad doesn't like to talk about it and mutters under his breath if it comes up in conversation.

'Have you ever heard of the Doppler Shift?' asks Granny

Mary.

I shake my head.

'Well, you may never have heard of it, but you *do* know what it is. It's when a hooting train speeds past. Just like that bloody thing a minute ago! As it comes closer, the note of its horn changes. That's because sound waves are being compressed by the speeding train.'

'Compressed?'

'Pushed together.' She scrunches her fingers into a knot to make her point. 'But the thing is, the Doppler Shift can also be used to work out the speed of galaxies. That's what your grandfather is interested in.'

I open my mouth to say something, then realise I don't know what to say. I know what galaxies are, but don't know why anyone would want to know how fast they're travelling. All I want to know is whether there are aliens living on them, maybe looking like I do in the photograph on the mantelpiece. Actually, I hope they look better than that.

Granny Mary is staring straight ahead. 'You see, if a galaxy is whizzing towards us, the light it gives out appears to be blue. That's called blueshift. Or, if a galaxy is speeding away from us, it gives out red light.'

I try to imagine my grandfather on a railway platform, and the speeding train which, according to Granny, would be horrible and messy. I know that he was not much older than me when he started to get his 'big idea' and wonder what he must have looked like without his moustache. I've never seen a picture of my grandfather without his moustache and have sometimes wondered if was born with it. 'Redshift, right?'

'Bravo, Emma! The bluer or redder the light, the faster it's moving. So, if you take a look at a galaxy, you'll see that some of it is redshifted and some of it is blueshifted.' Now that the London express has gone through, the little train from North Berwick can join the main line. I see it jink across the line to London and jink again onto the line to Edinburgh. Granny seems not to have noticed and is still staring straight ahead. 'That's because galaxies go round and round, so at any one-time bits of it are coming towards us and bits of it are moving away from us. By working out the speed at which a galaxy is turning, scientists like your grandfather can work out how much they weigh.'

This makes no sense. 'Does it matter what they weigh?'

'It does to your grandfather.'

The train comes to a stop. I open the door for Granny and follow her inside. 'Is that what his book is about?' I ask.

I know that Granny Mary has been saddened by the hostility to Alberto's book. Like him, she doesn't like talking about it. I suspect that I've learned as much as I'm going to learn, at least for now. 'Sort of,' replies Granny Mary and pats my knee.

Years later, I discovered that grandfather's theorem on virtually everything was met with widespread ridicule. Not being scientific, I can't say if it's complete bollocks, but I've always thought it nice that we have a theorem in the family and although he could be a cantankerous old git, according to my grandmother, my mother looking disapprovingly down the table, the epithet I most remember is *spherical bastard*.

Gramps is often wrongly credited with the discovery of dark matter and dark energy, but in the Rossini Theorem he goes out of his way to heap fulsome praise on the real discoverer, Fritz Zwicky, the Caltech professor who referred to every other physicist and astrophysicist as 'spherical bastards'. My grandfather was booming with laughter when he told me this. According to Zwicky, everyone was spherical because, from whichever side you looked at them, they were all still bastards.

It was Fritz Zwicky's study of the Coma Cluster that startled the worlds of physics and astronomy. The Coma Cluster is just over three hundred and twenty million light years away from us, comprises thousands of galaxies, and is some two hundred million light years in diameter. But, observed Zwicky, galaxies at the edge of the cluster were moving more quickly than galaxies at its centre.

That was odd because, like in our own solar system, the bits at the edge should be rotating more slowly. Also, the Coma Cluster was rotating at such a high speed that it should, quite literally, have flown apart. There wasn't enough mass to provide the gravity to keep all those stars together.

Zwicky looked at all those redshifted and blueshifted galaxies in the Coma Cluster and then calculated its mass. Zwicky didn't know what to make of this because, by his calculations, over ninety per cent of the Coma Cluster wasn't there.

Therefore, Gramps reasoned, if most of the universe was missing, it had to be somewhere. He decided to find out where it had gone.

His book also met with some ridicule in our family, as I discover one Sunday when Dad was home and we'd had a surprisingly good lunch. Mum is flushed with rare culinary success, but Dad hasn't complimented her or taken much interest in the food she put in front of him. He hasn't even put a hand on her bottom, which is very unusual. The real source of Dad's muted irritation is only revealed after lunch, when the three of us are in the kitchen: my mother is washing pots and pans, my father is drying up, and I'm putting things away in cupboards. This is to be one of our last meals in the semi-posh Edinburgh flat; the house in North Berwick is nearing completion and an army of builders, interior designers and security consultants has nearly finished.

There has been some local protest at the scale of the work, particularly the building of high walls, but those have been batted away by local councillors who have pointed out that no Hollywood A-Lister has ever made 'this crappy backwater of a bloody town' [Mum] their home.

She would much rather have stayed in Edinburgh or, at a pinch, endured a move to London. She feels safer in cities; there are more shadows in cities; more places to hide. She only likes the countryside for walking in. In cities, where there are lots of people, she can hide among them, anonymous. A small town, where everyone knows everyone – especially Hollywood A-Listers and their wives – is the worst kind of place to live. Mum isn't looking forward to the move but has resigned herself to it. She's even talked to the interior designer, chosen fabrics, been to galleries.

Don't get me wrong, Mum isn't completely useless, she can be practical when needs must. It's just that her nerves aren't made of steel. But in her heart of hearts, she knows that the semi-posh flat in Edinburgh is no longer grand enough; she understands that celebrity needs to flourish in richer soil.

She's already been asked to be president of the North Berwick & District Flower Arranging Society, although she's never arranged a bunch of flowers in her life. For some reason, she's accepted their "kind and generous invitation" and is "looking forward to attending your monthly meetings, when my schedule permits." 'Which will be absolutely never,' she tells me, sealing the envelope with a sweep of her tongue. I don't bother asking why she's accepted their "kind and generous" invitation to be president.

'I spoke to Sarah this morning,' Dad begins, a tea towel over one arm. 'Actually, she spoke to me.' I hang a saucepan on its hook beside the AGA and wait for him to continue. Sarah is his agent and conduit into the real world; his portal also to the parallel dimension in which he increasingly lives. Instead of more drying up, Dad has found an empty glass and a half-full bottle of wine.

He's also discarded his tea towel which means that, without cleaned and dried stuff to put in cupboards, I am also redundant. 'She's being asked lots of questions about

Dad's book, and what my views are.'

My presidential mother is wearing pink rubber gloves and is scouring a baking tray. She merely looks up but doesn't say anything.

'I thought that my father was writing a book about dark matter, whatever that is,' he says. 'That's what the old fool said he was writing about.' Dad is now looking out of the kitchen window, watching small birds flit between tree branches, his drying-up duties forgotten. He's also making sure that there are no delinquents or vagrants closing in on the Bentley. My father hasn't taken much of an interest in Granddad's book.

'He might be getting on, but he's no fool,' corrects Mum.

'Anyway,' he goes on in a louder voice, 'it turns out that Dad's book is a little more ambitious than I was led to believe. It's not just some mumbo-jumbo textbook on physics. According to Sarah, it's a bit more than that.'

'I see,' says my mother, her hands in water. 'And is Sarah a mathematician?'

'No, of course not!' snaps my father. 'It's just that she's had journalists onto her.'

'Asking questions,' says my mother. She is suppressing a smile. Dad takes his public profile very seriously, and only likes journalists when they ask the right questions.

'Exactly!'

Anyone wanting to find out anything about Dad has to go through Sarah's office. Nobody, but nobody, knows our phone number, even my school friends.

'It's the story of the universe,' I tell him.

He turns from the window, glass in hand. 'How the hell do you know that?'

'Granny told me.'

My mother peels off her rubber gloves. 'Emma's right, Paul. For heaven's sake, darling, Alberto's told you about his book often enough.'

'Well, yes, he might have done,' Dad concedes and picks up the tea towel. He looks at it, probably wondering what it is, then puts it down again. 'What I mean is, I didn't realise just how controversial some of his theories would be. Or, to be more precise,' he adds, pouring more wine into his glass, 'I didn't realise that his book would be of the remotest interest to anyone without several doctorates in astrophysics.'

My mother, having finished washing the dishes, now has no option but to pick up the tea towel and start drying the other pots and pans. 'It's a controversial subject, Paul.'

He slaps one hand on the Formica worktop. 'Except that, until Sarah phoned me, I didn't know just *how* controversial it was going to be.' He waves his other hand airily but doesn't need to amplify. His own career is too important to risk unwelcome attention, or journalists asking the wrong questions.

He marches off to the living room to resume reading the Sunday papers, leaving Mum and me to finish the washing up.

Two weeks later we're in our new kitchen, which has a gas cooking range – not a mere AGA – of the kind you might find in a large school or a busy restaurant. It has lots of gas rings and different ovens – including a pizza oven, hurray! – and an instruction booklet that's as big as 'a bloody telephone directory' – according to Mum, who flicked through it earlier, then put it down with the kind of sigh that means she'll never pick it up again. Does that mean she knows how the pizza oven works?

The kitchen has a marble floor and slate work surfaces, with discreet downlights that throw enigmatic patterns of light and shade. One end of the kitchen is a glass wall, with doors that lead out to a patio, onto which Mum has optimistically set out pots of herbs. In the hallway are boxes and more boxes.

The day had started in our old flat, Mum in tears, with

removals men in smart overalls carrying our possessions down to a waiting lorry. We'd then looked round the semi-posh mansion flat one last time, our feet clattering across rooms that I'd slithered across with greater speed. It was strange seeing our flat with nothing in it: the dining room, without its table and chairs, was just a room; the living room, without its chairs and settee, was no different from the dining room. My bedroom, pretty in pink, seemed much larger without its bed.

I said goodbye to the birds darting between branches in the big tree and followed my parents downstairs. With a dainty fingernail, Mum scraped off the *Rossini, Flat 3B* bit of paper on the outside buzzer. This made her cry some more; a final reminder that we no longer existed at that address and that, until we arrived with the lorry in North Berwick, didn't technically live anywhere.

I asked if I could travel in the back of the lorry with our stuff, but Mum said 'no'. She could have said that it would be dark in the lorry – because I'm still slightly scared of the dark – or that there wouldn't be any room – the lorry *was* very full – or that it would be dangerous with all that furniture. Instead, she simply said, 'Suppose you need the loo?' That's typical Mum: finding a completely useless reason when there are several better ones. But it's a particularly stressful day for her, and I can understand her anxiety, although Dad and I are mostly excited.

Mum has swallowed a couple of pills from the little bottle that she keeps not-very-well-hidden in her bag, so I know she's very nervous. Dad doesn't notice, and grins broadly as our possessions are heaved downstairs, grins even more broadly as he signs autographs for the removal men, then whistles loudly as he clatters down the stairwell to the waiting Bentley.

Mum had spent the morning gliding serenely between rooms – and between tears – not really doing anything except seemingly memorising every detail of every room, perhaps to decide how nice the flat actually was, or to decide whether she'd been happy in it. The removal men's eyes followed her every move, the utterly ravishing and supremely poised woman in tight-fitting jeans. To them, she was a picture of calm perfection; to me, she just looked medicated.

The new house was like stepping into a fairy-tale, but without bad witches or ogres in the tennis court. I've never played tennis before and I'm already dreaming about my Wimbledon debut. Last night I was tucked up in a familiar bed, with familiar city noises, with a familiar crack in the ceiling that looked like a badly-drawn question mark. There was the familiar spot of blood on the floor by my bed – nosebleed, never properly cleaned up – and my dolls and soft toys piled on chairs beside my familiar wardrobe.

I'm a bit old to actually play with them, but each one holds memories of tea parties, when they dutifully didn't eat anything, or comforting nights when they'd sleep in my bed and keep me safe from bad witches and ogres. (I used to believe in those as well.)

Now, my room has its own bathroom, with a bidet for washing my feet in, and overlooks a golf course and the sea. I stand for a long time by my bedroom window watching waves roll in, feeling like a princess in a tower, as if I'm standing at the edge of the world in a large and impregnable castle. I open the window slightly and listen to the sea and the call of seabirds. I half expect to see Viking ships or a fire-breathing dragon swooping down. Instead, closing my eyes, I hear the voice of the ocean, deep and rhythmic. It suddenly seems to be speaking to me and, for some reason, I really do feel at home, as if the sea and this house have been waiting for me.

That sense of being in an invincible castle has also been created by Chuck, who met us at our new house, and who introduced himself as 'our' security consultant. He was wearing a leather jacket and dark glasses, looking a bit like a Mafia hoodlum, which I supposed is an important part of his job. Under his leather jacket was an ominous bulge, which could either have been a packet of cigarettes or a gun – I didn't ask which.

He gave Mum and Dad two sets of buttons each; one to remotely open and close the wrought-iron gates at the end of our driveway, the other to open and close the garage doors. We have space for three cars in our garage, which means that Dad can buy another Bentley if he chooses. There is a door from the garage into a pantry beside the kitchen. Above the garage is a guest annexe.

Then Chuck took us inside and showed us how to access the TV monitor that films outside the wrought-iron gates, and how to open the gates if we decide that we actually want to let people in. There is another small screen that shows pictures from just outside the front door so that, if we change our minds about wanting to see them, we can refuse them entry at this point – although that might be a bit rude.

Chuck had to explain things to Mum several times, with Mum nodding sagely and then asking him to repeat it all again. Mum's eyes were a little glassy at this point, so I'm not sure that we'll ever have visitors.

The two stone lions are ceremoniously removed from the lorry and placed on either side of our red front door. In their new, grand surroundings they no longer look out of place. They look ready to leap to our defence in times of threat, although there is little chance of them being needed. The house is surrounded by high walls, with floodlights everywhere. The house itself has bulletproof glass, and intruder alarms linked to the local police station, which is just down the road. The police have already reassuringly told Chuck that they can have someone at the house within five minutes, although *I* don't find this particularly reassuring. A lot of bad things can happen in five minutes.

All the external doors to the house have been designed by Fort Knox, and the wrought-iron gates at the end of the driveway can't be climbed, according to Chuck. If the police do ever need to get in, it would be impossible without high explosive. There again, maybe that was reassuring, as it meant nobody else can get in uninvited – unless Mum presses wrong buttons on the security system, which is entirely possible.

We even have a panic room on the second floor, with its own air supply and secure telephone. One of the first things I did was to put my dolls in there. Well, you can't be too careful. It didn't take me long to unpack the rest of my toys and clothes and put everything neatly away – Mum's instructions – and saw with approval how much additional space there was in my chests of drawers – plural! – and fitted wardrobes – also plural! The chipped desk in my old room was replaced by a space-age glass table, on which someone had thoughtfully placed a bowl of flowers. (Could that have been Mum, trying her hand at flower arranging?)

For the rest of the day, I wandered about my new surroundings, from the manicured lawn in front of the house to the manicured lawn and flower beds at the back and then, further back, to the Wimbledon nursery of the tennis court. The house is built on a small slope so that, standing right beside the front door, I could look over the front wall, over the golf course, and glimpse the sea. Its breath was slow and measured, like an old man's.

The only confusing thing was how little of our old stuff has actually made it to the new house. Our much-loved settee on which I would bounce and jump has been replaced by two – two! – cream-coloured settees. There are new pictures on the walls, new beds in each of the bedrooms, new furniture everywhere. Most of our old stuff had gone to auction, I later learned. On my travels around the house, listening to its little noises, I would occasionally meet Mum coming the other way. She was looking happier now that the move was complete and that interior designers had finished everything to her specifications. But she also looked a little lost, as if she couldn't quite remember what was down the corridor, or behind a particular closed door.

On one occasion she found me looking at a new picture in our hallway. It looked like something a three-year-old would paint, if they were in a bad mood and didn't have much time. 'It's about the impermanence of life,' she informed me. 'It's called Art, apparently,' she added, giving it a capital A. 'He painted it in his own blood, apparently.' It still just looked like red squiggles. 'Do you like it?'

The thought of having someone else's blood on our wall wasn't very nice. 'No,' I said with a small shudder.

'Well, your father does, apparently.'

On another chance encounter, this time on the first-floor landing, she said that Dad had invited Granny and Gramps for supper, 'As if I haven't got enough to do.'

This isn't actually quite true. When we'd arrived in our little convoy – lorry and Bentley – we'd been met by several people. The interior designer, glamorous and bossy and carrying a clipboard, who took Mum on a final tour of inspection. Chuck, with his gun – or cigarettes – and remote-control buttons. A gas and electrical specialist who showed Dad the rudiments of the heating system, who clearly didn't need to be there but who did want an autograph and finally a Mrs Boyce and a Mr and Mrs Perkins. All had been lined up in front of the house like in an Edwardian film. I half expected them to curtsy to Mum.

These last three are to be Mum's little helpers. In Edinburgh we'd had a cantankerous old hag who came three mornings a week to do the cleaning and ironing, and who was forever complaining about the weather, the government, or her arthritis and who Dad hated; she never went to the cinema and didn't own a TV, and therefore had no idea who he was.

In North Berwick our support system has expanded to match our new surroundings. Mr Perkins is to be our gardener, Mrs Perkins, housekeeper who, it turned out, had put the flowers in my room, and Mrs Boyce, part-time cook, assistant housekeeper and occasional nanny. Mr and Mrs Perkins and Mrs Boyce have also signed confidentiality agreements that forbids them on pain of a slow and terrible death to ever speak about the goings-on in the Ross(ini) household. In other words, Mum no longer has much of anything to do, except learn how to arrange flowers.

Dad, of course, had better things to do than wander around the new house and admire pictures or furniture. He had retreated to his new study overlooking the golf course – for him, a perfect view – and had spent the day writing stuff on his computer. I looked in on him from time to time, even bringing him a cup of coffee. Each time, he smiled broadly, asking me again and again if I liked the place. Each time I reassured him by saying 'yes' and meant it.

The only thing I would miss from our Edinburgh flat was sliding down the corridor, and that was a small thing to miss. Every room in our new house has deep carpets, so you can't hear where anybody is. The one bad thing is that the alien blob photograph – me – has reappeared on our new mantelpiece. But it's a much bigger fireplace, with a much bigger mantelpiece, and my picture doesn't seem so prominent.

Mum, of course, had no idea what to do when the buzzer beside the front door discreetly announced the arrival of a car outside the wrought-iron gates. She jabbed at a few buttons, said 'fuck' several times – which Granny and Gramps unfortunately heard – until Dad came to her rescue and the gates slowly swung open. Mum stared at the little screen as their car advanced up the gravel driveway, as if it was a TV programme she had particularly wanted to watch.

Dad then dispensed with the computer and took his parents on a guided tour of the property, starting at the top of the house and working their way down to the basement areas: storage, wine cellar and cinema room. This took some time, with much laughter, and then we traipsed round the garden, with Granny naming most of the plants in the flower beds and Mum nodding sagely in a presidential way.

Then Gramps and I go for a walk on the beach. Like Mum, Gramps is a great walker and often wears a shabby woollen coat that, in a bad light, makes him look like a tramp. Today, with the sun shining, although now dipping to the west, he's wearing a shapeless cardigan and shapeless corduroy trousers. Gramps may be a master of the universe, but clothing doesn't much matter to him.

Dad, who believes that clothes maketh a man, would *never* be seen out in shapeless trousers or a cardigan. We have a little steel door beside the wrought-iron gates, with a 'Top Secret' security code that has to be punched onto a small keypad: *123456*, although that doesn't sound very secret to me.

We wait beside the fairway to let a foursome of golfers pass through, then cross down to the beach. It stretches away to my left and right and we are the only people on it. A light wind picks up sand and flicks it against my bare legs. Small waves are rolling in and breaking with a hiss. I dip my hand in the water. It is very cold.

I have rarely been on a proper beach before. Portobello beach in Edinburgh doesn't count because it's part of the city, and I was too small to remember the time we went to Tenerife. Apart from that, holidays have been spent visiting Dad in London or Stratford, where they don't have beaches, or to Pinewood Studios where I met Tom Cruise several times. He *isn't* in the Top Twenty, much to Dad's quiet satisfaction.

I have swum in London's Serpentine, but didn't think that

it was very hygienic, what with all those people probably having a pee in it – including me – although we do go to northern Italy every year, and I have swum in the local lake, which also doesn't have a beach. It's very big, so it's OK to pee in that as well. Apart from that, the only trip that stands out was a long weekend in Paris where we went up the Eiffel Tower. Well, Dad and I went up it. Mum sat stoically on a bench in its shadow and ate a croissant.

North Berwick beach reinforces my conviction that I'm standing on the edge of the world. The outline of Fife is clearly defined across the water, but that could just be an undiscovered land, full of strange and barbaric people, with Viking hordes being dive-bombed by dragons.

'I'm sure you'll be very happy here,' says Granddad, and opens his arms out wide. 'This beach, your new home. You're very lucky,' he adds with a wink.

'I'm not sure about Mum,' I say.

'Your mother is a worrier, Emma, but she'll be OK.' He seems certain about this, and we stand for a few minutes without speaking, with more sand being flicked against my legs and the same waves rolling in, one after another.

An hour later and Granny Mary is chopping salad and Gramps is finely slicing a small red chilli into tiny pieces. My grandmother looks indulgently at her husband, pausing with her knife, then scrapes lettuce into a glass bowl. We are in the new kitchen, illuminated under discreet lights. Dad is back on his computer and Mum is lying down in her room, once she'd managed to find it.

'In southern Italy, chillies are very important.' My grandfather makes a great show of kissing his fingers. His moustache is curled up happily at each end. His whiskers extend across his cheeks. 'No, more than important because, as in all civilised countries, food is almost a religion. There are chilli festivals at which priests are called to bless the chilli fields and sprinkle them with holy water. Children are taught how to recognise the different varieties and their individual properties. Oh, yes, Emma, my shining star!' he says, smiling broadly, his moustache creeping further upwards. 'Did you know that Mafia warlords fight over the best harvests? In Italy, venerating chillies is second only to venerating Christ and the Madonna – Jesus' mother, not the singer, by the way.' He smiles broadly again, having worked in a little joke and demonstrating that he knows that there is more than one Madonna.

'And, at the epicentre of all this is the gastronomic hub of Abbruzzo, a town I have never visited and probably never will, where the local chillies are called *diavolicchio*. Translated, that means little devil. It is a particular kind of chilli, known only to that part of Italy, and imparts a flavour that is absolutely unique.'

'Your grandfather often talks nonsense, Emma. Best just to ignore him,' advises Granny, winking at Alberto. I can't tell whether he is teasing me or not. Italians know things about food. My grandmother, despite being a good cook and being married to an Italian, was born somewhere in the Highlands. I don't know which one of them to believe. All I do know, and what is of real importance, is that we are cooking spaghetti, my absolutely most favourite food.

Mum joins us for supper, having found her way to the kitchen – probably by following cooking smells – drinks far too much wine and unexpectedly ends up in a good mood. We have *antipasti* to start and, after that, *fettuccine e ceci alla napoletana* and *panzanella alla minori*, according to my grandfather, who declares it to be excellent and hugs my grandmother. Granny Mary says in her gruff way that we've eaten pasta with salad but looks pleased to be hugged. Over supper Granddad waves his knife alarmingly, his moustache still curled upwards, declaiming against spherical bastards everywhere. He is also in a good mood.

Afterwards, my mother hums as she fills the dishwasher.

43

I haven't seen her so happy for a long while, despite having spent the day either in tears or swallowing pills. She straightens from the dishwasher and pats my head, then pours herself another glass of wine and absently starts to hum again. I lean against her, and put my arm around her, and give her a hug. She smiles down at me and hugs me back. Sometimes I like to let her know how much I love her; how much I worry about her. She smells of perfume and warmth.

Granddad, Dad and I then sit in the lounge while Granny and Mum gossip in the kitchen. The new lounge feels funny. It doesn't hold any memories, and I don't know where to sit. In our old lounge, Dad had his chair, Mum had hers, and I usually ended up on the floor beside the fire. In our new lounge, we have chairs and settees for a small army, but – old habits – I still end up lying beside the fire.

I can hear Gran laughing. Mum may have said something funny, or maybe Granny is laughing at one of her own jokes. Mum doesn't really do jokes, not ones that are funny. I have a jigsaw in front of me. It's a jigsaw that I'd forgotten I had, until I found it earlier in a box. I've nearly finished a picture of the Eiffel Tower, even though jigsaws are for losers. It also reminds me of Dad's first film, his big break, and I don't like being reminded about *that*.

Dad is intently reading through a sheaf of papers and mouthing words. I guess that he's memorising them. Dad is very good at memorising things and never forgets his lines – according to him. But he is also shaking his head and frowning, because I've just remarked to Gramps that I share my birthday with a friend in my class at school – well, probably now a former friend, in my former school. Will I ever see any of them again?

Granddad is reading a newspaper, but with less enthusiasm than Dad reading his lines, and doesn't seem particularly surprised by my observation. 'It's not really a coincidence, Emma.'

Dad lowers his homework and looks at his father. Dad is wearing reading glasses, something he has only recently admitted to needing, because it seems to undermine his status as one of the World's Sexiest Men. 'Of course, it's a coincidence,' he says.

'In which case,' continues Gramps, 'let me ask you a question.' Even after all his years in Britain, and as an eminent professor at Edinburgh University, my grandfather's accent is still distinctly Italian. I don't know if he is speaking to me or my father. However, Dad has raised his paperwork in front of his face and is invisible behind it. 'It's quite interesting, in an uninteresting sort of way. The question is this: how many people would you have to have in a room before you had a better than evens chance of two or more of them having the same birthday?'

I shrug. 'No idea.'

'Guess.'

'Hundreds and hundreds.'

He beams triumphantly. 'The answer is twenty-three.'

I know he must be right because he's a genius, but I still manage to look sceptical.

'And if you have a hundred people in the same room,' he continues, 'the odds are more than three million to one that two or more will have the same birthday.'

I know that Dad has been listening to this. The script in front of his face has moved to one side. He is looking at my grandfather round the side of it. 'Rubbish,' he says.

'Not rubbish, Paulo,' my grandfather corrects. 'You can't argue with mathematics.' Dad also hates being called Paulo. His name is Paul, so he keeps saying. 'OK, then here's a question for you,' says Granddad, but instead of asking it, flicks through to the sports section of the newspaper.

My father has sharply lowered his script and seems irritated. 'Well?' he demands.

'What's your handicap?' my grandfather asks.

My father looks nonplussed. 'Handicap?'

'Your golf handicap.'

Dad doesn't immediately reply. He doesn't like to admit to mediocrity in anything, far less golf, his favourite pastime. 'Eighteen,' he eventually concedes in a low voice. 'Why?'

'So, not a good golfer, but not a bad golfer either,' says Granddad, his moustache twitching like cat's whiskers. 'In which case, let me ask you a theoretical question. If, say, you were to play golf with Tiger Woods, could you beat him?'

My father doesn't even bother thinking about it. 'Don't be ridiculous,' he scoffs.

Alberto is still smiling. 'Nevertheless, given your golf handicap and his scores at the Colorado Classic, you have a probable chance of beating him once in every one hundred and seventy rounds of golf.'

My father then realises that his glass is empty, puts down his newspaper and walks to the sideboard on which are perched a whisky bottle and jug of water. He refills his glass and returns to his seat. I note that he doesn't offer his father a glass.

'Absolute crap,' he says eventually.

My grandfather pulls a face. 'In probability theory, even the improbable can sometimes happen.' He is smiling broadly.

'Not to me it doesn't,' says Dad, tipping back his glass and finishing the contents. This time he walks a little shakily back to the sideboard.

That night and I lie awake in my new room, feeling warm and safe. There are probably no ogres under the bed because Chuck will have banished them beyond our high walls and, if one does appear, I can hide in the panic room with my dolls. My window is open, and the curtains move slightly in the night breeze. In the distance I can hear the voice of the sea and I feel at one with it. It's a feeling I have never forgotten, of being bound to something infinite and eternal, in the place that is now my home.

$$\frac{2\Omega_0(1 - \cos\theta)}{R_f(\Omega_0 - 1)} = 4$$

Scale factor for a closed universe

The next week, with the last of the boxes unpacked, we're leaving our new house in the safekeeping of Mum's little helpers and going on holiday. Mrs Perkins comes out to wave the Bentley goodbye. She has a dishcloth in one hand, and she waves it like a large handkerchief as the gates open.

If Mrs Perkins had been a Mr Man, she'd be Mrs Splodge, because it's quite hard to tell if she's a little overweight or quite fat. Her clothes disguise her body so well that she is simply a rather unkempt shape floating from room to room, generally with a duster in one hand or a basket of washing under her arm.

But she is quietly and ruthlessly efficient and knows precisely what needs to be done, and precisely when it needs to be done. In our old flat, with the cantankerous old hag in charge, dust oozed from every crevice. Now, in our new palatial surroundings, dirt and dust have been abolished on the orders of Mrs Perkins. Mum, now with staff to do everything, has given up doing anything and, out of sheer boredom, has even been to a meeting of the flower arranging society, arriving home in a foul mood. 'They've asked me to be a bloody judge!' she announced, un-presidentially. 'What the hell do I know about flowers?'

Between moving in and going on holiday, there have been two trips with Mum into Edinburgh to buy clothes – mostly for me, my wardrobes and drawers filling up nicely – a visit to a posh restaurant and walks on the beach. Mum has also bought me my new school uniform, with a blazer which makes me feel grown-up, and I'm looking forward to the start of term and to finally making new friends.

Our holiday villa in the south of France belongs to a film director who is trying to persuade Dad to act in his new film. Dad isn't convinced. 'It's not the lead role,' he's explained to us, 'and I'm not sure if it's the right thing for me to do.' Dad no longer likes being number two on the credits, or being killed ten minutes in. The film has been the subject of several late-night calls between my father and his agent, his study door firmly closed, and my mother surreptitiously listening at the keyhole.

The director suggested a holiday in the sun to think it over and, as further inducement, offered us his villa. Dad, now as wealthy as Croesus, still loves to get things for nothing and, not having any immediate film commitments, readily agreed. My mother's plans for a family holiday in Greece have been quietly shelved.

'I've got you both a surprise,' says my father as we arrive at an unfamiliar part of Edinburgh airport. Mum not only doesn't like travelling in the Bentley, she, like me, doesn't like surprises. I can see the muscles on her face contract.

During the flight, Dad sleeps and Mum nervously pretends to read a book. On top of her other neuroses, she doesn't like flying. I watch a film then stare out of the window. It's the first time I have ever flown in a private jet. The seats are huge and, at the press of a button, can swivel or turn into a bed. Mum puts down her book, turns her seat into a bed, and also goes to sleep, having now had several gin and tonics. While they sleep, I get the stewardess to show me the plane's extensive selection of crisps and sweets so that, when we land, I'm feeling a bit sick.

We're met at the airport by one of Dad's people, who is holding up a sign saying ROSS. Dad seems to have people usefully dotted around the world, just in case he drops in.

49

'Goodness!' says Mum, as we leave the terminal. 'What's that bright light in the sky?'

'It's the sun, Mum,' I reply, not looking up. I've found out the hard way that it's better not to respond to Mum's attempts at humour, because if you do something silly like laugh, it only encourages her to be funny again, and it never is.

Dad's south of France representative, immaculately dressed in a neat grey suit and chauffeur's cap, drives us to our villa outside St Tropez, deposits our bags inside the front door, and crisply salutes before driving off.

In some respects, our villa in France isn't that dissimilar to our house in North Berwick. Both have large gates with remote control buttons to open them – which make Mum sigh – and both overlook the beach, although not a golf course. Every room has a marble floor, even the bedrooms. It also has air conditioning, which we don't need in Scotland, so that I shiver when we get inside.

By the time I come downstairs in my swimsuit, Mum is already in her bikini and sprawled on a lounger by the private pool, with a glass of white wine in one hand and her book open on a little table by her head. I am reminded again how beautiful she is, with her long hair and big eyes and perfect figure. Even Dad is looking at her in a predatory way, which is a little unnerving.

Not wanting to think about this, I splash around in the pool for a bit and then, needing a pee, go back into the house. The Serpentine was OK for a toilet, but our pool is too small. Then I walk to the front of the house – the pool is at the back – and stare out at the beach. It doesn't look the same as North Berwick's beach. The sea looks blue and tranquillised, as if it's been in Mum's handbag, and there are no waves crashing in. The sea seems tired and defeated, even though there are lots of people sitting in it, or near it on towels, and not wearing any clothes.

My small shriek brings Mum off her lounger. I point out the window to the beach. 'Holy shit!' says Mum loudly.

Dad also now appears and puts an arm around Mum. 'How charming!' he says with a fat grin on his face. Just then, an old man facing towards the sea, bends down to pick something from the sand. 'Holy shit!' says Mum again. Dad, however, has been looking at a couple of beautiful young women further along the beach and hasn't noticed the old man's bottom. 'Well, I think it's rather nice,' he says. 'It's what the south of France is all about.'

'It's not nice at all, Paul,' says Mum, still traumatised by the old man's bottom.

'It's very chic and bohemian,' says Dad, looking at the young women, who are now throwing a beach ball to one another.

'Paul, if you even suggest that ...' Mum gestures towards the beach.

'You would put them all to shame,' says Dad, and kisses the top of her head, his arm, like a boa constrictor, now encompassing her thigh. Mum, of course, would never dream of taking her clothes off in public – just think what the *Daily Mail* would do with those photos!

I go and splash in the pool some more. I don't mind being an only child. I'm used to it, although I would like a little brother to boss around. It's what my friends in Edinburgh told me about their little brothers. If you do something wrong, like put paint on a wall or tread in dirt, there's always someone else to blame – and little boys usually can't remember if they have actually put paint on the wall or trodden in dirt.

They might be a bit smelly, but they also do what older sisters tell them to do because, like a wonky computer, that's how they're programmed. I think about this, swimming up and down, although it would also mean having to share Mum, and I don't want to do that. She needs me to take care of her, and not to have to care for someone new.

51

Mum and Dad have gone for a lie-down upstairs. I have no idea what they're doing, but when you're married to Number Eighteen they must be up to something.

Our holiday involved a lot of swimming in our villa's pool and no swimming whatsoever on the public beach, although I did peek from time to time at all the naked people. Some – very few – were close to Mum's class and looked OK with no clothes on; most weren't in Mum's class and should have been wearing a Mrs Perkins smock. I didn't like looking at the men.

We went on small excursions to local towns or into the hills, and Mum bought locally made jewellery for us both, and some dubious-looking cheese that made it back to Scotland and then into the bin. Mostly, however, we stayed at the villa, Mum on her lounger reading several books – in sequence, not all at once – and me in the pool. It was sunny every day. Dad spent most of the time in the film director's study, which overlooked the beach, on the phone to wherever, or maybe just staring at all the naked women outside.

On one of our last days, Dad learns that he has won an award and, to celebrate, we eat lunch at a pavement restaurant in town, Mum marvelling at the prices – as if prices were of any importance anymore – and trying to look anonymous behind her dark glasses. Dad, on the other hand, has his hair gelled back. His dark glasses are in his top pocket. All through lunch he's accosted by passers-by. Some merely take photographs, others thrust out pieces of paper for him to sign. Dad smiles obligingly and signs whatever he is proffered, even signing the back of a small child's T-shirt.

Mum's glasses are pushed firmly up her nose and she shoves salad around her plate, but hardly eats anything. Over coffee, an elderly woman in tight white trousers comes to our table, apologises for interrupting us, and says how much she respects my father's work. Dad is in seventh heaven. The woman is Brigitte Bardot.

When the woman leaves, Mum asks if we can 'get out of here, now!' and, to reinforce the point, she stands up, even though we haven't yet paid. It is clear that she has had enough of being famous, if only by association, and sits silently in the front passenger seat of our car on the way back to our villa and doesn't look at my father. Dad refuses to acknowledge this, dark glasses now propped up on his head, and waving at anyone who recognises him.

To make things worse for Mum, we are in the film director's red Ferrari, which ostentatiously growls its way through small streets and attracts everyone's attention. This is a worse nightmare than the Bentley.

Over the few days that we've been in France, Mum's complexion has changed for the better. Her skin is bronzed and the lines on her face seem to have flattened out. Her natural beauty has emerged in its full glory: she looks radiant, and I am so proud of her. But on the drive back to the villa, having experienced her very own kind of hell, I see that the lines have reappeared.

That's when I started to worry that, as her daughter, I might grow up to be as barking mad as she was. I also sensed that, despite fame and fortune, our own little world was crumbling at the edges.

I never wanted to grow up and follow in Dad's footsteps. I never wanted to be like him. Full stop. I could never figure out what the big deal was in being an actor. OK, if you're very, very lucky, you can make a living, but most don't. I also don't see why actors are considered important. Someone else writes your lines, another someone tells you where to stand, and lots of other people film you. All Dad had to do was 'look pretty' – his words – and be convincing. Do those meagre talents add up to the millions and millions he was paid?

OK, Dad was also very good at reading scripts and

making changes to them. He could quickly get under the skin of a character and know how that character should sound. He could turn the two-dimensional into a real person. But did he ever have an original idea in his whole life? He was very good at criticising scriptwriters, sometimes to their face, but could he ever write a film script? I rather doubt it. Everyone else did the hard work; Dad just turned up, said some words, and then got huge sums of money and lots of awards. Nobody saw the shadows behind the tinsel. But we did, Mum and me.

But I did want to grow up and become a great wizard like my grandfather – without the moustache – and to be able to understand the magical and indecipherable formulae that filled his notebooks, his crabbed hand recording a sort of genius.

He was writing his own words and symbols, and it had to be genius because he was my grandfather, and I always believed in him; his impossibly-long calculations suggesting that everything in the universe could be explained by mathematics, and that every problem had a precise algebraic solution. I sometimes thought of him as a kindly wizard, with a magic wand in one hand, lightning jumping from its quivering tip, casting spells to make everything right, including us.

Every year, the five of us – my parents, grandparents and me – would spend a week in northern Italy, in the village where Granddad was born. It was his way of reconnecting with his roots and of keeping in touch with a place in which everyone seemed to be related. It was a trip that Dad dreaded because, no doubt, it seemed a pointless waste of time. But it was a trip he had made from boyhood, when Alberto was the family star and Dad was just a rather good-looking small boy.

Mum, however, was only too happy to go, and utterly insisted that Dad still went along too. I later found out that,

54

in Dad's struggling years, when money was tight, it was Granddad who paid for those trips back to his homeland, and for a lot else besides; this was Mum's way of ensuring that the debt was never forgotten.

In the days leading up to the annual pilgrimage Dad would grumble and mumble, like a child trying to evade going to school. However, once we actually got there, Dad quite enjoyed it. The younger villagers would ask for autographs and photographs, but the older folk, who have known Dad for years and years, simply think of him as Alberto's son. Dad can therefore have time off from being famous, Mum can have a holiday from being the wife of someone famous, and I can eat lots of *real* Italian food.

Bellagio Ripano sits in the hills above Lake Como, nestling in pinewoods and with tantalising glimpses of the water. From the village you can look across to the lake's only island, Isola Cernobbio. It's never been much of a village, with only a modest road from the lakeside town of Moltrasio, and with none of the amenities that tourists and travellers expect.

It's therefore quaint and relatively unvisited although Darth Vader once ate lunch in the village. *Risotto con zucchini e fiori* followed by *fichi secchi al vino*. In Bellagio Ripano such visitations are rare and therefore much discussed. They were, of course, on location nearby, filming *Star Wars: Episode II – Attack of the Clones*. The balcony kiss after the wedding, the achingly beautiful view over a lake? That's Como in all its glory.

Like Dad, I viewed each visit with a mixture of anticipation and alarm. I was both a person and an exhibit; a relic from a distant land who was also the granddaughter of a local lad made good. That made me everybody's property. I also seemed to be related to almost everyone through a complex web of intermarriage that I've never properly understood. Intensely shy, I was known to everyone, with old crones inviting me to their homes for hot chocolate and *pane al miele* and conversing with me in Italian, which I didn't understand.

It was on one of those trips that Granddad revealed himself to be a great wizard. We had a rented small villa at the top of the village with a veranda fringed by pear trees. It was springtime. The days were warm, but the nights could be cold. Clouds gathered over the mountains each morning and would slowly boil away. From the veranda I could see down to the water.

We kept discussing whether to go down to the lake and swim, but we hadn't yet bothered; the lake looked dark and cold. The veranda was the sanctuary on which we would gather: Mum and I reading, my grandmother with her knitting, and Granddad snoozing. Dad smiled a lot, I remember. He had every reason to be cheerful. There was talk of a plum role in a forthcoming blockbuster, and he was still in the top twenty of the World's Sexiest Men – but only just: number twenty this year.

It's Mum's birthday and Dad had promised to take us all out to lunch. But Granny Mary doesn't feel too well – an upset stomach, something trivial – and declines. Granddad says he'd better stay and look after her. That just leaves the three of us and we drive down the hillside at high speed in Dad's rented Mercedes, my mother forever telling him to slow down; my father driving with one hand near the steering wheel, one eye on the road, his other hand on Mum's knee, and neither foot anywhere near the brake.

We have been discussing where to have Mum's birthday lunch. There are several good restaurants in Moltrasio; some set back into the hillside and some overlooking the water. It's a discussion that had started the evening before and which had continued through breakfast, until Granny said she wasn't feeling too well and patted my mother's hand and said that she'd rather have a quiet day.

We therefore have no destination when we screech off and none when we arrive at the foot of the mountain. The car's roof is down. The lake sparkles under a warm sun; Isola Cernobbio hangs in the lake, wreathed in mist. The alleyways of the village stretch back up the hillside.

'It's your birthday, Cat, you decide,' says my father.

'Well, I don't know, Paul,' replies Mum.

Neither of them think to ask my opinion.

'OK, then what about Passalacqua?' suggests Dad. 'You had the fish last time, remember? Turbot, or something. You said it was tasty.' He isn't really asking Mum's opinion now; he has made up her mind for her. The car is already weaving its way to the lakeside, its horn scattering villagers and tourists. Dad thinks if pedestrians don't immediately get out of the way, even profoundly deaf ones, they deserve to be run over.

Being early in the season, the restaurant is hardly full. There's a family at one table – a father, mother and two small children – and an elderly couple who spend the entire meal without saying anything, but maybe communicating telepathically. Apart from them, nobody; and nobody recognises Dad. We eat on the terrace under a striped red awning. A speedboat carves its way across the lake. The Passalacqua is my least favourite restaurant in the village; it is too opulent, too hushed, and it serves food with names I don't understand and vegetables I don't recognise. Worse, the portions are very small.

I stare over the water while my parents drink white wine. I drink Coke through a straw. The waiter knows us from previous visits; he is charming and attentive; with a flourish, he presents us with menus. He is wearing a white waiter's jacket with gold buttons. The leather menus have faded to brown. I look blankly at the pages. Nobody in the Passalacqua seems to know English.

Dad orders another bottle of wine, making Mum frown, and it comes in a silver bucket with clinking ice. My starter consists of small parcels of pastry stuffed with cheese and ham. Mum had said that I'd enjoy it, and usually she knows what I'll enjoy. Today, perhaps distracted by being a year older, she is completely wrong. I excuse myself and go to the end of the terrace and, kneeling, trail my fingers in the water. It feels cold, small waves slapping at the terrace edge.

My main course is worse – veal in a sauce made from fruit. It tastes sweet and sickly like Jelly Babies – which are nice because they're *supposed* to taste sweet and sickly – and so small that I eat it in a couple of mouthfuls. I would much have preferred spaghetti, but the Passalacqua doesn't seem to realise that it's Italy's national dish and it wasn't on the menu. But my parents seem happy enough, Mum once again eating fish and my father eating steak.

'How was the veal, darling?' Dad asks me. His cheeks are flushed, either from the sun or the wine – or both – and he has that look in his eye that I've come to recognise. The kind of look that means that he and Mum will soon need to have a quiet siesta, with Mum reappearing some time later looking happily dishevelled.

'Little,' I reply.

We drive more slowly back to the villa, Mum chatting about who we still have to see and who has been invited for drinks tomorrow, and how she'll need the car in the morning to go shopping. My mother likes mundane activity, she likes making ordinary plans. Granny is making tea when we arrive back. She says that she's feeling much better, reaching down teacups and setting the kettle to boil. 'How was lunch?' she asks.

'It was lovely,' replies Dad in a commanding voice, just in case Mum or I dare to disagree, which I would have done, because I'm still hungry. 'We decided to try the …'

'… we know where you went,' says Granddad who has

appeared in the kitchen with a newspaper in his hand. He is grinning like a Cheshire cat; his moustache bristling.

'How do you know?' asks my father.

'Alberto worked it out,' says Granny, filling a jug with milk.

There's a piece of blank white paper on the table that Granddad now turns over. On its other side, written in blue ink, is a mass of calculations – line after line of algorithms, 'x's and 'y's, numbers multiplied and divided. At the end of the calculation is: = Passalacqua

Mum and Granny Mary laugh. I laugh as well. But it's noticeable that Dad isn't laughing. He takes the piece of paper from the table and frowns at it. Then he frowns at his father.

Granddad's moustache is still enjoying itself. 'I merely calculated all the variables, Paulo.' To me, it seems like a kind of magic. While there are only a small handful of *trattorias* in the village, the lakeside is dotted with many more. We could have chosen any one of the village restaurants or, if we'd driven a few miles from the village, the odds would have been astronomical.

'Variables?' my father echoes.

'What food you enjoy, that kind of thing.' Granddad gestures to the window. 'The weather and whether it was nice enough to eat outside.' He is beaming, proud of his handiwork. 'I simply worked out the variables and calculated the probability of where you'd eat.' He doesn't need to ask if he's right; he only needs to look at our faces and my father's frowning eloquence.

I look again at the piece of paper. It looks like something that only Merlin, or another great sorcerer, could have written. The calculations are precise; nothing is crossed out. There are no smudges. Numbers and letters are lined up in precise formation.

But of course, as I realised much later, the Passalacqua

was the most expensive and exclusive restaurant for miles around, so it wasn't a difficult calculation to make. Given a choice, Paul Ross only ate in the best restaurants. But at the time I thought it was magic, because it had to be.

Back home from the south of France, the living room has miraculously sprouted a Steinway baby grand piano. Neither of my parents plays the piano, so I don't see the point of this, although it does handily fill an empty space at one end of the room, so maybe that is the point of it. Even more curious, the top of the piano is now littered with family photographs in silver frames.

There's another one of Mum and Dad on their wedding day, with confetti swirling like snowflakes around their heads. Dad is carrying a top hat; Mum is holding a bouquet of flowers and staring rather intently at Dad. Dad's other arm is nowhere to be seen and I wonder what part of Mum's anatomy he's touching, and if that's why she's looking a bit intense.

There's another of me, taken the year before in Italy, on Mum's birthday, sitting at our lakeside restaurant table. There's an empty plate in front of me and I can still remember how hungry I was. In the background are water-sparkles from Lake Como. I'm wearing sunglasses – mimicking Mum – and making a peace sign at the camera. Mum was taking the photo; Dad only likes having his picture taken.

There's another silver-framed picture of Dad in a tuxedo, shaking hands with the Queen – he's bowing slightly - then a picture of Dad shaking hands with Tony Blair – Tony Blair is bowing slightly - and one of the three of us on a red carpet in London. Dad is beaming into the camera, Mum is smiling bravely, despite experiencing an underwear malfunction, and I have my chest puffed out. I'm wearing a red dress and Mum is wearing a black Dior dress and holding tight to my hand. Someone's shoulder is intruding into the photograph that I know belongs to Judi Dench, who was very nice but kept calling me Emily. I've never seen those photographs before, and I wonder where they've suddenly come from.

If we ever move out, Mum has said that the house will make the perfect bolt-hole for 'a drug dealer or pornographer' – although I don't know what a 'pornographer' is. I am still pestering them to install a swimming pool, without any success. Neither of my parents much likes swimming. You can't swim and speak on the phone – which rules Dad out – and Mum doesn't like to get her hair wet. (How does she wash it? Maybe she doesn't).

Strangely, despite her worries about virtually everything, Mum thinks all our protective devices are a complete waste of time. For some reason she believes that the east coast of Scotland is quite safe, far from the reach of terrorists or kidnappers, and doesn't see why we need cameras and bulletproof glass. Maybe she feels that, because she and I aren't movie stars, we're therefore safe, or maybe she still can't quite believe that Dad is really that famous and is stuck in a kind of nervous denial.

In the early days, Dad's life meant treading the boards at provincial fleapits and living in B&Bs, later rising up through layers of theatre, staying in increasingly lavish hotels, until the Royal Shakespeare came calling, and Dad departed for London and a season of *Othello* and *King Lear*, seven performances per week, and only Sunday off.

It was a summer when we didn't see much of him; instead, Mum would spend weekends in London or Stratford, leaving me in the care of Granny Mary who, she confided, quite liked to spend time away from Alberto. My grandfather, I learned, could be quite crotchety, particularly when colleagues contradicted him, as they often did.

Once I went with Mum to London and watched Dad, with beard and dagger, pace the stage. Mum, eternally nervous that Dad would fluff his lines, sat rigid to attention in the seat beside me. I wasn't allowed to eat popcorn, which has always put me off the theatre. But I was also acutely aware that the father I knew was also other people, and I gradually realised as the years passed that Dad was generally a better person on film or on the stage, speaking other people's words, than he was in real life trying to speak his own.

My parents met when he was a RADA drama student. He, the talented student with a huge ego; she, a retiring secretary who did something in administration. My father must have been overwhelming, like a tidal wave. I have a picture of them taken soon after they met. He's wearing jeans, an open-neck blue shirt and has long hair. She's wearing a sensible knee-length brown skirt with an equally sensible cream blouse.

Mum is not quite looking into the camera. You can tell that her smile is a little forced; it doesn't quite reach her eyes. Dad, despite his easy grin, is also looking menacing; the actor's innate ability to be different people all rolled into one. It is a talent that over the years has served him in good stead. I can see why Mum fell for the charming rogue; but, despite my love for her, I can't see why he fell for her.

She is beautiful enough in the picture, with wavy hair and fine features: but she's also awkward and uncomfortable among people she doesn't know. She never dresses in bright colours or seeks the bright lights. Walking on red carpets terrifies her. She doesn't much like parties; my father loves them. The things she likes are not the things he likes. They are opposites and I can't discern the magnetism.

They moved from London to Edinburgh soon after he graduated when small parts dribbled in. It was where Dad had grown up, and where he'd always wanted to return. Or that's what he said. Mum was born in London and had grown up in London; it must have been a wrench leaving the city she knew for a smaller city she didn't know.

It also explains her aversion to North Berwick; she'd much

rather be a small fish in a big pond than a whale in a puddle. But in those pre-Bentley days, Mum would stoically drive Dad to Edinburgh airport, kiss him goodbye and, probably, secretly wonder when or if he'd return. In his absences, I grew closer to my mother. We went walking together in those semi-posh mansion flat days, usually into the hills, and would watch clouds scudding on weather fronts. I was happy in her company, and secure in my conviction that she would never, ever disappear.

Mum decided on our French holiday, and to our relief, to finally leave all the cooking to Mrs Boyce if, that is, she turned out to be any good. Happily, Mrs Boyce has heaps of culinary certificates – which are why she was taken on – and is *very* good at cooking, although Mum has insisted that she'll bake a special cake for my birthday. Mrs Boyce either stays late if we have guests, which have included our local MP and his wife – who basically invited themselves, and who tried to engage Mum in a political discussion on social care and community development, without much success – and several film people up from London, bringing in each course on a big tray; or, if we don't have guests, leaving something in the kitchen that can either go into the oven or microwave.

Despite not having to cook, Mum has, to my surprise, semi-mastered the cooker and its knobs and functions including, so she says, the pizza oven. Neither Mum nor Mrs Boyce has cooked pizza yet, although it's on Mrs Boyce's to-do list.

But Mum hasn't mastered everything. She may have learned how to use some buttons and knobs on the cooker, but she still struggles with the door entry system. Other devices she ignores completely. The house burglar alarm, that Chuck solemnly said must be activated every night and every time we go out hasn't, as far as I know, ever been turned on. However, even Mum can remember the secret 123456 side-door entry code.

As the summer draws to a close, and my arrival at my new school looms, we often leave the house in Mum's sensible little car – a mere coastal patrol boat to Dad's battleship – and drive to favourite places by the sea, then pick our way across sand and rocks, cold water sloshing at our feet. When we are safely out of North Berwick, Mum can then take off her sunglasses. She only wears them for protection against other people's attention; she doesn't need them for the sun.

In Aberlady Bay, a nearby small village, scoured by a squally wind, is the wooden skeleton of an old sailing barge; further out, in shallow water, are the rusting hulks of two midget submarines. On one occasion, when the tide was out, I walked out to them with Dad. He said that they had attacked the Tirpitz, which was a big German battleship – even bigger than the Bentley.

When I asked him about this, clambering across the flaking superstructure, and wondering how sailors could have fitted inside, or if they used actual midget sailors, he admitted that he didn't know if it had been *these* actual submarines or just ones like them. He didn't know why they had ended up as scrap metal in the middle of a bird sanctuary. Mum, on the other hand, took no interest in the submarines. I doubted that she even knew they were there.

We walk round the bay and out to the headland. Here, Kilspindie golf course hugs the coastline, although there is a path between the rocky beach and the fairways. Mum, timid in most things, has no fear of golf courses. I don't think she understands that golf balls are hard and can travel at high speed. She dawdles along the pathway, oblivious to golfers waiting to tee off.

I stop and point. On a sandbank is a group of seals.

'They're always there,' says Mum, 'at least when the

tide's out. Then when the tide comes in, they go fishing and catch their lunch.'

'Stupid looking things,' I say.

'They're lovely, Emma,' says Mum. 'Don't be so silly.'

I used to think that East Lothian was made from golf courses, in the same way as Wales was made from coal and steel and Birmingham was made from cars. The fairways are 'as God made them', said my father once, instructing me on the Glen putting green, the only time he ever took me near a golf course.

I look inland. Over my shoulder is another golf course and, on the hillside by Gullane, another three courses. I think that it is nicer having golf courses and stupid-looking seals than steelworks and smoke.

'Your father's in New York again.' The way she says this, he might actually be in Rome, or playing golf just behind us.

'He's doing a film,' I remind her.

'And the rest,' she says sourly, biting her lip and then bumbling off again, bumbling briskly now, and smiling sadly at the sandbank on which the seals are clustered. They are brown and dappled-white and always huddle in the same spot. 'Gracious!' she then exclaims. 'What the fuck was that?'

A small white object has sailed over our heads and landed harmlessly in the sea. The seals have paid no attention. Mum, who shares their disinterest in golf, walks on oblivious, hunched into the west wind, but I can see that she has started to cry.

Suddenly she stops, a tear hanging from the end of her nose. 'I can't go on like this,' she says, her voice trembling.

'Like what?' I ask, mystified.

'Like this!'

She says it softly, almost stoically, and I slip my hand into hers and she gives me a hug. She is warm and soft, and we walk back to the car holding hands. It's parked, probably illegally, in the golf club's small car park, but Mum doesn't care. She's a radical anarchist when it comes to driving and believes that she should be allowed to park anywhere she chooses.

We stop in Gullane on the way home and have tea and chocolate cake in the village bakery. The man behind the counter speaks in a German accent which probably means, Mum says, that he is German. I think about the small submarines in Aberlady Bay and wonder if the German man knows about them, or whether he cares. Mum is laughing by the time we leave the bakery, normal humour restored. But I can understand her bouts of unhappiness. Our new home, with its pretensions and grandeur, marks us as a breed apart and Mum likes travelling with the herd.

Looking at it from a different perspective, there are two schools of thought about dark matter.

The first believes that the stuff is concentrated in brown dwarfs or black holes, and is made up of ordinary material, particles of matter that we know about, simply compressed under huge gravitational forces.

The second school believes that dark matter is both within us and around us and is made up of something else entirely – stuff we don't yet understand because, for all we know, it might be a hundred thousand times smaller than an electron.

My grandfather drew together all those strands of relativity theory, particle physics and quantum mechanics, and then added his own quirky genius. A different kind of universe, a universe in which nothing is quite as it seems: parallel universes filled with despair and hope, places of infinite change and rebirth where nothing quite disappears.

To Mum, our house represents a portal to a parallel dimension that she doesn't really want to occupy.

$$\frac{5\Omega_0(\cosh\eta - \eta)}{2R_r(1 - \Omega_0)} = 5$$

Scale factor for an open universe

It's my first day at my new school and I'm proudly wearing my new uniform for the first time. I twirl and pout in front of the big mirror in my room, as if on a catwalk, sizing up how I look. The blazer is a bit big, my skirt a bit long, and my shirt a bit loose around the neck. But nothing that could be considered a complete fashion fail, if school uniforms can be considered fashionable. My small backpack is filled with pencils, rubbers, a ruler, notepad, chocolate biscuits, a box of paper hankies, more pencils, and an apple. The apple is Mum's idea, although she knows I don't much like apples, so why she's put one in my bag I don't know.

Mum makes a great fuss of me: brushing my hair; making sure that I've got everything; dabbing at a speck of dirt on my shirt; and telling me over and over how grown-up I look. She even makes me a bacon roll for breakfast, which she only does on special occasions because she likes pigs and doesn't like cooking them. Mum says that pigs are very intelligent and make very good pets, although I'd much prefer a dog. Mum says that she's allergic to dogs, which I don't believe as she's always petting other people's dogs without sneezing. I just think that not having a pet gives her one less thing to worry about.

Mum then drives me to the school gates and waves me off. I take a deep breath and march in, following the uniformed tide of other children, all of whom are chatting and shouting at each other. I have nobody to chat to or shout at.

My first day passes in a bit of a blur. In a way, it's not

unlike my old school in Edinburgh. For a start, it's filled with kids my age – surprise, surprise – with teachers who are mostly old or ancient. It also has a bell that sounds exactly the same, and I quite enjoy its tyranny: how its punctuation marks time between classes, shepherding us between classrooms and subjects, between things we enjoy and things we would rather forget about. The school is quite big so that it's a bit difficult for me to find my way around, but I've been given a map of where everything is and manage to navigate without getting lost too often.

The day starts with assembly and a roll-call of who's here and who can't be bothered to come to school. When my name is called, I say 'Here, Miss' and am immediately aware of chairs scraping and lots of heads turning in my direction. North Berwick's jungle drums have obviously been busy during the summer although, cocooned behind bulletproof glass, I clearly haven't heard them. Feeling like a closely-scrutinised botanical specimen I turn bright pink and stare at my shoes.

In morning break, without anyone to talk to, I wander into the playground to eat my chocolate biscuits – and *maybe* the apple – and watch small boys play football on a fenced-off bit of the playground. There's a table-and-bench seating area in the playground and I sit by myself and watch the football match, although it's not clear who is on what team or where the goals are. It just seems like an exercise in running about and shouting.

'Hello,' says someone behind me. I turn to see a small girl with red hair who, strictly against regulations, isn't wearing a tie. She is smiling and I recognise her as someone from my new class. 'I'm Patsy.'

'I'm Emma,' I say.

'I know who you are,' she informs me. 'My mum fancies the pants off your dad. But maybe she's joking,' she adds, not looking convinced, and not seeming to care.

A lot of people fancy Dad, at least until they get to know

him. But maybe that's also being unfair. I don't say anything, then hold out my packet of chocolate biscuits.

She takes one and sits beside me. 'Why did you come here?' she asks. Strands of hair have blown across her face, and her nose is a mass of freckles.

'It's the local school,' I reply.

'No, I mean here. North Berwick.'

'Dad liked the house,' I say lamely.

Patsy takes another of my chocolate biscuits and devours it in a couple of bites. She points across the playground at a gaggle of other girls. 'See her with the long black hair? That's Georgia. Don't talk to her. She's a cow.' She points again. 'See her with the straggly mouse-coloured hair? That's Victoria, like the dead queen. Don't talk to her. She's also a cow.' She pauses. 'Actually, that part of the playground is moo central. They're all cows.'

I found myself warming to little Patsy with her freckles and red hair and unruly attitude. 'Is there anybody I *can* talk to?' I ask.

'Very few,' she says.

'Because it's my birthday next week,' I reply, feeling a sudden need to unburden myself, 'and I don't know who to invite to my party.'

'Me,' says Patsy, and with a wave disappears off into the throng, with chocolate biscuits in both hands. I'm reduced to eating the apple.

The last class of the day is with Miss Frobisher, the maths teacher. Unlike the old or antiquated teachers, Miss Frobisher doesn't look much older than the oldest pupils. She's written stuff on the blackboard, handed out books – my school bag now weighs a ton – and has explained what we'll be learning this term. As she warms to her subject, she stops speaking English and lapses into Mandarin or Punjabi, or into something mathematical that makes no sense whatsoever.

I am towards the front of the class, Patsy at the back;

when I look around, she seems to be asleep, but wakes up when the bell rings and is out the door before the bell has stopped ringing. The rest of us scrape back chairs and heap books into bags.

'Right, everyone sod off!' says Miss Frobisher, in a husky voice. 'Go somewhere else, learn something new! Actually, just go home. Except you, Emma. A word, please.'

The classroom door closes. Miss Frobisher has marched to the window and is lighting a cigarette. She inhales greedily, pluming smoke through the open window. After a couple of puffs, she then grinds out her half-smoked cigarette and throws the butt into the car park.

I know that some of the senior pupils are prefects who patrol the school to catch other pupils smoking. I wonder if there are teacher-prefects who patrol the school for smoking teachers. 'Thing is, I'd like a quick chat, if you don't mind.'

That's the trouble with teachers. They make requests like this sound as if we have a choice, which we don't. The bohemian Miss Frobisher doesn't wear a wedding ring, is wearing strange beads and drives a clapped-out 2CV Citröen. I'd seen her arrive in it at the start of the day and park it in the staff car park, the car looking both wonderful and ridiculous as only a 2CV can.

Miss Frobisher pulls out a chair and sits on the other side of my desk. She has a stack of exercise books in her hand that she sets down on the table. 'And how has your first day been, Emma? A marvellous and enriching experience? Perhaps the best day of your life?'

'It was OK,' I reply, not convinced that *marvellous* or *enriching* would describe it, and not sure how serious she's being.

'Well, "OK" is a start, I suppose.' She drums her fingers on her stack of exercise books for a moment. 'I gather you're related to someone rather well-known,' she then says, looking at me evenly. I lower my eyes to the desk which is covered with indecipherable squiggles and a pencil drawing of an erect penis.

'My Dad's an actor,' I tell her. Well, she must know that what with all those jungle drums.

'Is he indeed?' she says, making her eyes go all big and innocent looking. 'Actually, I didn't mean him.'

'Then I don't understand, Miss.'

'June, for God's sake! Let's give the "Miss" a miss, shall we? I mean your grandfather, assuming that Alberto Rossini *is* your grandfather?'

I nod rather uncertainly. I didn't know that anyone outside our family and a few spherical bastards had ever heard of him.

'I haven't actually read his theorem, you understand. I'm but a simple maths teacher. But my brother has. He's the clever sod in our family. Oxford University. He's a physics lecturer.'

I nod again. Over the years I've become good at nodding. I'm nearly as eloquent at nodding as my grandfather's moustache is at speaking in sign language.

'My brother thinks that your grandfather's name might one day be bracketed with John Lennon and Einstein. Please tell me you've heard of them! I was just wondering, as your maths teacher, if you might have inherited any of his arithmetical ability?'

I now see that the erect prick has little ink-blobs of stuff being squirted from it, presumably drawn by a giggling boy-idiot who thought it would be funny for the rest of us to see. 'I rather doubt it, Miss,' I say.

'June! The month after May!' She looks at me with her eyes half closed, a small smile playing at the edges of her mouth. 'In which case, you will be my special project for the year, Emma. It just wouldn't do for the granddaughter of an eminent scientist to fail her maths exams, now, would it?'

'I'll try not to,' I say, without much confidence.

'Incidentally, I thought your father's last film was crap. Now sod off somewhere else, Emma.' By the time I've

71

reached the door she is already back at the window, a lit cigarette in her hand, and drumming her red fingernails on the window ledge.

Mum is waiting for me outside the school gates and is surrounded by several other mothers who, like hyenas, all seem to want to devour her. *How do they know who she is*, I wonder? They're all talking to her at once and Mum is gamely trying to smile and engage in several simultaneous conversations. Mum, as always, looks like a million dollars. Mum sees me and waves, extricates herself from her tormentors, and ushers me quickly towards her car which is partly parked on the pavement and mostly on a pedestrian crossing.

'From now on, Emma,' she immediately says, once we're safely inside and buckling up seatbelts, and before she's even asked me how my first day has been, 'I will either meet you further down the road or leave you to walk home. I do not want to go through that again.' She looks in the rear-view mirror, just in case the hyenas are snarling and whooping and giving chase.

It turns out that she's already been asked to join the Parent-Teacher Association and, being a parent, has felt obliged to accept. But, in the mêlée outside the school, she's also been asked to be honorary chairperson of something else and didn't really hear what she was being asked to be chairperson of, or if she's said 'yes'. It happens to her sometimes. Her mind just goes blank, thoughts and words wafting around her head and then drifting from her ears.

Mum's worried that she might inadvertently now be in charge of the North Berwick & District Paedophile Society, or something worse. It turned out that she hadn't said 'yes', but hadn't said 'no' either, so the Pottery Club assumed that she meant 'yes', which amounts to the same thing. She did attend a couple of their throw-downs, an expression that neither of us had heard of before, coming home with a well-turned if rather wonky bowl, with only a couple of small cracks, and decorated with painted flowers nicely arranged in a vase: Mum's presidential way of neatly killing two birds with one stone.

From then on, I generally walked home after school.

I've not been looking forward to my birthday party because, despite Patsy's warnings, I've invited everyone in my class, including 'the moo brigade' which, according to Patsy, sums up virtually everyone. Strangely, Patsy is very popular at school, with her impish charm, and complete disdain for rules and regulations. She's not part of any particular group, and therefore doesn't seem to have best friends or worst enemies. I just didn't know who not to invite, and I don't want to store up trouble. As the new girl in town, my strategy is to be friends with everyone, or at least to try.

Some of my old friends from Edinburgh have also been invited although I no longer think of them as friends. Funny how people can so quickly fade from affection and memory. Only a couple have been down to North Berwick since we moved in and it felt a bit awkward, as if I didn't know them anymore, and we didn't know what to say to one another. I showed them the dolls and soft toys of my younger childhood, now safe in the panic room. They didn't laugh, as I thought they would. They hadn't seen a panic room before and didn't know such a thing existed.

More positively, Mum, Mrs Perkins and Mrs Boyce have been doing a lot of baking in anticipation of the party. The three of them get along like a house on fire – hopefully not literally – and our home has, for days and days, been filled with cake smells and the incessant whirr of extractor fans.

I should be more excited than I am, except that I've invited a bunch of people I've barely met, most of whom already think of me as a bit of a freak because nobody, including me, can understand why we we're in North Berwick and not Palm Beach or Los Angeles. That said, most of them are friendly enough to the freak – me – if only to have the chance of meeting Dad.

The teachers, except Miss Frobisher, also regard me as a freak, although a very delicate freak. A Ming porcelain freak, and they keep a wary eye on my every move. If I ever take up smoking, it would be impossible to light up on school grounds. I would be discovered in a nanosecond, if not sooner. I sometimes feel that binoculars and telescopes are trained on me from every direction, and particularly from the staff common room. Even the school cat has taken to following me along corridors, its erect tail hiding a secret transmitter that signals my precise whereabouts. How have they trained it to do that?

I cut my knee playing hockey this week, and I know that angry questions were asked of the PE teacher as to why I hadn't been swaddled from head to toe in cotton wool. Basically, for most of them, I just shouldn't be here. ACTOR'S DAUGHTER SLIGHTLY CUTS KNEE PLAYING HOCKEY. PRIME MINISTER DEMANDS POLICE ACTION. I can see their point of view: I should be at a posh school that has more experience of dealing with the offspring of the rich and famous.

To be honest, it's probably the only time that Mum has ever won out over my father. She wanted to keep me close, and she wanted me to have a normal schooling, like she had. I don't suppose it made any sense to Dad but, as it didn't impact on his career, and might even reflect well on him as a 'man of the people', he acceded to it readily enough. Frankly, I don't think he much cared where – or if – I went to school.

The invitations were printed off Mum's computer which sits in her new study on the first floor. Now that Mum is Honorary President of virtually everything in town, she feels that she needs her own space – somewhere to read the minutes of previous meetings and correspond with other office bearers. It's a peaceful room that overlooks the beach. No nudist sunbathing here or, for most of the year, no sunbathing of any sort.

Her new study also has a bookcase (one book: *Flower Arranging for Dummies*), a couch for quiet contemplation and a picture of me taken on our French holiday. I'm wearing a cream sun dress and eating an ice cream; a little blob of it is stuck to my nose. I'm laughing at the camera, and Mum was laughing as well when she took the picture.

In the background is a town square with tables and chairs and people sipping beers from under striped awnings. I look at the picture and remember the throb of cars going round the square, the smell of fruit from a nearby market, the oppressive heat, and the vanilla ice cream that mostly melted down my hand. (I wonder if Mum would notice if I swapped this photograph with the alien-blob picture on the living room mantelpiece.)

The party invitations helpfully suggest: "If you have a tennis racquet, bring it with you!!" This has probably alerted even the most stupid kids in my class, and there are a few, that we either have a tennis court or a deranged sense of humour. Still, it means I can finally get on the Wimbledon ladder.

Mum has already bought "tennis bats" and balls from the town's sports shop but playing with Mum hasn't been a success. Although she can move about the court with surprising speed, she too often lapses into bumble-mode and trips up; she's also not very good at hitting the ball over the net. She either hits it into the net ("Fuck!") or over the high surrounding chain-link fence onto the lawn ("Shit! Fuck!")

I haven't therefore had much practice, as Dad hasn't been around. He's filming in London, although he has faithfully promised to be back for my birthday. So far, there's no sign of him and Mum keeps looking at the big clock in the kitchen and tapping her foot, faster and faster.

First to arrive is Auntie Fran, Mum's sister, churning up the driveway in a fancy sports car that she's hired for the week. She's a year younger than Mum, but could only be

Mum's sister, because they look almost the same; she's also tall with dark hair and feline eyes and is strikingly beautiful. But not quite as beautiful as Mum, although maybe I'm biased; Aunt Fran looks like someone who needs to preen; she's constantly brushing her hair, or looking at herself in mirrors to check her make-up.

Mum doesn't preen, doesn't look in mirrors and doesn't need make-up. Mum looks beautiful first thing in the morning, and last thing at night, and doesn't need potions and creams. Beside Mum, Aunt Fran looks a little manufactured, like a Mr Kipling cake.

By now, Mum has partially mastered the door entry systems, but has decided that, for today at least, we'll simply leave the wrought-iron gates and the front door open. If terrorists or kidnappers chance by, at least we'll outnumber them. A police car regularly drives past, keeping a close eye on our front gates, driven by the father of a girl in my class, one of the bovines, and I expect he's got nothing better to do. There's not much crime in North Berwick.

If Mum has been given the best of the beauty genes, Fran's been given the brain genes. She's a deputy editor on *The New Yorker* and spends her time flitting around the USA – and other bits of the world – interviewing politicians, artists and social commentators. She's very clever, although you wouldn't know it, because when she gets together with Mum they talk rubbish to one another, laughing like adolescents. As an adolescent, I'm *allowed* to laugh like that, but Mum and Fran's laughter would make a vicar blush.

But I also like to hear Mum laugh, because she doesn't laugh very much and, lately, very rarely. For someone so prudish, except for her swearing, she has a very dirty laugh. A copy of Fran's magazine regularly arrives in our letter box, and Mum dutifully reads it, or pretends to. Dad flicks through it, if he's around, and makes grunting sounds, which he sometimes does if he's bored.

Fran used to be married to a film producer that Dad

76

knows vaguely, but no longer sees. He didn't want to move with Fran to New York, being quite happy at the BBC, so that was that. Fran doesn't have children. She says that she's married to her job, which must be nice because you don't have to cook the job supper or share a bathroom with it. Actually, it was Fran who said that, but wistfully, as if she misses her husband just a little bit but doesn't want to admit it. She's in the UK to see friends, stay with us for a few days, and meet a variety of political leaders – to 'get a sense of the special relationship from this side of the pond,' as she put it.

Mum takes Fran for a quick tour of the house, both sisters screaming with laughter at nothing in particular, and then they make their way to the sauna of the kitchen where final preparations are under way. Cakes and little sandwich triangles are being loaded onto plates. There are biscuits – none shop bought! – sausage rolls, sausages, crisps, and slices of pizza from our very own pizza oven! It amounts to a feast of gargantuan size and both Mrs Boyce and Mrs Perkins are sweating profusely, even with the French windows open.

In case you're wondering, Mum's pots of herbs are doing rather well on the patio, although that could be down to the attentions of Mr Perkins who regularly waters them and sprinkles on plant food. I can see him now as I wait for my first guests to arrive. He's bent over a distant flower bed which probably means that he's weeding. Mr Perkins spends a lot of time weeding.

Aunt Fran has bought me a beautiful gold watch for my birthday, and I clip it on, watched indulgently by Mum, her sister, and Mum's little helpers who seem to be more excited about the party than I am. Mrs Boyce is particularly taken by my watch and grasps my arm and twists it in different directions – some rather painful – so she can see it from different angles. The kitchen is Mrs Boyce's domain: even my mother is only allowed in the kitchen on sufferance, with Mrs Boyce keeping a close eye on everything Mum does, so that Mum gets nervous and leaves, often without doing what she originally came into the kitchen to do.

But my birthday seems to have changed that dynamic, with Mum and her staff all laughing and joking, and Fran making it a quartet, with cakes and sandwiches now being carried to the big refectory table that dominates one end of the kitchen. Mum and Fran are also drinking large gin and tonics.

Patsy is the first proper guest to arrive – Fran doesn't count – slightly out of breath, having run most of the way. I'm not sure if Patsy has learned how to walk yet, or simply finds it more convenient to travel at warp speed. She has a towel over one shoulder and hands me an empty box of chocolates. She explains that she was peckish on the way over and ate them, but that the empty box might come in useful and 'if you have to write thank-you letters, you'll know what I gave you,' and then, remembering, wishes me a happy birthday.

She has a look round our large hallway and tells me that it's probably bigger than her whole house. She then sees the red squiggle picture and squints uncertainly at it, much as I had done. 'It's Art,' I tell her. 'The artist used his own blood.' Patsy doesn't seem to find this gross, nods in an appreciative way and then strips off her T-shirt to reveal a pink bikini top. 'Right,' she says, 'where's the swimming pool?'

It takes me some time to convince an incredulous Patsy that we don't actually have a swimming pool because, as she says, 'everyone thinks that you do.' I try to explain that it doesn't really matter what people think because thinking it won't make a swimming pool magically appear. 'But you do have a tennis court?' she asks, looking doubtful.

By now, other guests have arrived – some also with towels, and a few with towels and tennis racquets – most of whom have come with at least one parent. You'd think we lived miles and miles out in the country, rather than at the edge of a small town. One has brought both parents *and* a set of grandparents, as if my birthday party is a family day out.

Rather than just drop their offspring at the end of the drive, most are now inside our house and itching to have a good look around. Mrs Perkins, perhaps wisely, has discreetly positioned herself with a tray of soft drinks at the bottom of the stairs to prevent any incursions upstairs.

Mum and Fran appear from the kitchen, looking almost identical in blue jeans, long dark hair, and cream polo shirts. The audience in our hallway, momentarily confused, doesn't know who to say 'hello' to first. Which is the famous actor's wife, and which is the irrelevant imposter? Mum thrusts her hand out to the closest person, one of the hyenas I remember from the school gates on my first day. 'I'm Cat,' she says, with her best smile, and everyone breathes a sigh of relief. Fran can now be safely ignored.

Soon everyone is in the kitchen, mostly drinking tea or Coke, although Mum and Fran are still swigging back gin and tonic. Mum's dirty laugh can be heard all over the house, making everyone wonder who is telling her filthy jokes. Mrs Boyce is kept busy at the pizza oven – the pizzas have gone down extremely well, and who else in North Berwick has a pizza oven? The pizzas have smoothed out some of the non-swimming pool disappointment.

A few of the mothers have already been on a close kitchen inspection, mentally noting the fancy Italian names on our appliances – no doubt for Google price searches later – and marvelling at the opulence of it all. Several mothers have also been on a tour of our garden – maybe searching for elusive fountains, rainforests or waterfalls – and are now sitting on chairs on the patio. I find their behaviour extremely rude because they haven't actually been invited, but Mum doesn't seem to care, now pouring herself and Fran another large gin and cackling at something her sister has said.

It's a very warm day, unseasonably so, and several mothers have removed brown and sage green coats to expose their most clingy and revealing summer dresses in anticipation, no doubt, of seducing Dad and then living in

Hollywood. But I can also see how they look at Mum, and how they now privately realise how utterly beautiful she is, and how they couldn't possibly compete with a creature of such slightly-pissed perfection. 'So, why did I put this dress on anyway?' they're probably all thinking. How could their wobbly bits possibly be as attractive as Mum's non-wobbly bits.

It's all down to attraction, I think, which I've never understood because I don't understand why Mum and Dad got together. Did she discover something about Dad that's so awful that he had to marry her to shut her up? Does she do things to him in the bedroom that nobody else will? I don't like to think about this, although it's entirely plausible.

Maybe Gramps could explain it to me, if I ever dared to ask him, because in his book he discusses the strange science of attraction. The example he gives is the Great Attractor. It lies millions and millions of miles away, but nobody has yet figured out what it is because it sits in what Granddad terms the 'zone of avoidance' – which is a clever way of saying that the rest of our own galaxy is blocking our view of it.

The Great Attractor is important to Gramps because it's such a gravitational anomaly. Lots of galaxies in the area are being attracted to it, without even having been properly introduced.

It gets worse. According to Gramps, hundreds of thousands of galaxies, including the Great Attractor, are also being pulled towards something even more attractive, which astronomers call the Shapley Supercluster.

It contains more than eight thousand galaxies and has a mass of more than ten million billion suns and is – apparently – the biggest galaxy cluster within a billion light years. The bad news, like it or not, is that Earth, our Milky Way and every other galaxy in our small corner of the universe are all travelling to meet it – at over two million kilometres per hour. That's faster than Dad drives, and that's saying something.

It's all down to either dark matter or dark energy, the pheromones of the cosmic kingdom, because the stuff we can see – all those galaxies! – makes up only about five per cent of the universe. It kind of sums up Dad as well, and why normally sensible women feel compelled to wear revealing dresses and their very best underwear on the off-chance that they'll meet the great attractor.

$$\frac{9}{4\pi G\rho}\left(H_0^2 + \frac{kc^2}{R^2}\right) = 6$$

Friedmann equation

A few of us then play tennis, while everyone else lounges on the grass. Fran is in charge of music, a task she takes seriously, which is blaring from speakers in the living room, with the windows open. It's therefore impossible to be anywhere near the living room, otherwise your ears would bleed. Fran is surprisingly good at knowing all about contemporary music – well, being 'cultural', it's her job – and everyone on the grass seems happy with her choices.

I'm paired up with Georgia – 'Black-Haired Cow' – with Patsy paired up with Vicky – 'Mouse-Haired Cow'. It turns out that Patsy is good friends with both of them, and just likes to be rude about people behind their backs. By now, I'm probably 'Rich Cow' or 'Rich Bitch'. Black Cow turns out to be very good at tennis, with a commanding serve that even *looks* like a proper serve – she's had lessons – and which usually wins us the points without any needless return of serve or volleying. I'm mediocre at best – Wimbledon dreams slowly fading – but Patsy is even worse than Mum, and after each game we have to search the flower beds for balls that she's managed to knock out of the court.

Mouse Cow tries her best to make up for Patsy's ineptitude, but Black Cow and I win handsomely. I then decide to do some mingling and leave them to another game. A few others have also drifted to the tennis court, so a tournament of some sort looks inevitable.

Back in the kitchen, insulated from the music that is still blasting from the living room speakers, Mum and Fran are at the refectory table holding half-empty glasses. Several other mums and one dad are at the other end of the table, not entirely sure why they're still there, but determined to stay on until the elusive Paul Ross makes an appearance.

Mum has said that he's due back at any time, which she shouldn't have said, because it's glued the gawkers to their seats. When I venture into the living room, there's a very old person – probably female – asleep in an armchair. I'm not sure who it belongs to, or why it's there, but I assume it's deaf. It's wearing trousers, sensible shoes and has short hair, so it's difficult to tell what species of old person it is. These days, earrings are no more than a guide.

I'm just wandering back to the kitchen when I come across Oz. He's looking at a painting in our hallway – not the blood-squiggle.

He's a bit of an enigma, according to Patsy, because he keeps to himself, except when he plays rugby when he becomes a monster – again according to Patsy. Standing in our hallway, with a can of Fanta in one hand, he doesn't look much like an enigma or a monster. He has furrowed eyebrows, as if from too much frowning and long piano-playing fingers.

'A Picasso print,' he says, indicating the painting in front of him. It's full of strange shapes, with eyes and mouths in odd places. I haven't really studied it before, and we both stare at the picture for a few moments, trying to figure out which mouth goes with which eyes. I hadn't seen Picasso's signature on it either. 42 out of 50, the label at the bottom says. 'At least he signed it,' I say eventually.

'So did a lot of other people,' he replies with a small shrug and apologetic smile. 'Happy birthday, by the way.'

On the hallway table is a stack of birthday cards that I haven't opened yet. Patsy is the only person to have brought me a present, even if it was an empty box. But I hadn't expected any presents, being the Rich Bitch, and would have been embarrassed if anybody had brought one. The birthday cards will go up on the mantelpiece and temporarily obscure the blob-alien photograph.

I'm about to walk away when he suddenly says, 'I can see you, you know.'

I stop, confused. 'See me?'

'On the beach,' says Oz. 'You go there nearly every evening.'

I don't say anything. I know that other houses overlook the beach but didn't think that anybody would be watching.

'We're almost neighbours,' he now says, and gestures with his can of Fanta. 'We live two houses down, in the poor part of the neighbourhood.' He smiles again, a little embarrassed. 'Why do you do that?' he asks. 'Just stand there. By yourself.'

'None of your business, Oz.'

'Temper, temper.'

I'm not sure why he's irritated me, but I'm distracted by two small children – who the hell do *they* belong to? – who are trying to feed cake to Romulus and Remus. The two stone lions, noble and stoic, don't seem to like cake, and marzipan and icing are stuck to their faces. 'Maybe I just like the sea,' I say eventually.

He's looking at me with his head to one side, and I'm not sure whether he's being enigmatic or monsterish. He doesn't look like either; just inquisitive. Strangely, his gaze makes me feel a bit gooey inside.

'Sorry,' I say brightly, turning for the front door, and stepping over the unidentified small children, who might simply have wandered in off the beach and through our open gates, with anxious parents now scouring the shoreline and desperately phoning the coastguard. 'I'd better see how the tennis tournament is going.'

Not well is the answer. A sizeable crowd is now gathered around the perimeter of the fence, with much catcalling and witty banter. A few boys are throwing a Frisbee. Someone is snogging Black Cow but, because her hair has blown forwards and across their faces, I can't see who the lucky boy is. I feel a touch of jealousy; nobody has even tried to snog me, not that I would have let them. A few others are laid out flat in bikinis, having tried and failed to locate our swimming pool. Mr Perkins is still weeding a flower bed, oblivious to everything. Patsy and an oafish boy called Lance are playing two of the many cows.

'Deuce,' says Patsy.

'It's not deuce, it's forty-love.'

'It's deuce,' says Patsy, more firmly.

'How the hell can it be deuce! You haven't won any points.'

'That's not important.' Patsy seems quite sure about this.

'That is *precisely* the point,' says Mouse Cow, exasperated, and marches off the court, handing her racquet to someone else. Patsy does a little victory dance, as if she's just won the match which, by default, I realise, she probably has.

Back in the kitchen, most of the hangers-on have left, having eaten their fill of free sandwiches, pizza and biscuits and finally admitting defeat in the hope of meeting Dad. Mum and Fran, however, are made of sterner stuff and are still at full throttle, still at the refectory table, with Fran talking loudly about a US senator who dared to make a lewd suggestion. 'He had the imprint of my hand on his face for a week,' she finishes, as Mum starts cackling.

Mrs Boyce and Mrs Perkins are at the other end of the kitchen, also gossiping but quietly, having only drunk tea. The old person in the living room seems to have vanished, leaving only a small wet patch on the armchair cushion. Romulus has an upended ice-cream cone stuck on his head and looks rather jaunty.

Then pretty soon everyone has gone, and the wrought-iron gates have closed. I've waved everyone off and thanked them for coming, and I think that almost everyone has had a good time. All in all, it's been quite a grown-up party, without any tantrums or fights – or none that I saw – and no doubt will be a source of delicious gossip for weeks to come.

All traces of the party also seem to have vanished. The kitchen floor has been mopped, plates retrieved from the garden, and Mum has even walked erratically to the tennis court to retrieve balls and tennis bats. The stone lions have had their faces washed and are once again looking menacing.

I have eaten far too much cake – which was delicious, one of Mum's finest – and can't stop burping (too much Coke). The sun is low in the sky and I'm wondering what to do when the driveway gates open and a familiar Bentley noses its way in. Dad has also brought Granny and Gramps with him, and Alberto, as always, kisses the stone lions.

Mum and Fran are asleep in the living room; Mum stretched out on a sofa, her shoes kicked off, and Fran in the chair recently vacated by the old person, her jeans no doubt mopping up residual spillage.

Dad kisses me and winks. He must have known the fuss that the party would cause and with rare consideration has kept well clear. He wanted me to be the centre of attention and for a few moments I'm grateful, then realise that it doesn't really matter: even by not being here, Dad was still the centre of attention.

After a decent interval, Mum and Fran are woken up; both come into the kitchen wearing sunglasses and not looking well. Dad pours everyone champagne, including me, the Perkins duet and Mrs Boyce. This is uncharted waters for Mum's little helpers who don't quite know whether they're employees or guests and end up being neither; nervously sipping their champagne and grinning inanely at one another.

Dad has also bought me a gold watch, having failed to listen to Mum, who had told him repeatedly – according to her – that Fran was buying me a watch. Dad doesn't seem to care. 'Can't have too many of them,' he says with another wink.

Mrs Boyce conjures up roast chicken and salad and

we all sit around the giant kitchen table consuming more champagne. After a few glasses, Mum and Fran perk up and take off their sunglasses and start cackling again. The little helpers also loosen up and Mr Perkins discusses gardening tips with Mum, who tries to look interested, while Mrs Boyce discusses the iniquities of British foreign policy with Fran who looks bored.

I tell Gramps about my chat with Miss Frobisher and how he might one day become another John Lennon or Einstein. He laughs and leans back alarmingly in his chair. 'We'll see,' he says, 'and then maybe I'll find out if I really am spherical.' He doesn't say 'bastard' because he knows that Mrs Boyce is quite religious and can barely tolerate Mum's bad language. He says this quite loudly and everyone is now looking at him, mesmerised by his moustache which is curling happily towards his ears.

'Or whether you're macho or a wimp,' I suggest.

'That as well!' he booms. 'You've actually read my book, Emma?'

'It's gibberish, Gramps. I've only looked at the pictures.'

Basically, there are two schools of thought. Some astronomers think that dark matter is concentrated in brown dwarfs or black holes. These are termed as Massive Astrophysical Compact Halo Objects, with the acronym MACHOs, which makes them sound like a tasty snack. Or, like my grandfather and other particle physicists, you believe that dark matter is both within and around us and takes the form of Weakly Interacting Massive Particles, or WIMPs, although to describe them as 'massive' is, of course, utterly misleading.

The WIMP theory is interesting because it does, in part, explain our very existence. If the Big Bang actually did happen, and nobody was around at the time to witness it, then the entire universe started off as a singularity made up from space, time and energy and which then, magically and instantaneously, became the universe.

Incidentally, physicists hate the term 'Big Bang' because it suggests that the universe started off as a blob of stuff which then blew up, which it didn't, but which is what I'd always thought, and which is why I'll never be a cosmologist.

Although not universally accepted, the Big Bang theory explains a great deal. But it doesn't explain the formation of stars and galaxies because, as we now know, the universe is expanding at a faster and faster rate. Something had to be supplying the gravity for all that space junk to get together and form the universe as we know it.

For Gramps it wasn't enough that dark matter and dark energy were the culprits; the answer had to lie beyond our own universe, in parallel existences, in other universes of space and time, in places that dwarf our own meagre galaxy and render us meaningless.

Gramps abruptly leans forwards and plants his elbows on the table. 'There are a few astronomers who are now taking an interest,' he concedes, then grins.

The three little helpers are looking at him blankly. Dad has turned his chair around and is looking out the window, engrossed in thoughts that don't include his family. Granny is looking pensively at Alberto, but it's hard to tell what she's thinking. Mum and Fran have their heads together and are twittering about god-knows-what. 'Early days, Gramps,' I say. 'Early days.'

After supper, Mr and Mrs Perkins and Mrs Boyce exit by the Top Secret 123456 gate, and Mum, Fran and Dad decide that a bottle of brandy needs to be drunk. Granny and Gramps take themselves upstairs, to leave 'the young ones' to it, although that could be a euphemism for not wanting to spend any more time with their very inebriated daughter-in-law and her sister.

After all the champagne, Dad is once again looking predatory, casting an eye between his wife and her sister, perhaps wondering whether he chose the right one and who, given the chance, he would like to invite to his bed. In his films, Dad has done quite a lot of inviting, and always to women who can't wait to get their clothes off, sometimes striding naked into his arms, with Mum making growling noises and demanding to know 'if anything actually did bloody go on, Paul!'

In the dim light of the living room, to which we've moved, it's a little hard to tell the two women apart. But Mum, of course, is looking radiant, if quite drunk, and Fran's make-up is looking a little tarnished around the edges. Dad hands round generous measures of brandy in crystal goblets and is about to sit down when he suddenly pauses and looks over my shoulder.

'And who the hell might you be?' he asks in his commanding voice, the one that carries over the stalls, the grand balcony and up to the cheap seats at the top.

'Sorry,' says Patsy, who is standing uncertainly in the doorway and still optimistically carrying her towel. 'I fell asleep upstairs.'

Mum ushers her to the kitchen and fixes her a chicken sandwich, and they phone Patsy's parents to reassure them that she hasn't been abducted. Mum still doesn't know if she's chairperson of that particular society, if it exists – or drowned in our Olympic-sized swimming pool, and then Patsy rejoins the rest of the brandy brigade in the living room, her big eyes and freckled nose pointed at Dad. 'You're not as tall in real life,' she informs him between mouthfuls.

'That's what they all say,' replies Dad, who has heard that particular line many times.

Patsy nods. 'Mum also quite fancies you,' she now says. 'But I think she fancies Sean Connery more.'

'That's also what they all say!' cackle Mum and Fran in unison and everyone except Dad laughs. Mentioning Sean Connery is not a good thing to do because Dad is slipping in the World's Sexiest Men charts while Sean Connery is still in the Top Ten, although Dad's antipathy really dates from

The Hunt for Red October when he'd been tipped to play the lead role but, for some reason, didn't get it.

Sean Connery is not therefore someone that Dad likes to hear mentioned because 'who's ever heard of a Russian submarine captain speaking in a Scottish accent?' Dad would have studied Russian and learned every nuance of accent and intonation. He was therefore a bit miffed, and likes to bear grudges, and was even more miffed when the film was a huge success.

A bit later, the level in the brandy bottle rapidly falling, Fran suggests playing a game of charades, which Patsy hasn't played before, so the rules have to be explained to her by Mum, who is too drunk by now to explain anything lucidly. Fran is also very inebriated, and so doesn't bother to help Mum, while Dad, lolling in his chair and grinning broadly, is enjoying his wife's inarticulate attempts at English too much to intervene.

Patsy is therefore left none the wiser about the intricacies of charades. It doesn't really matter anyway because the phone rings, and Dad answers it, and then disappears to his study, and Fran yawns, says that she's tired, and immediately falls asleep. Mum takes Patsy's empty plate and totters to the kitchen where we hear her drop the plate, hear it smash, and hear Mum swear very loudly.

It appears also that Patsy has been asked to spend the night with us, which is nice because I haven't had a friend to stay in our new house yet but when we go upstairs it isn't clear where Patsy is to sleep, or if there's anybody sober enough to sort out sleeping arrangements, so she sleeps in my bed, which is very big. As always, I open the window and we lie under the covers and stare quietly at the ceiling and listen to the soft breathing of the sea.

As Christmas approaches, the unseasonably good weather is replaced by seasonally cold weather. Normal climatic service resumed, the school's heating system clanks into life, teachers start wearing jerseys or cardigans under their jackets and the school cat has stopped following me about. I search him out and find him asleep under a radiator, his radio antenna curled up and, presumably, switched off. I conclude that MI5 now has better people to follow.

On Friday lunchtime after school, I walk home through the town, intending to buy a baguette from Greggs and eat it on the beach. There are angry clouds on the horizon and a tugging west wind is bringing them closer. Winter is setting in, the trees scrubbed of leaves; soon there will be storms, with great waves hitting the harbour walls. This is when the sea will sound primeval, wild and untamed, exuberant. I've always liked the not-quite winter before Christmas, when the days are short, and the air feels full of ice.

To my right is the Scottish Seabird Centre, another reason to come to North Berwick apart from golf courses, beaches and charity shops. In it you can play with toggles, like on a computer game, and control cameras on the Bass and the other smaller islands, and zoom in and out on a particular puffin or gannet. I've always liked puffins, with their clown faces and stripy beaks, and the way they live in burrows, like rabbits, seemingly not quite sure whether they're birds or should be performing in a circus.

I'd never really liked gannets; they looked big and fierce, like seagulls on steroids, with angry eyes. We went to the Seabird Centre on a school outing, and I suggested that its small café should attach sniper rifles to the cameras so that people could choose their gannet, shoot it, and then have it for lunch. In the old days, I know that people did eat gannets, although I don't suppose they tasted very nice. I also know that Queen Victoria liked to eat their eggs, which seems a bit odd considering that gannets aren't posh. I'd have thought that queens would only eat peacock or eagle eggs.

A few people laughed at my sniper rifle suggestion, but not Mrs Dove, our teacher, who even looks like a dove with grey and white hair and corpulent stomach. She told us that gannets return each year to the Bass to nest with their partner from the year before. They're faithful to each other for life, she said. I then decided that, despite looking angry and fierce, they must also be quite nice birds, and I started liking them and not wanting to find out how they tasted.

Mrs Dove isn't the only teacher with an appropriate name. We also have a Mrs French, although, disappointingly, she teaches German; a Mr Hill, who teaches geography; and a Mrs Lamb who teaches domestic science. I wonder about people's names sometimes, and if they can influence what you do in life. My own name, Rossini, comes from the Italian for 'red' but doesn't really signify anything.

'Hey, Emma.'

It's a cliché, but it's true. I nearly jump out of my skin and then my heart misses a beat.

'Oz! God, you gave me a fright!'

He seems to have materialised from nowhere.

'Sorry about that.'

'Ditto,' I say, because I've seen *Ghost*, and that's what the man and wife say to one another, even when one of them is dead. I'd liked the film, but didn't like the thought of ghosts suddenly appearing, particularly if I was in the loo.

'You don't happen to have the time, do you?'

I look at my watch, the one that Fran gave me, because it's the one that I usually now wear. Dad's watch is a little too fancy and a little too expensive to wear on schooldays. 'Nearly two,' I say.

Oz's real name is Mike Clarke, but he was born in Australia, so everyone calls him Oz. He doesn't seem to mind or, if he does, knows that it's too late to do anything about it. Sadly, you don't get to choose your own nickname. 'Train to catch,' he says. 'Thanks, Emma.'

'That's what watches are for, Oz.'

'Big game tomorrow. You coming to watch?'

Oz is the star of his rugby team and I've watched him play a couple of times. 'Might do,' I reply. 'Who's it against?'

92

'Bunch of posh Edinburgh bastards,' he says, clearly uncertain what team the posh Edinburgh bastards actually play for.

'Nice name for a team,' I suggest.

'Anyway, maybe see you,' he says and ambles off. The next train isn't for ages and ages so he can afford to amble.

I walk slowly into town, meandering slowly towards Greggs. A car horn flutters a pigeon into the air, towards the cloud nine on which I am floating. I have now spoken to Oz twice and find that my abdomen is making unusual gurgling sounds, although that might just be hunger pangs. I've never really thought about boys before, because most of them are smelly and think that farting is funny and draw silly pictures on desks and walls.

But Oz isn't smelly and, despite his long fingers, isn't good at drawing. I know this, I'm in art class with him. His useless efforts, worse than mine, deserve to hang in our hallway. I don't suppose that Mum or Dad would notice if I substituted a bit of crap Oz art for the Picasso print.

If someone had actually told me that my dinosaur Rolex didn't have a battery inside, and that it needed to be wound up, things might have turned out differently.

Unusually for him, Dad has been at home for a few weeks, ever since arriving at the tail end of my birthday party. But being at home for long periods doesn't suit him; after a few rounds of golf, several visits to restaurants in North Berwick and Edinburgh, having Ronnie Corbett and his wife round for supper, and lying in every morning, he's now bored. Forced inactivity makes him crotchety, and although he has no filming commitments, he needs to be doing something useful, which can only involve *not* being at home. Dad therefore disappeared off to the airport this morning, presumably to catch a flight to London, so that he can be bored somewhere else.

That evening, Mum and I are in the living room, having

eaten Mrs Boyce's lasagne, which was nearly as good as Granny's. I'm watching a film on TV, although I haven't really been paying attention and don't know who the goodies or baddies are. To complicate things, several good guys have turned out to be bad guys in disguise and are now planning a missile attack on a US army base that might be in America or the Middle East. I'm not really sure where Nevada is.

Mum's been reading a novel, lying lengthways along a cream sofa, with a glass of white wine on a small table within easy reach. Uncoiling herself, she closes her book with a snap, drains her glass and stands up. 'Right, that's me off to bed,' she announces. 'Probably time you were as well,' she adds.

'Tomorrow's Saturday,' I remind her. Having very little to do, Mum isn't very good at keeping track of days.

'So it is,' she says, retrieving her shoes from under the coffee table and carrying her empty glass through to the kitchen. When she reappears I am idly flicking through her book.

'Why do you read this stuff?' I ask. It's an old paperback by Jackie Collins, whoever she is. The front cover seems from a bygone era, with a picture of a man and women dressed in out-of-style clothes. The man is wearing a sports jacket and is smoking a cigarette. The woman has a bouffant hairstyle, a party dress and elbow-length white gloves. In the background is a city street, with big old-fashioned cars. The book's pages look well-thumbed, with crinkled yellow edges.

'Because it reminds me of when I was young,' replies Mum with a smile. 'Before I became a wife and mother, and all that stuff. Before I met your father, of course. You wouldn't like it,' she adds.

'Were you happy then?' I ask. 'I mean, before you met Dad.'

'Good gracious, that's a question and a half! Yes, of

course, I was!'

'Happier than now?' I persist, remembering our walk round Aberlady Bay.

'No, of course not! Life is what you make it, Emma. I'm happy now, and I was happy then. It's just become a different kind of happiness,' she says, her face in profile. 'For starters, I've got you now, haven't I? Whatever made you ask that?'

'Nothing really.'

Her book certainly looks well-loved, with its battered cover and its depiction of people old enough to have walked with velociraptors. I don't bother asking her why I wouldn't like it. The man on the cover doesn't look like a spy, and the woman, looking at him coyly over a cocktail glass - in the street, for God's sake! – seems either to be simpering or simple-minded. I doubt whether it will have guns or double-agents or anything interesting.

'You're right, I probably wouldn't enjoy it,' I concede, returning my gaze to the TV. A bomb has just detonated, or it might have been a missile. Dead bodies litter the TV screen, but whether they are goodie or baddie bodies is hard to tell.

'Then goodnight,' she says, bending to kiss the top of my head. She half-turns, then pauses. 'Love you,' she adds.

I nod. 'Ditto.'

'Then I'll see you in the morning,' Mum says.

I hear her climb the stairs, her footsteps soft and measured, and then across the upper hallway to her bedroom. On the TV, one of the good guys – maybe – has broken into the evil warlord's secret laboratory and accidentally knocked over a test tube.

Inexplicably, this small and insignificant accident is now threatening to engulf the whole laboratory complex in flames. There are more explosions, with lab technicians being blown over railings. The good guy – maybe – has also found the heroine and is leading her to safety down a long tunnel, pausing occasionally to shoot bad guys – probably

– who are all wearing yellow boiler suits. Behind them is a rolling wall of flame. Even by my standards, the film has become complete nonsense.

I switch off the TV and for no reason pick up Mum's book again. I let it fall open, then start to read.

"*He took her to the bedroom and undressed her slowly, he made love to her beautifully. Nothing frantic, nothing rushed. He caressed her body as though there was nothing more important in the world. He took her to the edge of ecstasy and back again, keeping her hovering, sure of every move he made. Her breasts grew under his touch, swelling, becoming even larger and firmer. She floated on a suspended plane, a complete captive to his hands and body.*

"*He had amazing control, stopping at just the right moment. When it did happen, it was only because he wanted it to, and they came in complete unison. She had never experienced that before, and she clung to him, words tumbling out of her mouth about how much she loved him. Afterwards they lay and smoked and talked.*"

This confuses me because, until then, I hadn't known that girls' breasts could grow like that. But Jackie Collins, the author, is a grown-up woman and presumably does know. Mine still need to grow quite a lot, and I'm very jealous of Patsy's boobs that are already an impediment on the hockey pitch. Jackie Collins, from the picture on the dust cover, also seems to have big boobs. Does that mean that lots of people have touched them? Or just one person, lots of times? And, after being touched, do they stay big, or revert to normal size?

Mum's boobs have always looked much the same, even after Dad's predatory expeditions, but I don't like to think about that. I close the book and lay it down on the coffee table, wondering what my mother was thinking about when she read that passage. About her youth, she'd said, before we'd become a family.

My bedroom is at the other end of the house from my parents. From the top of the stairs, I have to navigate a long passageway that is also lined with Art. There is light spilling from under Mum's closed door. From my bedroom I look across fairways to the sea.

On clear nights I can see the shapes of oil tankers anchored in the Firth and the sparkle of water under moonlight. Below the window is the glass desk where I sometimes do my homework if I can be bothered. Beside the desk, pinned to the wall, is an old-fashioned calendar and neat crosses obliterating the school term, marking the approach of Christmas.

Then, still confused by all that boob-touch-and-grow, I start to think about Oz, the shape and smell of him, how he moves. I lie on my bed, my hands behind my head and for no reason am gripped by a strange and unfocused sense of purpose.

Something drab that I don't understand seems to have been dribbling into my family and I need to find something else: something bright and luminous to soothe away the uneasiness.

$$\sqrt{\frac{196GMd_{\mathrm{OV}}}{\theta_{\mathrm{H}}^2 c^2 d_{\mathrm{V}} d_{\mathrm{O}}}} = 7$$

Einstein radius

Oz's rugby team is indeed playing a match against a posh Edinburgh school, and I've arranged to watch it with Patsy and several other cows, although Patsy is a little suspicious of my sudden enthusiasm for boys kicking shit out of each other. I have only ever been an occasional supporter, usually when there hasn't been anything else to do. I couldn't tell her about actually speaking to Oz although, being honest, it hadn't *exactly* been a proper conversation.

But for some reason I still feel churned up inside; for a brief moment I had been the centre of his universe before telling him completely the wrong time. But on such trivialities are false hopes built. Patsy grudgingly agreed to meet me on the touchline unless it was raining. Patsy hates the rain. I have decided not to ask her whether lots of people have been touching her boobs. I don't know her well enough yet, and I don't want her to think that I'm stupid or odd, or both.

I realise, in hindsight, that I must have fancied Oz for some time, but didn't think much about it, because I wasn't interested in boys, unlike most of my classmates who were forever fluttering eyelashes and puffing out their meagre chests (except Patsy). Oz looks older than the rest of us, his frown is more eloquent than ours; he moves with a languid grace that is more grown-up than adolescent. He has blue eyes, floppy brown hair and an infectious smile. He has small dimples on his cheeks which deepen when he smiles and a small cleft on his chin that's like a scar.

He seems untamed, or untameable, or enigmatic – maybe Patsy is right – and it seems odd that his first girlfriend was Catriona MacIntosh, a rather plain and dumpy girl who is also rather shy, but good at hockey. It was her hockey stick, crazy bitch, that cut my knee. Maybe it was her athleticism that attracted Oz to her, or her Siren-like entreaties from behind the bike shed, which she's well known for. But it didn't last long.

Patsy found Catriona sobbing in the girls' toilets, and Catriona – under conditions of strict secrecy – told Patsy that Oz had dumped her, which Patsy immediately then spread around the entire school – she'd have used the school PA system if she'd had the key to the school secretary's office. Oz rose several more notches in everyone's estimation: not only had he been one of the first boys in our class to have a proper girlfriend – even if it *was* just Catriona – he had been the absolute first to ditch a girlfriend *and* make her cry. Around his flame, the cows began to circle once again.

On Saturday morning I walk up to the High School and stand shivering on the touchline by myself. Patsy and the other girls haven't shown up, probably because it's a drizzly day, so I stand alone and feel conspicuous. By half-time, North Berwick is comfortably in front, to the annoyance of the visitors' coach who is screaming abusive four-letter words from the touchline, which isn't something you would expect from a posh Edinburgh coach. Without consciously meaning to, my eyes are following Oz, the way he darts and glides, confusing defenders; how he can change position on the field in the blink of an eye, linking up moves, or spotting a gap and charging through. On those charging runs, his face changes; it becomes a grimace of determination, almost something fearful or monsterish.

Then, just after half time, and just as I've made up my mind to go back into town – probably to Greggs, because I like Greggs – and definitely out of the rain, Oz is scythed down in an off-the-ball tackle. The opposing player is sent off; Oz limps away, casting dark glances at the opposition player, who is now being given a very loud bollocking by his coach. He even uses some words that I'm a little unclear about.

Oz pulls on a track-suit top with NORTH BERWICK RUGBY on the back and his leg is closely examined by the team physio, Mr Collins, who usually teaches music, and who I know has only completed a weekend course in first aid. Oz then limps along the touchline heading for the showers. As he passes me, I throw a cautious smile. 'How's the leg?'

'No big deal.'

I turn my attention back to the game, then realise he's still standing next to me. 'I missed my train because of you.'

I shudder inside. 'Ah, sorry. Watch malfunction.'

'You always wear a broken watch?'

'I didn't *know* it was broken. Actually, it wasn't broken. Christ, Oz, why would I do that? I just hadn't wound it up,' I finally confess, feeling stupid. 'I didn't fucking know that it needed to be wound up.'

'Temper, temper, Emma.'

I purse my lips. It's the second time he's said that to me. Oz has an uncanny ability to turn my insides to mush and rile me at the same time.

'Anyway, thanks,' he now says. 'You got me out of a shopping trip.'

'Is that a good thing?' I ask. I mostly like shopping trips because Mum usually buys me stuff.

'Very good thing.' I no longer feel riled. My legs have gone wobbly. 'Hey, maybe we could meet up or something?'

I can't immediately believe what he's just said. 'Um, yeah …' I reply, hoping that this doesn't sound like a desperate YES.

'The new cafe at the end of the High Street?' North Berwick mostly specialises in charity shops and coffee shops, so that you have the choice of cheap clothes or expensive coffee.

'OK, Oz.' My voice has also gone wobbly. I am in danger of falling over, or dribbling, or falling over and dribbling.

'In an hour, yeah?'

'You must like long showers.' I smile a wobbly smile, one hand in front of my mouth in case I really am dribbling.

'Is that a bad thing?'

'Good thing, Oz. Good thing.'

I watch him limp back to the school as a warm thrill wells up and infuses every part of me. It takes a while for all the wobbles to calm down.

An hour later, in the vastness of space and time, among all those countless billions of stars, another Great Attractor was sliding himself into the seat opposite me, a can of Diet Coke in one hand and a bacon roll in the other. I had thought myself in the zone of avoidance, someone to be ignored because I'm only a little bit pretty – no Top Twenty for me – and not therefore in his league, so I have no idea why Oz and I are now sitting at the same table and why he is smiling at me, a smear of brown sauce on his chin.

Or is it maybe who my father is? Am I to become an anecdote girlfriend – someone to be mentioned at dinner parties in decades to come? I decide to banish dark thoughts, if only for the time being.

'Leg OK?'

He takes a bite of his roll. 'That dickhead should be banned forever.'

I have a straw in my can of Coke and sip at it, trying to appear demure, like the woman on the front cover of the Jackie Collins novel. 'Must be about the last game of the year,' I suggest. 'Lots of time to get better.'

'That's not the point,' he says with some venom. 'Things like that shouldn't be allowed.'

'He did get sent off.'

'He should be shot.'

'Maybe a bit harsh, Oz.'

It was then that Patsy and the other two girls who should have been at the rugby match come in, see me and Oz, and immediately walk past, giggling, to sit at a corner table. They all have their heads together, but keep turning round to watch us, and laughing in an annoying way. Patsy points her phone in my direction, and then taps away on its keypad. I do my best to ignore them.

A little while later, after a second bacon roll – him – and another can of Coke – me – Oz says, 'I was hoping you'd come to watch.' He says it quietly, but is looking at me evenly, making the words seem more important than they are. It's the most romantic thing that anybody has ever said to me, although nobody has ever said anything remotely romantic to me before. 'Then I'm glad I did,' is all I can think to say in a dribbly-slurry way, trying to figure out whether I should add or multiply the probabilities.

In Granddad's book, he talks about probability theory and that the most likely explanation of something is usually the right one. But he also talks about independent or mutually exclusive events, how some events just happen, while others can only happen if something else has happened first. Like Oz asking me for the time, and me having a watch that told the wrong time. Going to the rugby match. Patsy and the others not showing up. Oz getting injured.

Granddad had tried to explain it to me as I completed the jigsaw of the Eiffel Tower and my father pondered the impossibility of beating Tiger Woods at golf, a script in one hand and a whisky glass in the other.

Once you've decided how independent an event is, you can then either add or multiply the probabilities. According to Alberto, probability theory is behind a lot of stuff that is actually useful, like weather forecasting, clinical trials for new medicines, determining the likely odds of winning the Lottery, or the chances of a monkey typing Hamlet without tuition – one in 15,625,000,000, apparently, although some monkeys must be cleverer than others. But I'm no good at maths, despite Miss Frobisher's best attempts, and I wouldn't know what to add or multiply.

'But, because of you, my mother's cancelled shopping trip is now today's shopping trip.'

'Because of me?'

'Because *you* made me miss the train,' he reminds me.

'Ah yes, bust watch.'

'You'd forgotten to wind it up.'

'I hadn't forgotten to wind it up. I thought it had a battery inside. Christ, all watches have batteries inside them! Except mine, as it turns out.' I'm not sure if he really is angry. 'You could say you're injured,' I suggest.

'I am injured,' he says, slapping a hand onto his leg for emphasis and wincing. 'But fat lot of good that'll do. Mum's got a list of things to get for Christmas and she needs me to carry stuff.'

'Then just ask Santa Claus. That's his job, isn't it?'

'We've got central heating. No chimney to come down. Anyway, Emma, Santa Claus doesn't exist.'

'God!' I reply, putting a hand to my mouth. 'You're joking, right?'

'Sorry, I kind of thought you'd know.'

'Jesus! Please tell me that the Tooth Fairy is real!'

He's looking at the table and scrunching up the little paper napkin that his bacon roll came in. 'Anyway, it was nice to finally talk to you.'

'Ditto.'

'Away from school, I mean.'

I don't know what to say but feel that I have to say something. 'We could sort of meet up again,' I suggest.

'Sure, yeah. Somewhere.'

'Somewhere?'

'Then why don't we meet up on the beach,' he suggests. 'You go there often enough.' He takes his can and plate back to the counter, throwing me a smile and waving airily to

Patsy and the other girls, who all immediately start giggling again.

I'm not sure if I now have a boyfriend, or what that really means. All I know is that Patsy is again busily tapping on her mobile phone and that, come Monday morning, I will be the talk of the school.

'Cat, we'll be late!'

'What? Speak up!'

'I am speaking up! I said we'll be late!'

'Then please don't confuse me with someone who gives a fuck!'

Dad is not only speaking up but shouting up the stairs in his best Shakespearian bellow. He's shouting up the stairs, and Mum is shouting down the stairs. I am sitting in the living room wearing my warmest coat and scarf. Although Mum hates to be late for virtually everything, she seems to have made an exception for the school's Special Christmas Concert: *Everyone welcome! Tickets at the door! Only £5!!*

Happily, I am not performing in it and don't much care if we're late or not. Dad, on the other hand, who is generally late for everything, is being unusually organised. He's shaved, showered and is dressed in a grey suit with open-neck blue shirt. His hair is neatly combed. He looks every inch the film star which, I suspiciously conclude, is probably his intention.

'Cat, please get a move on!'

'I am getting a move on! I'm drying my hair!' Wet hair? Mum does wash her hair! 'Look, just go without me! I'll see you there.'

'I'm not going without you!'

'Then shut the fuck up! I'll be down in a minute.'

It took very little persuasion to get Dad to come to the school's annual Christmas concert, which will feature the 'very best from our incredibly talented school community' – according to the headmaster at assembly, casting a beady glance at Mr Collins, the Head of Music, who didn't seem to hear, perhaps dreaming of a new career as a sports physiotherapist.

Mum appears a few minutes later dressed in black jeans and a Chanel cream jacket. As always, she looks stunning; elegant but informal. Dad wolf-whistles when she totters down the stairs, which makes her smile. I give her a hug; I'm very proud of her.

The school's concert is being held in the gym-cum-theatre-cum-assembly hall and we're met at the school gates by the headmaster himself, who takes us in a side entrance and into the school's large administrative office, where a trestle table has been set up with bowls of crisps and peanuts and bottles of red and white wine.

Standing round the trestle table is a fat man wearing a chain of office – the town provost, apparently – a very fat lady in bright red lipstick – provost's wife, I learn – our local MP and his wife, and several very old people who have crisp crumbs down their cardigans who we're informed are former senior members of staff.

I obviously shouldn't be in here with the VIPs, but I'm hungry and I've also seen a plate of mini pakoras. The headmaster takes his leave, backing slowly towards the door like a junior emissary, bowing like Tony Blair in the photo on the piano, while Dad pours wine into two glasses and hands one to Mum. He doesn't pour me anything, even though there's a jug of squash on the table.

The very old people are looking at Dad blankly, perhaps wondering if they're actually at home watching a TV programme with a vaguely familiar actor in it. The MP takes a step towards Mum, maybe intending to engage her again in political debate, before thinking twice about it and stepping back.

Instead, it's the provost who steps forward and extends a podgy hand. 'And you, sir, must be Paul Ross. A pleasure

to finally meet you and to welcome you to our small town.'
Dad shakes his hand, mutters something under his breath,
and introduces Mum and me. The provost shakes our
hands as well, which is rather nice of him, although we still
don't know what he's actually called. His wife, who also
hasn't been introduced, wearing an iridescent green dress,
is shimmering like a chameleon, with barely contained
excitement. I eat a second pakora.

Various teachers have, of course, tried to persuade me
to take part in the concert, but I resolutely held out; it's not
that I'm against being on stage, it's that I don't want to be
on stage under false pretences, with the school letting it be
known that the daughter of the internationally acclaimed
Paul Ross *will also be performing, with tickets now only
£500!!*

Still, getting Dad along is a much greater coup, and I
rather sense, from the hubbub in the corridor, that the
assembly hall will be rather full. I look at him now as I munch
my way through another pakora – have I eaten *all* of them?
He has charmed both the provost and his wife. the very old
people are smiling in a vacant, but happy, way and the local
MP seems to be at a loss for words. Mum is standing by his
shoulder, smiling, and then sweeps back her long, *dry* hair
with one hand and surreptitiously winks at me.

Despite his laid-back demeanour, I don't think Dad has
been looking forward to the concert. He doesn't really like
small children and won't countenance appearing in any
film aimed at younger audiences. Tonight, Dad needn't
have worried. Most of the squealing horde in the corridor
are adults, mainly young mothers, although I can also see
Mr Semple, who teaches chemistry, simpering from the
sidelines. Dad is also something of a gay icon, although I'm
not sure why.

The headmaster and four members of the school's 1st
XV rugby team clear a path through the hall for Dad, where

we have seats in the front row. The rest of us – Mum, me, provost, MP, VIP wives – tag along unscathed in his wake. I'm not sure what's happened to the very old people; perhaps they've been forgotten about and will still be here in the morning when the administrative staff arrive for work.

We take our seats as the house lights dim and the headmaster strides onto the stage carrying a microphone which, inevitably, doesn't work and he's left in the spotlight doing his best to *ad lib* until another microphone is found. Nobody minds this enforced interlude: the headmaster's embarrassment and inept attempts at wonky microphone humour – which few people can actually hear – are highly entertaining. Then, with his new microphone, the headmaster explains that each class year will give a small performance that 'will showcase the many talents of our school community and conjure up the spirit of Christmas.'

The first performance is a bit of a fiasco, given by a bunch of primary age children, incongruously dressed in wigs and silly hats. None of them quite knows where they're meant to be on the stage; they're obviously supposed to be purposefully strutting, but they resemble a badly-organised mini-Hitler Youth gathering, and keep walking into one another. Few seem to have entirely learned the words to *Merry Christmas Everybody*.

Off stage, a plinky-plonky piano tries to jolly them along, without much success. Nevertheless, the audience claps raucously, with fathers taking flash photographs and whistling.

A second bunch of primary children then shuffle on reluctantly from stage left, looking unnerved by the preceding disaster, the camera flashes and huge and unruly audience. They rather timidly sing *Santa Claus is Coming to Town*, while dressed in ridiculous animal costumes, presumably hand-made by mothers lacking neither aptitude nor a sense of humour. The reason for this becomes apparent when they then enact a scene from the Nativity with Mary and Jesus – a rather scary doll, with big eyes that randomly open and close – sitting on a straw bale surrounded by all the animals of the field, including several animals that don't actually *belong* in fields. Didn't the child's mother know that an octopus lives in the sea?

Mary simply stares dumbstruck at the audience, eyes desperately seeking out someone she knows, and doesn't notice when the baby Jesus' head falls off, which makes a couple of young children in the audience burst into tears.

The best bit, after they've sung *Away in a Manger*, is when all the animals crowd round the baby Jesus. Mary is still staring at the audience, oblivious to a cat – or I think it's a cat – that is helpfully screwing her son's head back on.

'Moo,' says the cow.

'Baa,' says the sheep.

'Woof,' says the dog.

'Miaow,' says the cat that re-capitated the head.

'Hisssss,' says the snake, who is hidden inside a series of linked hatboxes painted in brown and green stripes, with a train of green fabric across the floor, also painted crudely in green and white stripes, and which may have been curtain remnants. The snake has a forked tongue in green felt and lurid blue eyes, with holes in the centre for a little someone to look out from.

The snake, out of all the animals is the most ridiculous – even the octopus – because we've all seen the *Jungle Book* and know what snakes are supposed to look like. The unicorn probably feels the same way and, sight impeded by a stupid papier mâché horse's head with one wobbling antler, is standing on the snake's tail so that, when the snake takes a step forwards, it falls over with a loud shriek. The snake's arms are inside the hat boxes, so that it falls over in slow motion. Now horizontal, the snake is writhing quite realistically on the stage and sobbing.

I look sideways at Dad who is trying to look concerned, although I know he's doing his best not to laugh. Mum, more humane in every way, genuinely looks concerned. Two teachers have rushed to the rescue and manhandle the python, or whatever species it is, to the wings where sobs continue for some time. We can all hear the sound of hat boxes being ripped apart.

It then takes a short while to sort out all the other animals who, like real animals, have been rather spooked by this unexpected turn of events and aren't quite sure what to do next. Mary, mother of God, is now absently turning her baby's reattached head round and around like a scene from *The Exorcist,* which makes the same small children in the audience burst into tears again.

'Roar,' says the tiger, after a couple of prompts from an offstage teacher.

'Miss, Miss,' says the unicorn, which seems to have evolved to speak English.

'Quack,' says the duck.

'Roar, roar,' says the tiger, again, and is kicked by the horse.

'Woof,' says the dog, again.

'Roar, roar,' says the tiger very loudly and kicks the horse.

'Moo,' says the cow, again.

'Neigh,' says the horse.

'Miss,' says the unicorn, again. 'Someone's peed on the floor.'

After that, once the stage has been cleaned and disinfected, things improve. A very little Chinese-looking girl comes on stage and gives a virtuoso performance on violin, two boys with guitars sing *Letter from America* rather well, and then a large group of my class year shuffle on to sing *Bridge Over Troubled Water*, with lots of harmonies and descants. I am glad to see that Oz doesn't once look at Catriona MacIntosh, and that she doesn't once look at him.

Since the rugby match when Oz was injured, we've been to the beach several times. Like me, he's good at listening to the sea, but hasn't pressed me on what I look at when I'm there by myself. Like me, I think he's a little lonely, and only yesterday I slipped my arm through his and, together, we stood and looked out at the shifting waves, listening to seabirds and the rhythmic thump of falling water.

Afterwards, Mum and Dad – and me – are ushered to a nearby classroom that has again been laid out with glasses of wine and soft drinks – but no pakoras or crisps. Only VIPs and members of staff are allowed in this classroom, with burly rugby players guarding the door with folded arms, trying to look menacing. On the way from the front row, Dad is surrounded by a doughnut of adult female admirers, no doubt hoping for an invitation to our grand home. Despite my birthday party, local legend still insists it has a squash court and underground swimming pool. Someone read it in *The Sunday Times* apparently, so it must be true.

The aged teachers from before the school concert don't reappear, and I wonder what's happened to them. Do they live in a secret wing of the school, and live off school dinners? If so, what happens during school holidays when the cafeteria is closed? Or is there a special home for old teachers, with bells to announce feeding time or bedtime?

The provost's wife is still shimmering and, having downed several glasses of wine – I was watching – is also making eyes at Dad, who pretends not to notice. Mr Semple is also still simpering, but from the wrong side of the doorway, having been refused entry by the rugby players.

Mum and the MP's wife are chattering on about the concert, and enquire about the wellbeing of the snake – who's fine, apparently, although the hat boxes are ruined – while the headmaster keeps thanking Dad for 'gracing us with your presence.' He's used the phrase three times in as many minutes, although he's never once said it to me for bothering to turn up to his poxy school.

Dad keeps repeating how much he enjoyed the concert and hopes that he'll be able to come to many more. I know Dad is lying when he says this. Something in the slope of his eyes gives him away; Dad's duties to his daughter's school are now complete.

Dad is then cheered out the school exit, with the rugby players forming a protective shield – do they carry guns, I wonder? – with Mum and me a few paces behind. Dad deigns to sign autographs, which takes some time, as more than a few people want multiple autographs for friends and relations in far-flung parts of the world. I know now from experience that they're probably lying, but Dad scribbles an approximation of his signature on everything. You can buy hundreds of Paul Ross autographs on eBay, some of which may be genuine.

But he does look tired, having only just returned from Mexico where he's been filming a drama about the Mexican Revolution alongside Sienna Miller, who keeps her clothes on throughout. (Mum demanded to know.)

'The first rule of theatre, old girl, is never to let your audience know that there's something wrong,' advises Dad. He has taken to calling me 'old girl' from time to time, usually after one of his long lunches, which is why Mum is driving. 'The unicorn shouldn't have said what he did. The first rule of theatre is just to say your lines, nothing else.' What do unicorns really sound like? We never found out. 'Stage fright as well. Happens to us all. But the first rule of theatre is just to carry on.' Dad seems unaware that he's just pronounced *two* things as being the first rule of theatre.

'Even you?' I ask. I've never seen my father being frightened by anything, except spiders, which he flattens with a rolled-up newspaper, and Mum when she's being particularly bellicose.

'Even me,' he confirms, folding his long body into the

111

passenger seat and closing the door.

'Did everyone notice?' I ask. Somehow, I don't think that the pee culprit is going to be in next year's Christmas concert.

My parents look at each other. 'Well, maybe a few,' says my father diplomatically, then chortles, passing streetlights streaking his face with light. Mum, both hands on the wheel, is looking straight ahead and biting her lip. She particularly hates driving the Bentley on small streets at night. 'God, I hate aeroplanes,' says Dad.

I look out the car window. There are Christmas trees in front rooms. The air is sharp and icy. Dad is leaving for America in the morning, on a short trip to Los Angeles. It's the last day of the school term.

'Couldn't I come with you?' I ask, although I'm not hopeful that he'll say yes.

Instead it's my mother who answers. 'You'd be bored, Emma. Dad has work to do.'

'Your mother's right, old girl,' agrees my father. 'America ain't no place for a little girl.' He has put on a homely Southern drawl to say this.

I am about to remind him that America is probably full of little girls when my mother adds quietly: 'He doesn't want you going with him, Emma.' I don't know what she means by this.

'But you will be back for Christmas?' I ask brightly. A trip to America should mean lots of presents. Although my father hates shopping, he is usually very good at buying things for me, or more likely getting other people to do the actual shopping. Dad's little army of useful people is wonderful at shopping.

'Of course, of course,' he replies, but his mind is already elsewhere. His eyes are closed. Our house is only a few minutes' drive from the school, and again I wonder why we're living here, in a small and unimportant town, in a house that Mum hates, and which is light years away from the world that Dad really lives in.

I don't see why we can't just move to London or Hollywood. He'd be nearer his work, we would see him more often, and we could have a real swimming pool. Film stars don't live in North Berwick. It's against all rules of nature.

That was the year that my father spent Christmas Day in Reykjavik. He was on a plane back from Los Angeles which, due to a technical problem, was diverted to Iceland where, on the day before Christmas Eve, bad weather then closed the airport for two days.

It may not have been his fault, but my mother was livid. Granny and Gramps were in Italy, and my mother and I sat grandly on Christmas Day at the dining room table wearing paper hats and, because Mrs Boyce had the day off, eating overdone turkey and burnt parsnips. Later, once the dishes had been washed and put away, she went to her room, where I heard her crying.

$$\frac{1}{60c}\sqrt{\frac{L_\odot}{4\pi F}} \simeq 8$$

How many minutes it takes light from the Sun to reach Earth

After her outburst in Aberlady Bay, watched incuriously by golfers and seals, I tried to protect Mum in my own way. Against him. I tried to be cheerful and make jokes, although Mum rarely laughed. I tried to involve her in my homework projects, with limited success. I told her, over and over, how lovely she was. I tried to make her realise that there was someone else in her life, apart from her husband.

But, of course, we weren't simply a family, like any other family. I was the daughter of Paul Ross, my mother was the wife of Paul Ross. Our existences were defined, not by who we were, but by our relationship to him. He was our star and we circled in uneasy orbit. Mum was a moon. I sometimes felt like a small piece of space junk. I hugged her often and held her hand when we went for walks.

A few months after Christmas – Dad had come back on Boxing Day laden with remorse and presents – I physically tried to protect her. Over the winter, waves had crashed to the beach, breaking and foaming over the harbour walls; now, the sea had calmed down, tired after its exertions, and spring flowers were beginning to poke through.

Dad was going to London for a few days, which he often did. We had an early supper, Dad's small suitcase packed and sitting in the hallway. It isn't a large suitcase because, for convenience and security, he's taken a long lease on a small flat in Green Park. It overlooks a quiet street lined with expensive hotels. Berkeley Square is just a short stroll away. He once made me stop and listen for nightingales. He didn't bother to explain why. His London flat is filled with everything that he could possibly want. The Gucci suitcase in the hallway doesn't therefore need to be very big.

On the other side of the dining room French windows, Mr Perkins is power-washing the patio, his hosepipe stretched across the flagstones. The parabola of water sparkles in cold afternoon sunshine. My mother has cooked fish pie, my least favourite of her staple foods – Mrs Boyce is off sick with 'dicky waterworks' – and for the umpteenth time she's asking Dad if he absolutely has everything he needs.

My father is off to make a car advertisement. Belatedly, Bentley have discovered that my father owns one of their cars. Their people have talked to my father's people and Dad was persuaded, although I don't think it took much arm-twisting. Dad's Bentley is a daily announcement of his success and if he can broadcast that success to an international audience then that's fine by him. My mother drives a small and sensible Ford, Dad would never agree to be in a Ford advertisement, however much they paid him.

The family meal is eaten largely in silence, with me wishing that we had a dog that I could surreptitiously feed the fish pie to. Dad is also pushing food around his plate, but not eating much, and only partly because the fish pie is borderline inedible. I suspect that he'll have another late supper in London, probably in a fancy restaurant that doesn't serve fish pie.

I spear a potato and examine the flower arrangement on the centre of the table. Dad is looking out the window at Mr Perkins, who is now coiling the hosepipe; water drips from its end makes a small river across the patio.

'They're nice, aren't they?' says Mum.

'What?'

'The flowers, for God's sake! I bought them yesterday.'

Mum is beginning to take her flower arranging presidency more seriously, and sometimes feels compelled to do some gardening. She holds her fork halfway to her mouth. 'Paul, are you sure that you've got everything?'

It's one of their rituals, my mother worrying over and over, and relentlessly trying to be useful. My father winks at me over the table and pushes away his plate. 'Delicious!' he says loudly, although he couldn't have eaten more than two mouthfuls, and is probably also wishing that we had a dog. 'Of course, I've got everything.' He nods towards the hallway.

'But you've not finished,' complains Mum.

Later, standing on the stone steps, the sightless lions still crouching on either side of the door, we wave Dad off. As he sweeps down the drive, he loftily waves out the window, as he always does. He is driving quickly, spurting gravel, as if he's late. As he turns onto the small beach road that will eventually take him to the airport, he toots his horn, as he always does. My mother and I turn and shut the front door, the big gates at the end of the driveway slowly swinging closed. My mother sighs, as she always does.

I watch TV for a while as Mum bustles in the kitchen scraping fish pie into the bin, and then I help her load the dishwasher. Dad will already be at the airport, hiding in the VIP lounge, and no doubt on the phone to London or Los Angeles, his family forgotten.

'When's Dad coming back?' I ask, once kitchen duties are complete and we're back in the living room.

Mum is sitting in her usual chair beside the fireplace and reading a book. The grate is filled with a large bowl of wildflowers, which she's also bought and haphazardly arranged. 'Next week, I expect. Why?'

'Because he's left his passport behind.' I indicate the coffee table on which is stacked glossy magazines, several theatrical publications, and my father's passport.

She smiles, her eyes bright, her book folded on her lap. 'He's only going to London, Emma. He doesn't need his passport.'

'Oh.'

I look at my wound-up watch. He might even be in the air by now, wearing dark glasses and with his hair parted the wrong way. But for some reason I feel uneasy. 'It's just that he doesn't usually leave it lying around,' I say.

'Like I said, lovey, it's really not important.'

'I suppose not.'

I watch my mother turning pages, her mouth framing words. Her feet are stretched out, her shoes kicked off underneath the coffee table. A glass of wine is perched close at hand. I now only have half my mind on the TV, because something unpleasant has crept inside me. My mouth tastes unpleasantly of fish.

Mum had earlier been out to buy the fish. She'd seen a recipe in one of the Sunday papers and, although fish pie is something she has relentlessly cooked for aeons, wanted to give this variation a go. Dad, who doesn't much like fish, merely grunted at my mother's idea. He was in the living room. Pages of a script were on his knee. Around his feet were other pages. In his hand was a gold pen and he was scoring out sentences and paragraphs and rewriting them in his big handwriting.

My father has a punctilious reputation; when it comes to his work, he knows his character better than the writer. He knows what his character has to say and how he should say it. Rewriting other people's words is part of his professionalism, but it also always puts him in a bad mood. 'It isn't what I'm paid for,' he told Mum, who nodded and then set out for the shops.

So, rather than disturb him or catch the end of his

117

bad temper, I go to the kitchen and do some geography homework. The phone rings and Dad answers it, sounding brusque.

'No, I'm not having a good day!' I hear him exclaim. 'It's this bloody script.' I have no choice but to listen; his baritone isn't designed to be ignored. 'The idiot who wrote it should be fired.'

I hear him grunt a few times, then sigh loudly and theatrically. 'That's not the point, Sarah. The simple fact is that the idiot has written complete crap!'

There are a few more grunts and then he laughs. 'You're damn right they should give me a car. Least they can bloody do!' He is chuckling and making happier grunting noises.

Then there's a lengthy silence before Dad speaks again. 'Look, why don't we get away for a couple of days? What do you say, old girl? Good idea?'

My mouth is dry, my stomach feels tied in knots. My father has clearly forgotten that I'm within earshot.

'No, I was thinking somewhere nicer. Paris, maybe.' I hear him say. 'Somewhere that's not here.'

My eyes have filled with tears. Although I know that he lives in two worlds, ours and his, I have never experienced them coming together like this. He has always been careful to keep dividing lines between his lives; now, his other life is intruding into ours. It feels like abuse, a casual cruelty. He is planning a trip away with his agent. He cares about her more than he cares about us.

I feel something take over me. I can hardly breathe; I can barely suck air in. I feel sick, for myself and my mother. I realise then how much I hate him; for excluding us from his other life, and for wanting to live it with someone else. I don't know how long I sit in the kitchen, my eyes fixed on the schoolbook and my chest slowly subsiding, before I quietly go into the hallway, open Dad's small suitcase, and take out his passport.

The last day of term before Easter is very warm and, after eating a baguette from Greggs with Patsy, I wander home and watch TV for a while. Later, I'm going to meet Oz on the beach and, at the thought of him, my knees go a little wobbly. Sometimes when I touch myself down *there*, I'm thinking about Oz, although I wouldn't let him touch me down *there*, because I know where things can lead. I've seen enough of Dad's films to know everything there is to know about where things lead.

As the afternoon wears on, the temperature drops and a breeze springs up. The sun becomes obscured by dark and angry-looking clouds. The first detonation of thunder is unexpectedly loud, followed by a wall of water. On the kitchen table is a page torn from that day's *Daily Express*. On it is a picture of Dad, dressed casually and walking down a London street. Big Ben is in the background, so I know it's London.

Dad phones later. He's still filming the Bentley advertisement, which has overrun because of technical problems. He now won't be back for a few more days. He then asks to speak to Mum.

'She's not here,' I tell him.

'Oh,' he replies, as if he expects her to be in the house at all times, just on the off-chance he might phone up. 'It's just that I need to speak to her rather urgently. Where is she, do you know? Shopping, I expect.'

My father makes no secret of his disdain for shopping; although he likes to be recognised, when it suits him, he doesn't like people knowing what he's buying: PAUL ROSS BUYS UNDERWEAR, PICTURE EXCLUSIVE. Mum does most of his shopping for him, including clothes, although most purchases are quickly returned.

Mum's idea of what would suit my father rarely meets with his approval. She isn't ostentatious; she likes muted colours. My father likes vibrant colours, striding across

Muirfield's fairways, golf bag over one shoulder, in lurid greens and reds.

'Her car's still here,' I tell him.

'Oh,' he repeats. 'Then she's probably gone for a walk.' He seems pleased to have reached this conclusion, his voice bright on the line from the film studio, although it isn't a difficult conclusion to reach. My father likes to walk on golf courses. It gives *purpose* to a good walk, he'll say. My mother likes walking on anything except a golf course, a game that she thinks of as a waste of time.

'I expect she'll be home soon,' says my father.

I look outside at the monsoon rain and the flicker of lightning. In the newspaper picture on the kitchen table, Dad is wearing dark glasses. He sometimes does when he's trying to be invisible. I wonder if he's wearing them now. 'I expect so,' I agree.

A little later and Dad is again on the telephone. On this last day of term, we've been given the results of a geography test. To my surprise, I've done rather well. Normally, I'm not much good at geography. I try to tell my father how well I've done, to make him proud of me.

Outwardly, I try to sound cheerful. Inwardly, I'm anything but cheerful because Dad doesn't seem very interested in my geography test results. To me, they are important; to him, probably swilling champagne on a film set and chatting to Bentley PR executives, they no doubt mean nothing.

'So, what's the capital of Peru?' he demands.

'I don't know.'

'The population of India?'

'I don't know.'

'The principle mineral export of South Africa?'

'Dad, do you know any of this stuff?'

'No,' he admits, 'but I'm not the one studying geography.' There is a small pause. 'I don't suppose your mother's back,

120

is she?'

'No.'

'Then where the hell is she?' he demands, as if it's my fault.

'Dad, I don't know. I've already told you that.'

'Well, it's not good enough,' he says. 'Look, old girl, I really have to speak to her. Is her car still in the drive?' I suspect that my father has had a long lunch. He sounds distant and hesitant.

'Yes.'

He sighs. 'Has she done this before? I don't like her leaving you alone.'

'Dad, I'm old enough to look after myself,' I remind him. I sometimes wonder if he even knows what age I am.

'I know that Emma. Sorry. It's just that I worry about her. When did you last see her?'

'Yesterday. We went to the cinema.'

'Yesterday!'

'We saw you at the cinema.'

We'd been to see Dad's latest film, with Sandra Bullock in it. 'Did you enjoy it?' he can't help but ask, as if my opinion matters.

'I don't think that Mum liked it very much.'

'Listen, old girl, I really do need to talk to her rather urgently,' he now says, although he's already said this in his previous phone call.

'About what's in the newspaper?' I blurt out.

I expect him to bluster or laugh. Instead, there's a small silence. 'Yes,' he says.

Mum positively hated the Sandra Bullock film. Given the sex scenes, that was only to be expected. But on top of that, she has grown increasingly withdrawn. The worry lines on her face have become more pronounced. She has friends, but doesn't see them so often now, staying at home, reading books, pottering rather aimlessly, even by her standards.

She's also taken to drinking orange juice in the afternoons, but once when she'd left the room to answer the phone, I took a sip from her glass. It wasn't just orange juice. I know she's lonely, and I can't blame her for that, or for having a husband who leads a different life in another galaxy. But for whatever reasons, they chose one another, and now have to live with the consequences.

I put down the phone, suddenly worried.

$$\frac{24\pi G\rho_f}{H_0^2} = 9$$

Critical density for the expanding universe

The four of us – me, Dad, Granny Mary and Alberto – are in Bellagio Ripano for our annual pilgrimage. It's a place of beauty but was no place for a go-getter with a large moustache. Bellagio Ripano, for all its rustic charm, could not hold Granddad: after posts at the universities of Milan and Rome, he'd headed west to Cambridge, then to Edinburgh to become the University's first Professor of Theoretical Physics. His greatest contribution to science is, of course, the Rossini Theorem, in which he postulates in several hundred pages of dense calculations, that there has to be something else making up the universe, apart from molecules and atoms. Widely ridiculed at the time, the Rossini Theorem is becoming a textbook for contemporary astrophysics.

My father's Italian was deliberately non-existent, a shame which became palpable on those annual visits. My father sees himself as British. OK, he's the son of an Italian émigré, but he doesn't aspire to complex genealogy; he only wants roots in the place of his birth. Learning Italian would be to admit a part of him that he denies. Bellagio Ripano is therefore full of relatives he doesn't need or want. As always, we fly to Milan in a private jet.

I am walking up a hill, the big hill behind North Berwick. There are wildflowers all around and grass is breaking against my legs. I seem to have been walking for hours and

I want to lie down and go to sleep. But I can't: the ground is still soggy from the rain and my shoes squelch in muddy patches. There are insects everywhere, and swallows darting, swirling and looping. It is early evening, and the sun is low over the Forth. As I climb the hillside above the town, I can see a sailboard on the sea and kites being flown at the water's edge. The school term is over. I have passed my geography test and the school gates have shut.

I'd always thought of my mother as one in a million. She had to be, to put up with my father. Prone to myriad neuroses and anxieties, she was also protective and good-humoured. After a few glasses of wine, she could sometimes be persuaded to sing. Blushing madly, she could belt out *When I'm Sixty-four* and never hit a wrong note.

She nursed me, put plasters on my knee, taught me the rudiments of chess and, without effort, offered an unconditional love that was so real it almost crackled like electricity. I remember her smile, her lips on the top of my head every night, telling me that she loved me.

At the top of the hill, I stop to catch my breath. Beneath me, under a lowering sun, is the estuary. Around me, the whine of insects and darting birds. My eye is caught by a fluttering bundle of old clothes on the hill's peak.

It's Mum, curled up as if asleep, with one arm outstretched. Her clothes are rain-sodden and steaming in the evening sunshine. But I know that she can't be sleeping. My mother never goes walking in the rain and would never, ever lie down on wet grass. In her outstretched hand I notice that she's holding something long and shiny. I prise it from her fingers and stare at it dumbly. Then, with all my might, I hurl it far down the hillside and watch it spin and catch the light as it falls.

I now know that in any one year, each of us has a one in 387 chance of dying from cancer and a one in 16,800 chance of being killed in a road accident. In a desolate place far from help, my mother was struck by lightning. It didn't kill her, not immediately. Maybe she could have been saved, except she was alone and there was nobody to raise the alarm. She wasn't now just one in a million. Statistically, she was one in 18,700,000.

I still don't really know why I went looking for Mum, or why I climbed the Law. Maybe just that she'd always been at home when I was around, and she never *ever* went out when it was wet. Her absence had therefore been unusual, and the Law was one of her favourite places.

Inevitably, every newspaper, radio and TV station in the world carried the story of her death: "*Film star's wife killed in freak accident is found by young daughter.*" For a while, I too was a minor celebrity.

Dad arrived home late that night. He was with Sarah Parker. They'd come up together on a chartered jet. Mr and Mrs Perkins were in the kitchen. Mrs Perkins was in tears and had been ever since I'd come screaming into the house. The police arrived soon afterwards, and a helicopter then lifted Mum from the Law. Anyone else would have been stretchered off or just rolled down the hill.

Dad, looking gaunt, hugged me perfunctorily but didn't say anything. Sarah kissed me on the cheek and squeezed my shoulders. She said how sorry she was, which was more than Dad had said. By then, Granny was also in the house, having driven at breakneck speed down from Edinburgh. Alberto was in London but was hurrying back. I wondered why Dad couldn't have picked up my grandfather, rather than Sarah Parker.

There was more bustle in the morning. Our wrought-iron gates were now firmly closed. Security guards had been called in, presumably by Sarah Parker. A media scrum was outside. I could see lots of people with lots of cameras.

I had no idea what they could be taking photos of. Later in the morning, Sarah marched to the front gates to read a statement to the throng, then marched back to the house with tears streaming down her face. The phone rang incessantly. My father ignored it.

I sat for most of the day in the kitchen, listening to the ebb and flow of people's voices, their footsteps up and down the hallway, the ring-ring of the telephone. A policeman was outside our front door. I couldn't see what possible duties he was performing. Occasionally, Mrs Perkins would take him a cup of tea. Granny mostly sat with me, without saying much. There was nothing much to say.

I felt like an outsider in what had happened. She might have been my mother, but she was also the wife of somebody famous. That made me irrelevant, a bystander; it was better to be in the kitchen than in the bustle taking place in other rooms: out there, funeral arrangements were being made while my father, now sedated, moaned from upstairs.

Later still, a detective came to interview me. He was small and round and was wearing a cream shirt. He was also wearing a tie and his shirt was too small for him. He kept sticking his fingers under the collar. It nearly made me smile; he probably never had to wear nice shirts, or ever to do up the top button.

It reminded me that we were a family apart, a black hole of a family, where the normal rules didn't quite apply and even this policeman knew that and had felt the need to smarten up. He asked me why I'd gone to look for her. Answer: because she never left the house for hours and hours without telling us where she was going. He asked why I'd gone to the top of the Law. Answer: it was one of her favourite places. He also squeezed my shoulder, but I didn't tell him what I'd found in Mum's hand.

Bellagio Ripano is united in grief for us. We'd travelled out

126

to Italy shortly after the funeral, having scattered Mum's ashes on the beach. My suggestion: I could be with her whenever I wanted. The funeral itself had taken place in North Berwick and was covered effusively by the media who were excluded from the church behind metal barriers and a phalanx of police officers.

In one photograph in the local newspaper, I'm holding onto Alberto's arm. He's walking with a stick and his moustache, still eloquent, is curled downwards. The caption describes him as a retired maths teacher. *The East Lothian Courier*, only ever dimly aware of local events, had clearly never heard of Gramps. A few stars were there as well, including Monica Bellucci, looking stunning in black, although Dad once said that 'she looks even better stark naked', which made Mum narrow her eyes and make growling noises.

In Italy, we are showered with kindness. Complete strangers who, in some unfathomable way, are also distant relatives coo and ruffle my hair, waxing lyrical about life's injustices, and crossing themselves against similar ill-fortune.

During the week, electrical storms have flickered across the Alps and Dad has locked himself in his room with the curtains closed, while I sit on our rooftop balcony and marvel at life's symmetry. On the mountains, the power of oblivion in bolts of lightning, and down the road, the classically-styled Tempio Voltiano which houses the artefacts of Alessandro Volta, the inventor of the electric battery.

I am aware of an awakening, a shift of an axis, but also of a gathering darkness. In the midst of personal grief, I am being drawn into a company of strangers who genuinely seem to care. My British mother is being mourned effusively in a place of alpine forests, none of which smell remotely like the alpine-fresh cleaning fluids Mum once used, and I sense that I am peering through curtains, with her still close by.

I think that the curtains mark a boundary, between the place where I live and the place where she now lives and that, if I concentrate hard enough, I'll be able to draw back the curtains and see her again. But I also know that between us is a dark universe filled with nothingness that, for the first time, I can feel against my skin.

The week passes; I grow bronzed, learning new paths up the mountains and following them to spectacular summits where the lake looks a million miles away. But I remind myself over and over, it's only a visit, an interlude. I know that I'm growing up; that my childhood is being extinguished. I sense my gathering maturity in my father's diminished frame. Gran says that I have to be strong for Dad, but I can't be strong for him because I can't even be strong for myself. It was Gran who suggested that we go to Italy to get away from the media frenzy and everything else. Dad had nodded his approval, as did Sarah Parker, but without any enthusiasm.

I go for long walks every day, lost in thought and memory, down through the village towards the water, or upwards to the soaring peaks. I am surrounded by the smells of the forest and the laughter of the living. But inside, never far away, are gathering shadows. 'He needs you,' says Gran once again, placing a hand on my shoulder. 'You might not know it, but he does. You're all he has left, Emma.'

It's our last day in Italy and Carla has cooked lunch and, even by her standards, this is something special. Insects thud against the window, and Carla is prattling on in her accented English about her arthritis. She has also said, repeatedly, how much she's going to miss us. She has cooked a meal in our honour, she tells us. *Risotto alla Milanese*, with the haunting smell of saffron; spaghetti baked in parchment paper; artichoke salad and, to end, green figs in strong wine and all effortlessly conjured to our table from her miniscule

128

kitchen. My father eats salad, and hasn't shaved for several days, and I notice how grey his beard has become.

Of all my distant relatives, Carla is my favourite. She drinks grappa, smokes little brown cheroots and, for reasons unknown, hates the local priest with a vengeance. I've always found her radical views bewildering and intriguing.

The nuanced antics of adults are still beyond me; but in Carla, despite her huge age, I sense a kindred spirit. She is widowed, without children, and treats me as the grandchild she might have had. Her *torta pasqualina*, Easter pie made with thirty layers of pastry to represent the years of Christ's life, is famous in the village.

At the end of the meal, Carla raises her glass and wishes us a safe journey home. She also hopes that we will come back soon. She is looking at me when she says this, and winks. She knows how much I like her cooking.

'But we're not really going,' says Granny Mary who, as eldest guest, is at the head of the table. 'We've been thinking about it, Ally and me, and we've decided to move here.'

My father, roused from his bed for this last meal, is outraged. However, even as a famous celebrity, he is a visitor in a relative's home. He has also been outmanoeuvred. 'You're *what*?' he manages after a few false starts. 'Move *here*?'

'Of course, dear. Here. This village. The place where your father was born. The place that we've been planning to retire to. Ally's decided that enough is enough, haven't you, darling?'

Alberto is at the other end of the table, drinking coffee and grappa. His cheeks are red. 'Until I'd finished my research, my plans were frozen in aspic. Now it's time to let others continue my work. I can finally retire. It's what we've always promised ourselves. You know that Paulo.'

'But it's ridiculous!' splutters my father.

Granny holds up a hand. 'Please don't be tiresome, Paulo.

Our minds are completely made up.' Dad winces at the use of his Italian name, and has half risen from the table. Now he sags back into his chair. 'But the idea's preposterous,' he announces. 'What on earth makes you want to move here? It's … it's just not *practical!* For a start, think about your house in Edinburgh? All your furniture? And what about your friends?'

My grandfather is enveloped in Carla's smoke. 'Furniture, fiddlesticks, and friends can visit. What's important is that the pawns and bishops all live in the same box. Our minds are absolutely made up.'

'But you can't just uproot yourself, not like this. At your time of life,' Dad adds for good measure. It wasn't clear which of his parents this is aimed at.

Carla's great-great-uncle had been married to a close relative of Alberto and, inexplicably, that makes us the closest of kith and kin. 'But we're also family,' says Carla in her thick English accent and reaches across the table to hold my grandmother's hand.

'Then what about us?' my father demands, although he is long past needing a mother's shoulder. 'What about Emma? She's just lost her mother and now she's going to lose her grandparents. Honestly, I don't know what's possessed you both.'

Granny Mary is looking to me, not her son, and I sense her need for my approval. 'Go for it, Gran,' I say quietly as Carla pours herself another generous measure of grappa, a brown cheroot clenched between stained teeth.

Granny Mary speaks faultless Italian that she learned at night-school, recognising early on that Alberto's extravagant romanticism flourished best in his native tongue. From him she picked up the regional dialect, almost a distinct language, and on trips to neighbouring towns is often mistaken for a local. This is also a source of grievance for

Dad. In markets, shops, restaurants and bars, he listens in silence as my grandmother discusses the weather, politics or food – always in great detail and winning endless plaudits for her proficiency. Her *bambino*, my father, grimly smiles, while people nearby take surreptitious photographs.

It isn't much of surprise to me that Gran and Alberto have now chosen to move to Italy. In the village, they have both always appeared more alive; in Scotland, in the rain, my grandmother seems smaller. The exuberant Alberto only truly blossoms in sunshine.

I lie on my bed in our rented villa, the window open, storm clouds gathering on the high peaks and wake up in an explosion of noise. A waiter across the street has dropped a tray of glasses, and is now being berated by the proprietor, Luigi, and several customers whose wine, coffee and grappa is now being swallowed by the earth. An Imperial Stormtrooper looks impassively on.

It is the village's only café-cum-restaurant and social centre and it was here that Darth Vader and his entourage had eaten. Luigi had declined payment in exchange for the Stormtrooper. Now released from terrorising the universe, it's new role is to stand outside the restaurant and hold a menu card. Members of staff are deputised to keep an eye on it.

At first, I was frightened by the Stormtrooper and didn't go near it. Then I felt sorry for it: this was no respectable retirement for a fearsome warrior: docilely holding a menu, with one foot chained to a drainpipe. *May the Force be with you*, I now say to him when I pass on the pavement, and I sometimes think his dark eyes follow me, fondly remembering the glory days of the Empire, although I'm probably mistaken.

Thoroughly awake, I find Granny Mary on the roof terrace, half-moon glasses on her nose and embroidery on her knee. My father's door is closed and I'd earlier heard

Gramps telling Granny that he was going for a walk.

She smiles but says nothing. I slide into a wicker chair and watch her needle at work. She's pencilled out a picture of the village, all rooftops from our vantage point, and is now filling in threads of colour. It's been her week's project and is now nearly finished. 'You don't have to finish it today, Gran,' I say. 'You could finish it when you get back.'

She looks at me over her glasses, grey hair haloed against the sinking sun. 'I suppose I could, Emma. But if I set my mind on something, I like to finish it.' Her needle is poised over the stumpy tower of the village church. 'I don't think your father approves,' she says after some moments. 'No, that's wrong. He *absolutely* doesn't approve. Sometimes I despair of him.' I've never heard anyone criticise my father before, except my mother, and I wait expectantly for her to continue.

'I first came here before your father was born. Back when Ally's parents were still alive. After that, we've tried to come every year. It was important to him, to keep in touch. A way of remembering where he was from.' Her fingers trace the contours of a rooftop, before selecting a new colour of thread. 'Once Ally retired, we were always going to move here. *Always!* Your father knows that. Ally wants to spend his retirement painting, and where better to do that than here?'

'So, he's not going to write another book?'

She shakes her head. 'No, no more books.'

I remember eating spaghetti and Mum humming as she filled the dishwasher. 'But at least he found the missing bit of the universe.'

She pauses. 'I suppose so, yes.'

'Won't you miss Scotland?' I ask.

'Of course, but here is also home. We'll come back often enough, and you'll come to visit, won't you, Emma? Even if your father doesn't.' Again, the piercing look over her glasses. 'And thank you for supporting me at lunchtime. It meant a lot,' she says and resumes her sewing, eyes cast down.

I have another question. 'What did Granddad mean about pawns and bishops?'

The needle stops mid-stitch. 'It's an old Italian saying. Quite a wise one, I suppose. It goes like this. *Quando finisce la partita, i pedoni, le torri, i cavalli, i vescovi, i due re e le due regine tutti vanno nella stessa scatola.*' She smiles. 'What the proverb says is that when the chess game is over, the pawns, rooks, knights, bishops, kings and queens all go back into the same box.'

'I don't think I understand, Gran.'

'It means that death makes us equal,' Granny Mary tells me, once more appraising me over her glasses. During that week, the 'D' word has been absolutely out-of-bounds, and it's almost a relief to hear it. 'Eventually, you see, it happens to us all. Your mother, bless her …even you, one day, Emma! After that there's nothing. Not on this earth anyway, and I'm not sure about heaven. I suppose I should believe in one, although Alberto doesn't.' After a pause, she adds: 'The proverb means that the only *really* important thing is life, and what we do with it. After we die, it's too late.'

'Is that why you're moving to Italy?'

'Precisely!' says Granny Mary. 'But your father doesn't play chess and wouldn't understand.' She looks at me sharply. 'You're smiling,' she says.

But I'm not really smiling: just moving muscles around my mouth. I don't bother to correct her, thinking instead about Gramps who once told me that the scariest thing in the universe is a black hole. It scours the universe, eating stars, always hungry. Time is meaningless inside a black hole because the laws of physics don't apply, and for the first days after Mum's death, that's what it felt like. The

133

sun would cross the sky outside my window but, inside and looking out, I couldn't tell whether it was the same sun I had looked at yesterday or last week or ten minutes beforehand. For a while, time lost meaning.

A black hole is the worst thing in the universe, and the best way to detect one is to see if there are stars circling around something that isn't there. In other words, a something that has gravitational force, but no actual presence. Think of a black hole as a predator; it eats galaxies, sucking them into a nether land of complete darkness.

The black hole at the centre of our galaxy, called Sagittarius A* – with an asterisk – is millions and millions times larger than our Sun. Stars circle, they get drawn in, they collapse. It's a scary thought; a hungry predator from the skies searching for unwary prey.

To put it another way, to reach space you need an escape velocity of 11.2 kilometres per second. At that speed, your mass and weight can break free from torpid Earth gravity. To escape the Moon, a much smaller lump of cheese, you only require 2.4 kilometres per second. But across a black hole's event horizon, escape velocity is greater than the speed of light, making escape impossible.

But one phenomenon is that the light from your doomed spaceship slows down. In black hole time, small particles of light from your afterburners will continue to be detected long after you have crashed and burned.

That's what Granny has seen, a faint afterglow in my smile. From the other side of the event horizon, its luminosity has completely faded.

Granny sighs. 'I know the last few weeks haven't been easy. Not for any of us, mainly for you. But believe me the worst is over, and time is a great healer.' She smiles, a pucker of the lips, and looks out over the rooftops. 'Time is the only thing that any of us has.'

From the perspective of the here and now, I know that it is threads of dark matter that connect us, woven over time into subtle tapestries of light and shade. We may believe that the pattern of our individuality is self-made, but no, it is the handiwork of generations, an ever-changing embroidery stitched by unseen and long-dead hands. That last day in Italy, watching Granny Mary's needle, I sense the futility of it all and, for the first time in my life, feel utterly alone.

Outwardly, I am coping, but not inside. It feels like being enveloped in a dark storm cloud and I lie on my bed, fully dressed, feeling that small fragments inside my head are breaking free. Soon I will be back in Scotland, in a grand house that will feel like entrapment, with a father who can't boil an egg, and isn't usually there anyway. Mrs Perkins won't exactly be an ideal substitute mother.

That night there is an electrical storm in the mountains. The air in my lungs seems heavy, and it's painful to breathe it in. I can feel the snap of electricity in my every breath, and in every lightning bolt hear the static hiss of its satisfaction. I've never been frightened by thunderstorms before, but I am now, and I find myself in the kitchen, looking upwards to the high peaks, watching lightning caress the mountains.

The storm seems to be growing closer, the noise shaking the house. I wonder why I'm the only person who can't sleep through it. My hands are over my ears; there are tears rolling down my cheeks. Mum's spirit seems to have found a way through the dark curtains and is all around me, carried by electricity. My ears are full of noise and fear.

I find a bottle by the sink and swig it back. It tastes of coffee and almonds and makes my head spin. It isn't unpleasant; it's what Gramps sometimes drinks after a meal, so it can't be poison. I drink more and more. I've never really tasted strong alcohol before, but I know what it does. Then I crawl under the kitchen table, shaking, willing the noise outside and the fear inside to stop.

It's there that Granny Mary finds me in the morning, lying in a pool of vomit, and a much larger pool of blood. Her scream brings Gramps at a gallop and my father at a controlled canter. Granny wraps tourniquets around my wrists and Granddad phones the village doctor.

Soon afterwards, I am in an ambulance heading for the local hospital by the lake. 'Why, Emma?' Granny sobs beside me in the ambulance, holding my hand, as we lurch down the mountain. But I pretend not to hear her over the noise of the siren, because I can't tell her about the blackness inside and how, unseen, it has devoured me.

And I can't tell her something else. That Mum's death was no accident, and that everything is Dad's fault.

$$-\frac{5mkc^2s^2}{E_W} = 10$$

Energy in a Newtonian homogeneous and isotropic universe

I spent four days in hospital in Moltrasio under the supervision of an elderly doctor in a frayed white coat, with whom Granny Mary would hold whispered consultations in Italian at the end of my bed. He had rheumy eyes, spoke no English and quite clearly had no idea what to do with me. There was talk of transferring me to a psychiatric unit in Milan; instead, I was prescribed tranquillisers and plastic cutlery. Brain medicine, I quickly decided, was quite nice. The pills quietened me and made me feel safe. They stilled my thoughts.

The bandages on my arm were changed regularly by a smiling nurse called Kara who seemed always to be there, always humming. She couldn't speak English either. At first, I could tell, they thought that I was just a stupid young adolescent: I was treated professionally but with scant sympathy. Then, when they found out that my Mum had just died, sympathy ratcheted up several notches.

At this point, I was in a small room with an Italian girl, who also couldn't speak English, who must have been ill, but looked fine to me. She would babble at me incessantly, as if I might suddenly become fluent in Italian, while I kept my eyes shut and fervently wished that she'd shut up, or die, or get better and leave.

The food was institutional, but wholesome. Then came the revelation of who my father was. Was it Granny who

137

told them? I suspect so. Suddenly I found myself in a room by myself, overlooking the lake, and the rheumy old doctor would actually bow as he entered the room. I was now given a menu card every morning, which Granny would translate.

I knew that I was at a new beginning, a singularity, from the moment my eyes popped open each morning, to the brain pills I was given by Kara in the evening. In between, on the hospital's opulent balcony, fringed with full-size Romanesque statues – the town's hospital had once been an aristocratic palace – were Granny's endless chatter, Dad's silences, and Alberto's sad-looking moustache. I felt sorry for having made his moustache unhappy; I didn't like to see it droop. I wanted to swim in the lake and on its surface were speedboats towing water-skiers; nearby I could hear shrieks and laughter from a public beach. But swimming wasn't allowed, Kara mimed to me, looking apologetic and gesturing at my wrists, although everything had mostly healed up.

Instead, at night I would fly over the lake, touching its dark surface with my fingers, then soar to the mountains where the electricity had also tried to find me, but failed. There was no fear in dream-flying and, so real was it, I could almost believe I was awake until, with a swish of curtains, Kara would start my new day of chatter, silence and disappointed moustache.

Granny also talked about *new beginnings*, saying how I had to be strong, how my mother would have wanted me to be strong, how she wouldn't have wanted to see me like this. I suppose Granny meant well, although she didn't get much help from Dad, who would look instead across the lake, his eyes half-closed against the glare, and say little. He didn't like being in the hospital and kept looking around furtively, not wanting to be recognised.

My hospital room also overlooked the hospital's formal gardens in which were scattered wooden benches. It was there where I'd sit during the day, warmed by the sun and aching to swim in the lake which lay at the end of the manicured lawn. One morning, standing by my window, I looked down at the wooden benches; as always at that time of day they were mostly occupied by old ladies who, despite the gathering heat, had blankets across their knees. Standing nearby were two female nurses in blue overalls. Both nurses were smoking and whispering to one another.

To one side of the balcony was a wall with trellis covered over with flowering blue bougainvillea. On the other side of the wall was a quiet residential street, where a gaggle of small children had been kicking a football. I stood by my window, not counting the minutes, listening to other people's lives. Then the kids over the wall drifted off; I could hear them but distantly now, still hear the fading thump-thump of the football.

Below, the old ladies were still sitting, each immobile and staring at the climbing bougainvillea. The two nurses had finished their cigarettes and gone back inside. I now realised that my curtains were the mirror-image of the bougainvillea outside, white blooms against a green background, and I wondered if my curtains had been chosen specifically or coincidentally, or if anyone else had ever noticed.

The brain pills stilled me and allowed the remnants of dark matter to seep from the wounds on my arms. But my mind still seemed filled with fragments; some small and insubstantial; others, like my mother's death, large and sharp and capable of inflicting pain.

But I sensed also that even the insubstantial fragments were joined together by other, smaller, pieces and that, between the bits that mattered and the bits that didn't, were microscopic fragments of not-quite nothingness.

It was Granny who signed the hospital discharge forms, because Dad didn't want his famous signature on a mental health form. Imagine what *that* would make on eBay!

Granddad's moustache was sending out conflicting signals. He seemed both pensive and sad, his moustache curling all over the place. I didn't like to see his moustache looking unhappy, and felt guilty, and I slipped my hand in his as we walked out to the hired car and the trip to Milan airport.

On our private jet back from Italy, Granny Mary holds tight to my hand and then comes to stay for several days in North Berwick, immediately taking over cooking duties, much to the confusion of Mrs Boyce who now has nothing to do except sit at the kitchen table with her arms crossed.

Dad eats little of what she puts in front of him, has lost a lot of weight, and doesn't say much to anyone. My uncharitable thought is that he's worried about the press getting wind of my 'little accident' as everyone now calls it. In his eyes, I have become a potential liability; in my eyes, he has simply become even more uncaring. That may sound harsh but consider this: I once found Mum watching the TV in tears. Dad was being interviewed by a well-known chat-show host. She hadn't known that her husband was going to be on the programme. He simply hadn't told her. His world found difficulty communicating with our world.

He once appeared in "A Day in the Life of ..." in *The Sunday Times,* although, from the article, I wouldn't have known it was Dad. According to the newspaper 'I get up at 6 a.m. most mornings and always swim twenty lengths.' *Twenty lengths of what exactly?* After reading that, I had to again check the basement to make sure that we still didn't have a swimming pool. 'I then work out in the gym and meditate for half an hour.' *What! Meditate?* And as far as I know, nobody has *ever* used the gym, and certainly not Dad.

'I have fresh fruit and camomile tea for breakfast and, if I'm at home between filming, I'm handling correspondence on the computer by 8 a.m.' When he's at home, Dad drinks strong coffee in his dressing gown and, unless he's golfing, doesn't normally switch his computer on until lunchtime. The article gushed on about how much time Dad devotes to his charitable foundation – bugger all, it's administered by Sarah for tax reasons – and how, if he's at home, his 'beautiful wife will cook something tasty and nutritious.' *What! Mum? Tasty? Nutritious?*

It was an article of falsehood, probably written by Sarah, to portray Dad as wholesome and family-centred; a paragon of personal virtue, working tirelessly for various charities and only managing, with great difficulty, to tear himself away from family life and reluctantly depart for Los Angeles.

The strange thing is that, when Dad read the article – as I suppose he did – he probably believed every word of it. He probably believed that we have a swimming pool and that he liked camomile tea. In his mind, the truth was malleable; it was whatever he believed it to be.

I've always enjoyed flying, in big planes before Dad became famous and then in the privileged splendour of a private jet – like dream-flying only real – but on the plane back from Italy I shrink down in my seat. The aluminium hull of our aircraft now seems fragile, a too-delicate membrane between us and the electricity above the mountains.

Dad once starred in a low-budget film called *The Art of Loss*, in which he played the role of a Vietnam war correspondent whose wife is killed in a car accident back in Britain. The film revolves around the horror of war, with soldiers deliberately killing other soldiers, and sometimes women and children, and the random carnage of one small traffic accident. In the film, Dad mourns his wife effusively, but then finds new love with his Vietnamese translator.

In *The Art of Loss*, Dad's performance was muted. He grieved, but not excessively. He cried, but he didn't lock himself in his room for days and days. He was able to organise a funeral, rather than having to rely on his own father and his agent to do it for him. There again, for years and years, my father has had other people to handle his life. Simple everyday things are now beyond him.

I doubt that my father has been inside a supermarket for a decade – except to open them. Every Monday morning Sarah Parker, his chief of staff and head of his publicity machine, sends him an email listing all his engagements for the coming week, as well as detailed instructions on how to get to his appointments, who he'll be meeting, what they're offering, and what he should say.

Cars, aeroplanes and hotels are all booked for him. It doesn't matter if my father is in North Berwick, London, Sydney or New York, the email must always find him. Without it, he's lost. In the film, Dad grieved but pulled himself together; in real life, he merely seems to have fallen apart. His grief is total.

I know he feels guilty and sad, but I don't really know in what proportion. His silences are towering; he won't now speak to Sarah Parker on the phone, and I doubt he's reading her emails either because the computer is in his office, and he never seems to go into it. Instead of speech, he now grunts: at Granny, who might have cooked him supper, at me, who might have said 'good morning', or at Mrs Boyce or Mrs Perkins, on their perennial cleaning duties.

Add to them his publicists on different continents, the secretaries who draft replies to his fan mail, all the people who make up his small army, and who are now rudderless on a Ross-less sea. He reminds me of Humpty Dumpty, and how all the king's men can't put him back together again.

The only error he made was to appear in a film called *Before Words*. At the time it was a ground-breaking concept. Set in prehistory, and therefore before vocabulary, it neither required a costume department nor team of writers.

The production company liked it because they believed, without need for translation, it would achieve international success on the cheap. It was mostly set around campfires or in caves, so no expensive sets; the action was about hunting, being attacked by neighbouring tribes or wild animals, or seducing each other and having little hairy babies.

In the film, the one thing that Dad did rather well was grunt. He was a method actor, his hero was Stanislavski; he might not have looked like a caveman, but he sounded like one. It didn't matter if you were from Timbuktu or Torquay, you knew exactly what he was grunting, it was eloquent, conveying pathos or good humour.

Since Mum's death, he has rediscovered the role and has been playing it magnificently. The grunting had started in Italy and has continued ever since. He barely says anything. What he seems to be communicating is that his wife, whom he didn't really love, is more important than my mother, who I absolutely adored, and that his grief is somehow more important than mine.

After her death, I'd wanted Dad's comfort, to feel his arms on my shoulders; some recognition that we'd both lost the person closest to us. But I never received that comfort or recognition. In his loss, there was no room for interlopers: his grief was monumental in its perfection. He couldn't console me because he couldn't console himself. He spent days in his bedroom, hardly moving from bed. I would see him sometimes, when he eventually ventured to the kitchen for a sandwich or a drink: gaunt, unshaven, the face of someone who doesn't know what to do.

A few days after our arrival back in Scotland an appointment had been made for me to see a Dr Madison in Edinburgh.

I can sometimes feel tiny pieces of darkness flowing through me and mostly out the other side. Only rarely do they get stuck inside, but when they do I have to find somewhere to be by myself, and close my eyes, and wait for the feeling to stop. I don't like it when the darkness comes, but it does sometimes, not often, and always reminds me that my mother's death was a crossing point: afterwards, when I was released from hospital, I was someone different. In the bundle of rags at the top of North Berwick Law, I'd seen a fate that could also be mine if I allowed it to happen. I'd cut my wrists with a kitchen knife, not deeply, but I still have the scars.

Dr Hermione Madison says that young girls often harm themselves. It's a way of coping, she tells me, although she doesn't have scars on *her* wrists. 'Even stupid people have more brain cells than stars in the universe,' she also says on our first meeting, sounding just like my grandfather, and making me wonder if they know one another. I make a mental note to ask Gramps if what she's said is true. I suspect it isn't and she's just trying to impress me with useless knowledge. All those cells, all wired together and fizzing with electricity, the same elemental force that killed my mother.

'It's not unusual for the brain to go haywire,' she continues. 'It's a complex piece of machinery. Like a car or washing machine, it can break down.' Granny Mary is in the waiting room; Dad is too terrified of recognition to ferry his only daughter to a medical appointment. If he had done, he'd no doubt be wearing a wig and clown's mask, or Islamic burka. The bandages on my arms have been removed, but the scars are red and vivid. I know that I have reached a point of singularity, but not what that new beginning is.

The picture of my father, the one that my mother cut from *The Daily Express* on the day she died, has not been mentioned in our diminished family. In it, he's walking down a London street, Big Ben in the background, and a woman is holding onto his arm and looking adoringly upwards at him. The *Express* referred to her as Paul Ross's "mystery woman," although she's no mystery to me. The woman is

144

Sarah Parker, his agent, and given how much he was paying her, she has every right to hold onto his arm and look at him adoringly.

I suspect therefore that my father is both grieving and feeling guilty, although it's not clear which emotion is proportionately greater. My father's grief therefore seems cynical and, while I've wanted him to show some tenderness towards me, I also shy away from the idea. Since her death, I've instinctively tried to keep a distance between us.

In itself, the picture proves nothing, but it doesn't stop me blaming him. I blame him for his absences and for not taking us with him more often. I blame him for not being there when I rode a bicycle for the first time. I blame him for not being there for my first day at school. I blame him for being in Iceland when he should have been with us for Christmas. I blame him for lots and lots of things, most of which aren't really his fault.

Being referred to a brain doctor hasn't entirely surprised me. I am old enough to know that everything comes with consequences and Dr Hermione Madison is one such consequence. She's a severe-looking woman of indeterminate age, with grey hair pulled tight from her scalp, whose consulting rooms in Edinburgh's New Town are discreet yet opulent.

It is filled with the same blobs-of-colour pictures that adorn our walls, leather armchairs in the waiting room, and a huge flower arrangement on the receptionist's desk. Mum would have been proud of it, although she'd have been unable to name any of the flowers.

Dr Madison has pronounced laughter lines, although she seldom raises a chuckle, but all I really know about her is that she has two grown-up daughters. She keeps a picture of them framed on a high shelf behind her desk. I wonder about this; she has to turn and look up to see them. Shouldn't the framed picture be on her desk, where she can watch over them? I guess, given the blobs-of-colour pictures and leather armchairs, that Dr Madison's services don't come cheap.

Hermione – on the first visit, she tells me to call her by her first name – asks how I'm feeling.

'Fine,' I answer. She is on one side of a desk in a large leather chair; I am on the other side in a much smaller leather chair. It reinforces the impression that I am somehow inferior. But, having taken brain pills twice a day for the past week, I also feel immensely peaceful.

Dr Madison makes a small squiggle in my file and pushes her half-moon glasses up her nose, much like Granny Mary does. 'It would help if you could define more precisely how you feel.' She sometimes wears her glasses, and sometimes doesn't, twirling them between fingers, or resting them at the end of her nose.

'I'm fine,' I repeat. 'Why keep asking me?'

'Because you hurt yourself, Emma.' Her voice is soft and lilting – she's from Ireland. 'We all have problems, you know,' she says, and then explains how, if you were to connect all the telephones in the world, you wouldn't get close to a brain's complexity. All those neurons sending messages to one another, all those chemicals ebbing and flowing and triggering small electrical storms. To function adequately, the brain needs its string section and percussionists, its trumpets and its woodwind. Give it a small tap, like your mother's death, and it's only to be expected that the conductor drops his baton. 'Don't worry,' she advises.

My eyes are drawn to the high shelf and the photograph of her two children, only a few years older than me. They are laughing, squinting into the camera. Their white T-shirts are smeared with sand. There seems to be a sea in the background; sparkling light making haloes around their heads.

I envy their laughter, the way they're leaning forwards to the camera, wanting to share their laughter with the person taking the photograph. Behind me is a white marble fireplace. In the space where the grate should be is a glass bowl filled with flowers. Some are lilies; I don't recognise the rest. The room smells scented. It could be my mother's scent, her favourite flower, the one that adorned her coffin.

Hermione leans back in her chair, which makes a soft wheezing noise, and twirls her glasses between long fingers. 'Your father's worried about you,' she concludes rather lamely, 'and your grandmother. Tell me, has the medicine helped?'

I nod warily. A sudden squall throws water at the window and, involuntarily, I flinch.

'Have you ever hurt yourself before, Emma?'

'Falling over, that kind of stuff.'

'But not intentionally?' she asks, still smiling.

I shake my head.

'You see, most people who do what you've done aren't trying to end their life, they're trying to cope with life.'

I close my eyes, smelling lilies. 'I just wanted to feel better,' I say, not knowing if this makes any sense.

'And did you?' she asks.

I open and close my eyes. 'Yes,' I reply, remembering the darkness pouring out.

'It calmed you?' she asks

'It was a relief.'

'OK, here's the science, Emma. Your brain is made up of chemicals and electricity, all joined together like an old-fashioned telephone exchange.'

'I don't know what you're telling me,' I say.

She ignores this, looking at me evenly. 'It means you have a condition,' she says.

'Like measles?'

'But without the spots.' She leans back in her chair and seems to be smiling. 'You see, Emma, when a stressful situation happens, two lots of chemicals are pumped around the brain. One lot simply informs us that there's an axe-murderer heading towards us. It tells us the facts, nothing more.'

I nod. This I can understand.

It isn't easy being me, I could have told her, but I suppose she knows that. She was probably young once, although because I still am young, I probably have a clearer idea of its sharp injustices. Hormones all over the place, all that stuff. Dad hasn't helped, traipsing in and out of our lives, disrupting things, taking Mum away from me.

Without him, she was mine; together, we were able to erect a wall against him, to be ourselves, a unit; when he returned, with red eyes, dropping his suitcase in the hall, pouring himself a large gin and tonic, and then falling asleep on the sofa, she was taken from me. I looked forward to his absences, and could sometimes hate him for what he was, and for what he wasn't, and for simply being there.

'At the same time,' Hermione is saying, 'in another part of the brain, a second lot of chemicals is released. These help us to make quick decisions about the axe-murderer. Is he definitely the axe-murderer whose picture was in the newspaper? Is he the same person who the police have told us not to go near?'

I am looking out the window as she says this. 'I don't know any axe-murderers,' I say.

'What happens,' she continues, speaking over me, 'is that in a split second of electrical discharge, we have to decide whether to confront the axe-murderer or run away as fast as we can.' She leans forwards and places her elbows on the desk. 'Does that make any sense?' she asks.

I don't say anything. Whatever secrets I have are mine to keep. I don't like it that electricity has killed my mother, and that my brain is filled with it.

'What's he called?' Hermione now asks, leaning over the desk. 'The axe-murderer? *Your* axe-murderer.'

'I still don't know what you're talking about.' My voice has risen, and I stare at her angrily.

Her glasses are pushed up her nose and light from the window has bounced against them, making her eyes invisible. 'Yes, you do,' she says.

Suddenly I am flustered. 'He doesn't have a name,' I stammer.

'Then what does he look like?'

I close my eyes tight shut, thinking about shifting patterns in the clouds. 'He doesn't have a face.' He's too small to have a face, I could have said. He's too small even for us to know that he exists.

Gramps concluded that there had to be parallel worlds beyond our own, undiscovered dimensions of time and space through which dark matter can pass. Only by accepting that multiverse does gravity and mass make sense: between the big stuff like black holes, and the teeny-weeny stuff like dark matter. My grandfather's theory of universal probability, supersymmetry and string theory is that, probably, we are a small and rather insignificant part of the real universe, that we occupy a dimension that is, probably, of no real importance to the much larger universes that we can't see and that, probably, if there is a god, he didn't create us.

It was during that period of grief that I finally started to read his great tome, not just look at the pictures, lying in bed with my knees drawn up, the book balanced against my legs. The mathematical gibberish still made little sense, but Gramps had also written it for a lay audience, with bits that even I could understand.

So, if my mother and father could occupy different dimensions, could I invent one for myself? But no, I concluded, we are what we are, that's the truth of it.

The only thing I *was* good at was English. I liked reading, unlike most of my school friends. I read books that were too clever for me, borrowing them from the school library, finding a curious comfort in words and phrases that someone had taken the time and trouble to think up and actually write down. It was the one subject at school where I didn't sit at the back of the class with Patsy. It began, I think, with a poem by Maya Angelou.

The caged bird sings
With a fearful trill
Of things unknown
But longed for still
And his tune is heard
On the distant hill
For the caged bird
Sings of freedom.

I first read it in primary school and was inspired by its simple eloquence, and immediately set up a Book Club which then met in our semi-posh mansion flat once a week where, with Mum's help, all we did was bake cakes. None of the other members were much interested in reading, but everyone knew about Mum's prowess with flour, butter and chocolate. So, did I even then think of myself as a caged bird?

There was another bereavement not long after coming back from Italy.

I'd spoken to Oz a few times, and we'd been texting back and forward, but it was the first time I had properly seen him since Mum's death. Before then, we'd been to the cinema, and to the same café where we'd met after rugby. Sometimes he brought his spaniel, Rolf, to the beach and we'd throw sticks and watch him bound in and out of the waves.

Oz is fun to be with and easy to talk to, although I still can't fathom why he would want to be with me, when there is a sizeable gaggle of prettier girls, most of whom are also more worldly-wise: brazenly holding hands at the school gates, sauntering down the High Street arm in arm and smoking cigarettes, or snogging down alleys where they don't expect to be caught. Is it my father he's after, I still think? A bit of reflected fame in being with the great man's daughter? I don't think so. He never mentions Dad and, apart from my birthday party, hasn't been to our house.

We'd arranged to go for a walk one Sunday afternoon and ended up walking across fields and then up what seemed, from a distance, to be a small hill. A stream wound round the foot of the hill, the run-off from a reservoir further up. Clouds were washing in from the west and the path up the hill steep and twisted.

'Not so fast,' I plead.

A valley we had traversed earlier now seems far below. A house in the valley that had looked so large and solid as we walked past it, now seems toy-like, with a wisp of smoke coming from its chimney, warming the toy people inside. I am wearing wellington boots with a jaunty flower design, and they're being sucked into pools of mud. We're both tired, and spurts of vapour are coming from Oz's mouth.

'I've got to stop,' I gasp.

'You're unfit,' he says.

'You're the rugby player,' I remind him.

'Yes, but you've got a swimming pool.'

We reach a white-painted gate with a sign saying, "BEWARE OF THE BULL".

'What do we do now?' I ask.

'Go on.'

'But there's a bull!'

'Do you see one?'

'No.'

'OK, so there isn't a bull,' says Oz.

'Christ, Oz! You really can be irritating.'

So we climb the gate and continue up the hill. I keep a good look-out for charging bulls, but only see a rabbit. The rabbit doesn't look worried. Although I know that bulls don't actually eat rabbits, I find the unperturbed rabbit comforting. The summit of the hill is much closer now, with a cluster of trees marking its peak. But something's not right. There's a shadow behind his eyes.

'What's wrong, Oz?'

'Nothing.'

'There's been something wrong all day.' I pick my way around a gigantic clump of sheep's droppings then come to a stop. 'I'm knackered.'

'Just concentrate on putting one foot after the other. It's what marathon runners do.'

'I'm not a bloody marathon runner,' I remind him, and we continue upwards towards the trees. We can hear the breeze whistle in their branches.

'But something's wrong, isn't it?'

'Why do you keep asking?'

'Because you're evading me, that's why.'

'Emma, I'm not evading you.'

'You fucking are!'

A bird screams overhead giving us both a fright, sounding like a pterodactyl, but smaller.

'Let's stop,' I suggest, stopping.

'But we're nearly there.'

'So bloody what?' I say, more angrily than I'd intended.

But Oz walks on and reluctantly I follow, and then flop down at the top of the hill. Behind me are the trees; below, far below, is the reservoir. It lies in a cradle between two hills and looks like a bowl of treacle.

'You can see the fort from here,' says Oz, sitting beside me.

'What fort?'

'See that hill over there?' He points. 'That's a Stone Age fort.'

'Really?'

'Really.'

We sit in silence for a minute. 'How the hell do you know that?'

'An uncle took me there. Years ago. He's an archaeologist or something.'

The hill he had pointed to is a small lump with concentric

rings around its summit. It doesn't look very impressive.

'The rings were its walls,' says Oz. 'Inside the walls lived the animals and the elite.'

'Lucky elite,' I reply.

'Most if it is buried, but it has been excavated. The old houses are now underground. But you can get the key from a local farmer. He's the custodian.'

Of what? I wanted to ask. *Of a grass-covered hill with some grass circles?*

'You want to go down now?' he asks.

'Christ, Oz! We've only just got up here!' I give an exaggerated sigh. 'What *is* wrong, Oz?'

'And that makes the third time.'

'It's just that you're being odd.'

'Odd?'

'Like you're thinking about something.'

A few leaves blow past us and up into the air. The clouds rolling in are darker now. 'OK, we'd better go,' I say reluctantly.

'Did you know,' he asks, once we're back on the twisty path, 'that more people get hurt going down hills than up them?'

'No, Oz, I didn't.'

We stay silent for the rest of the descent; my feet being sucked at by puddles. In a field at the bottom of the hill we come across a dead sheep, its eyes pecked clean. We circle around it. 'Probably attacked by the bull,' says Oz.

On the way back to North Berwick, crossing a field, he asks, 'What happened to your wrists?' He's not looking at my arms, but out towards the sea, which we can glimpse now, across a landscape of grass. I've told everyone that I slipped on rocks, and everyone seems to believe me.

'I cut myself with a knife,' I tell him.

'Thought as much,' he says. We are walking close together, and I can feel his warmth and the musty smell of him. He doesn't sound remotely shocked, or even surprised.

'It was just after Mum died,' I go on, wondering if honesty really is the best policy. Suppose he tells everyone at school? 'Things got a bit out of hand.'

'Are they still out of hand?' he asks, finally looking at me.

I shake my head, watching muscles in the sea tense and pull. 'It was just something I did.'

We reach a headland and look down on moving water. The collar of his jacket is turned up, and he has his eyes closed. Once again, I'm struck by how old he looks compared to the rest of us. Then he opens his eyes and looks at me and I realise that, for the second time, I am about to suffer loss.

His Dad, some kind of computer boffin, has been posted to Silicon Valley, and his whole family is expected to go with him. It's where I should be, in California, lounging beside a *real* swimming pool, with a beautiful maid in a neat uniform bringing exotic snacks and drinks, rather than Mrs Perkins in a shapeless smock making a cucumber sandwich.

But I'm used to goodbyes now, and losing him is smaller than losing Mum, and all I feel for a few moments is a cold numbness, and then he takes hold of my shoulders and turns me to him, and kisses me on the lips, a first proper kiss, a kiss of such intensity that nothing could ever match it again. For a moment it feels like first love and last love all rolled into one. He tastes bittersweet; of good things and all the perfect days we will never have.

Then he draws back and looks embarrassed, and suddenly I am in a world where the points of my compass have been removed.

'But I'll see you again, Emma. It's not forever.'

'Nothing is forever, Oz,' I say. 'When do you go?'

'Soon.' The wind has picked up and the long grass fringing the beach has set up a collective sigh. 'I would have told you sooner but, well … your Mum …'

We walk down the beach, both of us trying to be jolly and grown-up, and promising to write and text and email.

But after he goes off home, I stay on the beach by myself, not caring if he's looking from his house, and not caring if anyone sees that I'm crying. Out to sea is a sudden splash, but I can't see what's made it. A dolphin, perhaps, or a whale; they come here sometimes.

I then decide that I must still have all sorts of panoramas ahead of me, uncharted possibilities to be explored, and maybe that's what life is all about: to journey, rather than find landfall, because the sea is empty of bad intentions and the land is full of bad people. That's why I like to look at the sea, but I never told him that.

Then, for no apparent reason, Dad starts to perk up. He begins getting up in the mornings. He begins reading newspapers. He begins to shave each morning when, before, he could go for days without shaving. He's looking like a film star again, with the grey beard gone from his face. He's also begun to wear lurid golf trousers again, in loud greens or turquoise, although not actually to play golf. He's started to speak, monosyllables at first, then whole sentences. He has also accepted that his parents will be returning to Italy for good – and now seems to be encouraging it. He doesn't want his mother's constant judgement, and he's also remembered that he has an adoring public.

Although the grunting has stopped, I must admit that tragedy suited Dad; it has always been his best metier – in the early days, Shakespeare had been his inspiration. His *Othello* is still revered at the RSC.

He has resumed his conversations with Sarah, at first on the telephone then, later, as his full baritone returned, in person. He often refers to my mother, usually in loving terms, although never in such terms in front of Sarah. He pats my hair, calls me 'old girl,' and says that a child as young shouldn't be motherless. He makes out that theirs had been a great love, and that his loss is profound. He seems to believe it himself, even dabbing at his eyes from time to time.

Sarah often arrives in a hire car from Edinburgh airport and stays in the main guest bedroom at the top of the house – almost a guest apartment, with a kitchen, living room and en suite gym. Even now, I have no idea why my father thought that installing a gym at the top of our house would be a good idea.

I lie in bed, long into the night, listening for footsteps between bedrooms, but I never hear any. There again, the carpeting in our house is thick and exquisite and traps sound so effectively that armies could march around, and I wouldn't hear them.

Sarah's visits don't last long, a day or two at most, mostly spent locked in his study and no doubt weighing up what offers are in the pipeline or who she should talk to. He doesn't confide his plans to me, and I don't ask. The study door is kept firmly shut; my father's voice trapped behind its heavy oak. Unlike Mum, I don't bother listening at the keyhole. I don't want to know what they might be saying to one another.

I see Dr Madison for a couple of follow-up consultations, each the same; Hermione in her plush leather armchair and me, opposite, in the penitent's seat. It makes me feel small, makes me feel like a patient, a real loony; someone of lesser importance to the good doctor. It therefore makes me angry. But what can I tell her beyond the fact that my life has fallen apart? Just yesterday in French I realised that Oz's desk was empty, and I had to excuse myself and rush to the loo where I burst into tears.

I drink in the scent of Hermione's lilies but say little; I'm not old enough to judge myself, but old enough to not want the judgement of others. I keep looking at the picture of her kids on the high shelf, where she can't see them. I want to ask her about this: why ask her patients to look at her children, when she can't?

'You haven't told me very much,' she says.

'There's nothing much to tell.'

'There's always something to tell. After all, if you won't talk to me, I can't easily help you.'

'I don't need your help, Hermione.'

'Maybe you do, Emma.' She sighs and picks up my file, which she probably knows by heart. 'Therapy is about talking,' she suggests. 'Look, you had a traumatic experience … finding your mother like that. It can help to talk about things. Not keep them bottled up.'

'But I'm better now.'

'If you say so, Emma.'

Hermione, with her posh chair and discarded children, can ask whatever she likes. I see no reason to talk to her and our sessions peter out, as do the pills. I have learned how to cope, to smile again, to go back to school. It seems a better way of getting on with things, rather than discuss them for no purpose with Dr Madison. She wouldn't understand about the fragments I can sometimes feel on my skin, the course and flow of small particles. In any case, it seems to her that my mother's death was a singular catalyst and that I can now be trusted not to be stupid again.

I could have told her that a great many people are scared witless by spiders; not the little money spiders that scurry around, not the spiders you hardly notice. I'm talking huge and hairy, with big, long legs. If I see one that's managed to evade the cameras, bulletproof glass and intruder alarms, I simply pick it up and chuck it out the window; our security windows, by the way, are very heavy and difficult to open. It doesn't matter how big; I handle them all carefully and deposit them safely outside. But I know one girl who, if she sees one, will scream and stand on a chair. Otherwise, she is quite sane. What matters is perception. To some, spiders are a threat. To me, I know that the sky, when provoked, can generate limitless voltage. Otherwise, I'm quite sane, most of the time.

After my last appointment, Hermione wished me well.

Part Two: Antithesis

$$\sqrt{\frac{242GM}{rv_{\mathrm{h}}}} = 11$$

Escape velocity

'So, Maria, you have a degree in media studies.'

'Media and communications, yes.'

'Apologies. Media *and* communications.' John Salmond doesn't sound remotely apologetic and is holding my CV between finger and thumb as if it might harbour germs. 'As do a lot of other people,' he adds, not looking impressed or, frankly, very interested, and turns my single piece of foolscap over to read the other side. 'Many, I have to say, with better degrees than yours.'

I have been in his goldfish bowl of an office for less than a minute, and already I have an urge to get up and leave. A small pulse of anger is throbbing behind one eye. It may not be a very good degree, but it represents four years of my life; four years of listening to Professor Trish MacBeth explaining the societal impact of digital media and the democratic importance of a free press. Rather appropriately, Professor MacBeth often *did* resemble someone from a Shakespearian tragedy, with red eyes and tousled hair: the result of a messy separation.

The goldfish bowl is mostly glass and behind him, one floor down, is the newspaper's main editorial floor: journalists tapping on keyboards, a couple more on the phone, and several who appear to be asleep. John Salmond is deputy editor of *The Scotsman* and looks younger than I do. I wonder unkindly if his mother still makes him a packed lunch and picks him up from work every evening. This uncharitable thought makes me feel better. He's now holding my CV to the overhead light, to see if I might have written anything in invisible ink. 'Any particular reason why you think your CV is better than anyone else's?'

'I haven't seen anybody else's,' I tell him. He's wearing grey flannels and a blue open-necked shirt and is trying, and failing, for the casual-chic look. His trousers are too baggy and his shirt too big, perhaps hand-me-downs from an older brother. Half closing my eyes, I visualise him instead in shorts and a mucky T-shirt, the kind of clothes that he should be wearing.

He also seems to be made from leftover spare parts. His hands are too big for his skinny arms, and his head is too small for his shoulders. Nothing quite seems to fit together; his mouth is too wide, and his eyes too far down his forehead. The pulse of anger has become a rhythmic ache. I have spent four years earning a degree and I don't deserve to be patronised by a man-child in a shirt that doesn't even fit him properly.

'OK, then why do you think you are suited to a career in newspapers?' He also has a sing-song accent, which makes him sound Chinese, except that he's not. I can't make out his accent: he could be Scottish or Martian, and I rather suspect the latter.

'Because I'm curious and I know how to write'

'Most people know how to write.' He looks pained and swivels his chair round to look at the editorial floor. Several other journalists now appear to be asleep. It's mid-afternoon, the dead time when things that should have been written probably have been written, but before they're edited into tomorrow's newspaper or consigned to the bin. He then turns his chair back and places my CV on the desk in front of him. 'Any other nuggets in here?' he asks.

'None spring to mind,' I answer a little sourly, realising that my first-ever interview has hit rock bottom, before actually getting off rock bottom.

'Along with espionage, some say that we're the world's

second oldest profession,' he says in his strange voice, and I have no idea if his sentence has a question mark at the end of it. He's also looking at my chest, my slightly tight jumper, and my legs – knee-length skirt, so no luck there, mate. His goldfish bowl is actually a glass box, so that I can look into other glass boxes on either side, and through them to other glass boxes. All seem to be occupied by clones of John Salmond, which is unnerving. 'Almost as useful as the oldest one,' I reply, 'but probably not so lucrative.'

He doesn't smile. 'Then where do you see yourself in five years' time?' he asks, lapsing into proper interview mode, and asking the one question I have anticipated.

'To be a valued and trusted member of staff,' I reply, wondering what the difference between valued and trusted might be – I may have anticipated the question, but haven't come up with a coherent answer – 'and, of course, to have won a Pulitzer Prize.'

'Of course,' says John Salmond, without any trace of irony, and turns his chair to again look down on the editorial floor. Two large men are shouting at one another by a water-cooler and waving bunched-up paper at each other. Their faces are very red and they seem to be shouting rather loudly. The sleeping journalists don't seem at all disturbed, and everyone else just ignores them.

'Have you actually done any journalism?' he now asks.

I am swallowing mouthfuls of anger. 'A little bit of freelance stuff,' I reply and hand over my portfolio, which has several clipped-out articles all stuck into a ring-binder with double-sided Sellotape. He reluctantly takes it.

The altercation by the water-cooler seems to have ended, and I can't see any blood on the floor. One of the sleeping journalists has woken up, and is stretching and yawning, perhaps realising that he's paid to actually do things.

'"*Ten Things You Don't Know About Tom Cruise*",' reads John, looking at the headline in *Hello!* 'Did you write this?'

'Actually, it has my name on it,' I reply. He checks. It

does indeed show my name and has a small photograph of me.

He flips over a page. '"*At Home with Monica Bellucci*".'

'She lives in a very nice home. Well, several nice homes.'

John Salmond turns over another page. '"*Kate Beckinsale's Favourite Holiday Destinations*".'

'She goes on holiday quite a lot,' I inform him. 'Mostly to out-of-the-way places in Asia. She doesn't like to be photographed in a bikini. She also visits New York and Paris for shopping weekends.'

'Lucky her,' says John, closes my portfolio and drums his fingers on it. 'And how, may I ask, did you get to meet these people?'

'I spoke to their agents,' I tell him. 'Some agreed to be interviewed, some didn't.' I could have added that Kate Beckinsale stayed with us in North Berwick for a long weekend (nice but a bit snooty), that Tom Cruise is almost an uncle (but has never mentioned Scientology once), and that Monica Bellucci had a sex scene with Dad that was so torrid that Mum and I flew down to London to confront her.

Mum wanted to see 'the whites of her eyes,' or so she said, but, having found out that Monica was happily with someone else and had found the sex scene hugely embarrassing, ended up good friends with her.

'It usually isn't that easy,' he says. 'Or so our showbiz editor tells me.'

'Tenacity and persistence,' I tell him. 'Isn't that also what journalism is all about?'

'I'll remind our showbiz editor of that,' he replies, now looking thoughtful and flipping backwards through my portfolio. 'Is this the kind of stuff you want to go on writing?' he asks eventually.

'Bloody hell, no.'

He frowns, still turning pages. 'But you seem rather good at it.'

'I'd rather do stuff that matters.'

He closes my portfolio and pushes it across the table towards me. 'You also said in your application that you might have a story for us?'

In my application I did not use the word *might*. 'Actually, it's more like a series of stories.'

He's now looking both suspicious and intrigued. I hand over a small folder with a stack of A4 sheets neatly bound into it, all written in 12-point with double spaces, just as I was taught by the weeping professor. '"*Being Nearly Dead. The Doris Glimpton Story.*",' he says and frowns. 'The one and only Doris Glimpton?'

'The one and only,' I confirm.

'But she *never* gives interviews.'

'Well she gave one to me.'

'But she's famous for not giving interviews,' he says. 'That's also what our showbiz editor keeps telling me.'

'Tenacity and persistence, John.'

He's now looking more intrigued than suspicious, scanning through my A4 sheets. 'Christ! Did she really have sex with Prince Andrew?'

'I think she terms it a "failed romance".'

'Holy shit! And snorted cocaine with a shadow cabinet minister?'

'Apparently so.'

There's a small silence, while cogs in John's too-small head grind round and round. He places his too-large hands on his desk. 'Look, Maria, the London tabloids would pay a small fortune for this stuff. We just don't have those kind of budgets.'

I smile sweetly. 'I know that, but all I'm looking for is a job.'

Doris Glimpton has built her career around being Doris Glimpton. But, there again, you probably know that already. Most actresses would have changed their names, like Dad did, swapping a shell suit for a Gucci. But not Doris. She stuck to what she'd been born with and, amid sporadic tabloid derision, made it to the top. You may have seen her in *Four Weddings* – OK, a small part, but one that drew critical applause. She was also in *Notting Hill*, another cameo role, but well-received. In between the cameos were the bigger roles, several of which won BAFTAs.

It sometimes seems that Doris has been on our screens since TV was invented. However, we all remember her as the plucky barmaid in *EastEnders*, the unlucky-in-love fading beauty, the matriarch of her clan, who is run over by a jealous suitor – in a Bentley, although not Dad's – and who lingered in a coma for a whole season of episodes, while the writing team wondered what to do with her and the finance department worried how much their non-speaking star was being paid.

Despite entreaties that her Hollywood aspirations were at an end, and that *EastEnders* was where she really belonged, the feeding tube was withdrawn, shortly followed ten episodes later by the respirator that was keeping her alive. The death scene sent ratings through the roof, the funeral, which also saw a fight between her brother and the jilted suitor, sent ratings into the stratosphere. In sifting through clippings, according to *The Sun*, the whole nation mourned. I must have been out that night because, frankly, I don't remember mourning tragic Geraldine Grainger, her character in the soap, now having expired in slow motion for the benefit of the viewing figures.

Stubbornly, she had refused to change her name. I rather liked that, as someone who now has.

Her private life echoed her on-screen persona. She was briefly married to another star actor, which ended in divorce, after which she enjoyed short liaisons with, in descending order, a Premiership footballer, musician, well-known magician and a novelist. Her declining choice in men signalled that her professional career seemed in crisis, another interesting fact that *The Sun* paraded on its front page when news of her latest bust-up became the stuff of public gossip. However, as John pointed out, Doris is also famous for not giving interviews.

Personally, I found her charming. She once came to stay with us in Edinburgh. She was witty and bawdy, hugely indiscreet, and made both my parents laugh: Dad uproariously, Mum more demurely. She took me on a visit to the zoo and bought me an ice cream which I ate beside the giraffe enclosure. I remember that one of the giraffes kept looking at me. It was a hot day, and perhaps it wanted an ice cream as well.

Doris kept trying to imitate what each animal sounded like, squawking or screeching through cage bars. The monkeys thought she was rather nice and came over for a closer look, a lion opened one eye and then went back to sleep, and all the other animals ignored her. She didn't seem to mind.

Her agent passed on my message, and she phoned me back almost immediately. Of *course,* she remembered me. Of *course,* she'd help. She'd be *delighted* to help. 'Normally I don't do interviews,' she confided. 'But I'll make an exception for you.'

Her home was in one of those terraced south London streets where discreet houses open up, Tardis-like, to reveal mansions on the inside. She had Persian rugs on polished wood floors and a painting by Picasso over the living room fireplace that she assured me was genuine. So much for Dad's rubbish print, merely signed by someone who only *might* have been Picasso.

We sat at her kitchen table, a huge mahogany monstrosity that overlooked her small garden. She seemed wistful, detached. Like many screen stars, she was smaller in real life. Tricks of the camera to make them look taller. I drank coffee, having flown down early from Edinburgh. A grandfather clock in the hallway ticked the seconds and discreetly announced the quarters.

She was now, according to my research, approaching fifty.

She kissed me on both cheeks, saying the usual things like 'My, how you've grown!' and 'So sorry about your mother.' I thanked her repeatedly for seeing me, which she waved away, saying that it was the least she could do. We had the house to ourselves, except for a striped tabby cat which lay curled up at the end of the mahogany table and hardly moved, rather like Doris in *EastEnders*. She was single again. The novelist had gone to Bangkok for the purposes of research and now wasn't coming back. 'Research, my arse!' was her summary, with a sharp laugh.

'Couldn't you just say mid-forties?' she asked, refilling my cup from a hissing coffee machine. 'It sounds less daunting, don't you think?'

'This isn't really a proper interview,' I said. 'I'll write whatever you want me to write.'

'Then, maybe, *early* forties,' she suggested with a small laugh, running a hand through red hair and smiling across the expanse of wood that separated us. 'For women, everything dries up with the menopause. Personally and professionally.'

It was a nice line that I dutifully wrote down. 'And that's what you want, is it? To climb the greasy pole again?'

She inclined her head. 'It's my job, sweetie. I suppose I could retrain as a supermarket shelf stacker, but I'm not multi-talented.'

'So,' I said brightly, 'Doris Glimpton is open to offers.'

Her red hair, like fire, was framed against the window. 'It's a fickle game, acting. Well, you probably know that, don't you?' She ran a hand through her hair again and smiled. She could still have been in her early forties. Late thirties, even.

She saw that I was fingering a red stain on the table. 'I bought this thing in Kentish Town. God knows what I was doing there. Drunk, maybe. But I was after a new dining table, and I saw this thing in a bric-a-brac shop window. I wasn't particularly impressed by all its chips and stains, but the old Cockney in the shop told me to imagine all the parties the table would have seen. All that fun and debauchery! Aunt Mabel drinking too many sherries and knocking over her glass, happy children having knife throwing competitions on Christmas Day. That kind of thing.'

I looked back to the stain I'd been absently fingering, trying and failing to imagine Aunt Mabel. 'I could have walked out and bought a new table and started my own story in chips and stains. But the old geezer in the shop was right, why not just continue other people's stories.' She laughed. 'It was probably just sales patter bullshit.' The table looked polished and well-used, gleaming in sunlight.

At the other end, her cat suddenly scratched one ear and then went back to sleep. 'But it's what I've done all my professional life,' she now said, laying her wine glass down. 'Playing at being other people, telling their stories, pretending to be people who've never existed, or people I've never met. I suppose that's why I liked this table. Other people's lives, Maria. My livelihood has always been about other people's lives.' My father could never have been as eloquent or as whimsical.

She looked into the garden, full of jumping birds, a neat lawn and carefully-tended borders. At the bottom of the garden, a high wall topped with broken glass. Underneath the glass, what looked like new plasterwork: the price of fame, jagged shards to keep out the unwanted. 'I suppose what I mean is, if you think about it … which of us luvvies does *anything* that is remotely useful? We don't cure sickness, we're not looking for a cure for cancer, we don't risk our lives trying to help others, we don't even stack supermarket shelves …' She trailed off, looking into her garden, small birds threading between tree branches.

'How's your Dad?' she asked eventually. 'Sorry, that should have been my first question. Haven't seen him for years.'

'He's OK, I guess. Keeps himself busy.'

It's not much of an answer and Doris glanced at me sharply. 'It's just that I don't hear much about him these days. He's not done anything stupid like retire, has he?'

'No, not officially retired. He mostly paints.'

'Painting! Bugger me! That sounds pretty much like retirement to me. Is he any good?' She seemed genuinely interested.

'He's OK, I suppose, although I wouldn't really know. He's got an exhibition of his stuff coming up before Christmas in a Bond Street gallery. All proceeds to charity,' I added, just in case she thought that Dad was hard up.

'Just make sure I'm invited,' said Doris, 'and I might even buy one of his daubings.'

'Anyway, he's still open to offers.'

'Aren't we all, sweetie? Aren't we all.' Then she gave a short laugh, almost a hiccup. 'God, we had some fun, your Dad and me!' She looked wistful. 'We first met on the *The Octagon Project*. Christ, that wasn't yesterday!'

Memories came flooding back, all of them unpleasant. 'Mum took me to see it, but I screamed the place down when Dad was killed, so we had to leave.'

'So, you never saw the rest of it?'

'Just the first few minutes.'

She was almost laughing. 'But he wasn't killed. Badly wounded, but definitely not dead. Your Dad gets better, hunts down all the bad guys and, in the last reel, gets his girl.' She raised a finger and pointed theatrically to herself. 'I even had to take my clothes off. I wouldn't do that now, of course,' she confided, patting her stomach, which looked flat and firm enough to me. 'I'm sorry I couldn't make it to the funeral,' she said, with just the right amount of sincerity. 'I liked your Mum, although I don't think she liked me very much.'

She smiled, remembering something, but didn't say anything more. She didn't have to: nude scenes involving her husband and other women had a psychotic effect on Mum.

When I left two hours later, my notebook was bulging. Doris Glimpton had chosen to unburden herself, perhaps for the first time, about her life and loves, indiscreet beyond indiscretion, but knowing that I would only write what she wanted me to write, and that every word would be vetted by her lawyer and agent. I had been given that rarest of interviews; a true glimpse behind the tinsel smile, nuggets of gold from an actress desperate to taste success again and, if that was denied, to go down with all guns blazing.

But why had it taken Doris Glimpton to tell me that Dad hadn't been killed in that bloody film? Mum must have known. I suppose I'll now have to watch the film, no doubt containing at least one steamy sex scene, and imagine Mum making growling lion noises and wondering out loud – as she did – if 'all that flesh is really necessary?' It's a thought that makes me smile.

Clouds were scudding in as the train whisked me back to Heathrow, and that evening I posted my job application to *The Scotsman*.

Chaos theory. It's why weather forecasts for the next couple of days can be pretty accurate, but why they become less and less reliable, because somewhere an unseen butterfly is beating its wings and a hurricane is brewing on the other side of the world. All those little variations in air pressure or wind speed generate variables that make long-range forecasting difficult.

Or, putting it another way, you're having a dinner party and decide to invite your boss without realising that he has a nut allergy, an ambulance has to be called, and although he gets better, you lose your job, but then you find another job and meet the man of your dreams and live happily ever after. We all live in permanent chaos, however ordered our lives seem, with every innocuous action having lots of little

171

consequences that are completely unpredictable.

It's all about the science of surprises, and Granddad fulsomely admits that his theories are based not only on what can be observed, but on assumptions lurking in the chaos of stars and galaxies. The world is full of structure and organisation, but life is also filled with uncertainty.

I leave John Salmond's goldfish box to find that my car has acquired a parking ticket, which is disappointing because I'd parked it far down a side street off a side street and didn't think that traffic wardens would bother venturing so far off the beaten track. June Frobisher's Citröen 2CV is now my pride and joy. In my last term in North Berwick, I'd told her that if she ever wanted to sell her car, I'd buy it. A few weeks later, and just after I'd passed my test, she called.

She was now engaged to be married to a wealthy lawyer who was aghast at the thought of a clapped-out relic cluttering up their driveway, 'which probably means we'll get divorced,' she told me with, unfortunately, foresight.

I didn't quibble about the price, and I think there were tears in her eyes when I drove off. It took me several days to figure out the 2CV's idiosyncratic gears and the fact that it didn't have a stereo system – however much I looked for it.

I drive back to my ridiculously large flat in Leith which I once shared with a bunch of bohemian misfits. I suppose that makes me a misfit as well, although only one of the others knew that I have a trust fund in Switzerland and a movie-star father. Driving a clapped-out relic is my way of covering my tracks. As always, the 2CV attracts a lot of attention from the pavement. It's a relic, but a relic with brio and character, once the star of a James Bond film – and just as quick as an Aston Martin when driven down a mountain.

My flat forms the top floor of an old bonded warehouse, in a part of Edinburgh that they forgot to knock down in the 1960s, they've now realised twenty years later, that Leith was becoming rather chic, so tarted it up instead. Leith is now a place of reinvention where dockyard pubs, within which taciturn men silently drink beer and whisky, sit side by side with wine bars serving chardonnay on tap. It is a place in which I feel comfortable, and has a bohemian streak that tolerates most things, including 2CVs.

My phone rings and I pull into a bus stop. Mum would have approved. It's John Salmond and my stomach does a back flip. Surely, he can't have made up his mind already? It's late in the afternoon, and I'd assumed his mother would have picked him up by now, perhaps taking him to Swim Club or Pizza Hut, and ordering for him off the kiddie's menu.

'I was very impressed by your portfolio,' he begins. I don't say anything. I'm aware of a bus coming down the street behind me and it will presumably want to use its bus stop. 'But also a little bit confused.'

'Confused, John?' The bus is now flashing its lights and I have little choice but to nose into the traffic with one hand on the steering wheel, and the other on the quirky gearshift that comes straight out of the dashboard while trying to keep the phone against my ear.

'Maria? Maria?'

'Still here.' I've managed to squeeze the car onto double yellow lines outside a Chinese supermarket.

'I just don't see how you could have got all those people to talk to you. Big stars don't give interviews to media students.'

'Media *and* communications,' I remind him.

'My apologies. Look, can I ask you something?'

'Fire away, John.'

'You're not, by any small chance, the person I think you are?'

'I know precisely who I am, thank you.'

'I mean … look, Maria, could I ask who your father is?'

That was easy. 'My father's dead, John.'

There is a short silence, while the 2CV is buffeted by passing traffic. I have also attracted the attention of another traffic warden or, maybe, the same warden who's been spitefully following me. 'I'm sorry to hear that,' he says. 'In which case, can you start next Tuesday?'

$$\frac{6\pi Akc^3}{hGS_{\text{EK}}} = 12$$

Bekenstein-Hawking formula

After Mum died, I sometimes felt like a fairy princess in a gilded tower, and I kept wondering whether a prince on a white charger was coming for me. Not, obviously, a real prince on a real horse, because that would have been silly – and, anyway, they wouldn't have been able to jump over the driveway gates – but it was as if I was waiting for something or somebody, and I would stand for hours at my bedroom window looking out at the Forth, thinking about Mum and wondering where Oz was.

He did send a few texts when he reached the USA, and I texted him back, but they seemed arid, like the Californian weather. We never actually stopped sending each other texts, not consciously, but the intervals became longer and longer and, after a while, there didn't seem any point. I then lost my phone several times, and my number changed several times. I tried emailing him, but his email had changed, so unless Oz was psychic, we were now officially incommunicado.

I felt stranded, my compass still missing its north and south. Dad was sometimes there, and sometimes wasn't. We avoided each other when he was there, and I didn't miss him when he was away. Did he miss me? I rather doubted it. Without the gravitational pull of my mother, our galaxies had drifted apart. I liked it when Dad wasn't at home. When he was there, we made stilted small-talk, and I would go to watch TV in my room.

Patsy, for unfathomable reasons, remained my best friend. She is, according to her, of aristocratic Hungarian-

Jewish lineage, although I find that doubtful – for a start, she had red hair, she couldn't point to Hungary on a map – I tested her once – and that her parents are called Brenda and Kevin. But the best 'fact' about Patsy – which might even be true – is that she was conceived after three pints of beer in a guesthouse in Clacton, although which of her parents drank the three pints, or whether they split it equally, or what they were doing in Clacton, is unclear. I'm quite jealous of her conception; it seems ordinary and banal – three pints precisely! – and a beginning that you can pinpoint and maybe even visit the guesthouse.

I have no idea where my journey started, and I absolutely don't want to know. I prefer to believe that I'm the product of Immaculate Conception or artificial insemination. I don't like to think of Dad looking predatory and Mum having to do unspeakable things, whether in London, Los Angeles or the semi-posh flat in Edinburgh. Her memory is what I hold dear.

Mr and Mrs Perkins moved into the little flat over our garage and, although she wasn't as good a cook as Mrs Boyce, I didn't starve. Mr Perkins continued his weeding duties, forever bent over flower beds, stoic and stooped. Mrs Boyce, tearfully, decided that the Ross household no longer needed her services and resigned. This came as a surprise to Dad who didn't really know what she did around the house and assumed it must be important. He generously gave her six months wages – I suspect to keep her mouth shut, as if she might be considering a kiss-and-tell exposé.

It seemed to me that my childhood had been taken away in a charge of electricity landing on the unfortunate coincidence of my mother. Since then, I now look fearfully upwards, watching the sky: it claimed Mum and might now be looking for me. The terrors are crafty that way; they give no warning. When they do come, I can feel their footsteps on my skin. That's when I keep a watchful eye on the sky. Usually it is grey and formless, with sinuous clouds woven together, tumbling from west to east. But within their muscular formations I can sometimes discern faces; eyeless, blind – but somehow searching.

That's when I keep the windows closed, shutting them out, and close the curtains. When I see the cloud-faces, I am under water, trying to draw breath, ankle-deep in stinking mud. It is dark under the water, impossibly dark, yet sunlight sparkles on the water's surface, and I want so much to break free and float upwards to the light. But my feet are held fast, and I don't know what to do.

I struggled through school, and could mostly be found in the library, still reading whatever was to hand. June Frobisher did try to jump-start some mathematical aptitude but didn't succeed. Maths remained a foreign language and I failed every exam.

Granddad didn't seem to mind, telling me that we're all good at something, and that I just had to find out what I was good at. They have a small house above Como, under the Alpine peaks, and I go out for a week every Easter. The Imperial Stormtrooper is also still there, although a bit mildewed, perhaps still waiting for the Death Star to reappear so he can unchain himself from the drainpipe and resume his proper duties.

Like everyone else I pat him on the arm when I pass by. Ironically, despite his previous profession, he's become a good luck symbol and a tourist attraction in his own right. Luigi now has a CCTV camera pointed at the Stormtrooper, and his restraining chain is tungsten steel. Tourists take selfies beside the Stormtrooper and then guiltily feel that they have to stay for lunch. The Empire is proving good for village business.

Gramps did take up painting: local scenes of trees, flowers, and rooftops and many of our extended family have his paintings on their walls. I also have one, painted from the top of the village, with a panorama of sky with the village below. It reminds me of Granny stitching her tapestry and talking about pawns and bishops.

I scraped enough Highers together to make good my escape, although Queen Margaret University wasn't a big jump geographically, being in Musselburgh, a town on the eastern edge of Edinburgh and therefore, even in a 2CV, only a short drive from North Berwick. Nevertheless, it was an escape; the princess packing her treasures and moving to a new castle.

I left my dolls in the panic room; I think they feel safe there. Queen Margaret University sounds posh, but it exudes a permanent sense of surprise that it has been awarded university status, as well as the quiet satisfaction of knowing that very few students, if any, are expected to fail, which is mainly why I enrolled there. Or, more precisely, why they accepted my application.

I entered university in much the same way as I'd left school: without much expectation. Sure, I could write, but who can't? I wasn't particularly talented at writing, and I'd never done anything as fanciful as write even a short story. I just knew that during all those hours in the library I had absorbed other people's ideas and that, somehow, all those wisdoms were now mine. Somehow, I could put them to good use.

Nevertheless, I felt myself to be one-dimensional: a dog with no discernible tricks; someone suited to walking in shadows, as Mum preferred. The flower arranging society didn't ask me to take over her duties, although the chairperson of the PTA did write me a nice letter after Mum's death. I had fallen between lineages of greatness, with only curiosity and a love of words to call my own. It amounted to a skill of sorts, or so I liked to think.

My first year at university was a dawning realisation that media and communications is not exactly biochemistry or astrophysics. Quite frankly, much of the course could have been distilled into a few weeks, despite tutors and professors trying to make the course seem erudite and complex. It was also a course without much practical application: newspapers were going out of business and new media was making everyone a blogger or Facebook publisher.

The digital age was doing away with journalists and replacing them with Twitter trolls. The only beneficiaries of all this were PR agencies able, so they claimed, to make sense of it all. It seemed to me in that first year that proper journalism, the kind of journalism I wanted to pursue was being usurped by men and women in expensive clothes able to talk bullshit.

The weeping professor only added to this air of professional melancholy, although she only discovered her husband's infidelity in my second year and the messy divorce would grind on throughout my time at Queen Margaret's. In my first year she was still moderately sane, with piercing eyes and a mane of hair that wasn't quite mouse and not quite grey. She was tall and slim and wore bright red lipstick, and believed that, to achieve a coveted degree – did anyone ever fail? – the blindingly obvious had to be learned through intellectual gibberish.

For example, "*cultivation theory being the mechanism by which people who watch a lot of TV absorb media messages more readily*" i.e. couch potatoes see more adverts. Or, "*framing theory is the belief structure that the media pays particular attention to certain events and then places those events within wider contexts*" i.e. the media reports news.

More depressingly, Professor Trish MacBeth seemed to believe this nonsense and tried hard to use very long words, backed up by societal or psychological research from dubious academic institutions, mostly in small-town America. It was clear from the start that my media and communications degree would consist of several weeks of proper study and several years of needless waffle.

My despondency was made worse by no longer having a proper home. I was sort of living in student accommodation in a rabbit hutch of a bed-sitting room, but mostly still living in North Berwick. During that first year, Dad was mostly away filming, or so he said, but was coy about what was actually being filmed. I suspected that, like a medieval monarch, he was actually promenading around the globe and visiting his menagerie of mistresses.

Or maybe not. Maybe I'm being unfair. On the brief occasions I saw him, and asked where he'd been for the past month, he'd say things like 'here and there' or 'mostly Europe' – which didn't answer my question, because he was always looking suntanned, and even 'mostly Europe' has winter.

Frankly, I didn't want to know where he'd been or who he was being predatory with, and was glad of his absences, and enjoyed having the house mostly to myself, if you didn't count Mrs Perkins. If I knew Dad was coming home, I would move back to my rabbit hutch until he'd left. It was nice not having Dad around and, most evenings, I would sit at the kitchen table and eat whatever Mrs Perkins had cooked for me while making sense of the day's nonsense.

I also found that Mrs Perkins and her husband had discovered ballroom dancing and I would open the kitchen window and listen to waltzes and polkas being played from the flat over the garage. However, despite this nightly activity, I never saw either of them actually dance and was left to imagine this unlikely pair, stooped and bowlegged, shuffling gamely around their living room.

It was also clear that the other students in my class were similar cast-offs like myself: a rag-tag bunch of no discernible talents, for whom media and communications was the best or only option for higher education. I was therefore both pleased and disappointed – although not surprised – that Professor MacBeth's arid lectures on the dynamics of mass communication or the interplay between social media platforms in popular culture were as much above their heads as mine. However, I was, as far as I could fathom, the only person on the course who did actually want to become a journalist.

The others all saw the course as a useful way of whiling away a few years of their lives. Several of them had barely moved beyond Enid Blyton and found the concept of writing sentences with nouns and verbs quite daunting. I suspect most of them aspired to work in PR, which doesn't require such advanced literary skills.

I hadn't seen much of Patsy during that first year at university. The occasional coffee, the occasional drink, but nothing more. My rabbit hutch was on campus, and nowhere near the city centre, and – with Dad away – I'd taken to shutting myself in North Berwick and taking long walks on the beach, except during thunderstorms. I wasn't being unsociable – I still went to parties and got drunk with the best of them – but I was also finding a comfort in my own company. Mum was long gone and scattered, but it was only during that first year at university that I started to get over it.

Patsy was studying at Edinburgh University, a *real* university, doing a business degree, a *real* degree, having decided, perhaps for the first time in her life, to be sensible. Actually, that's a little unfair. Despite sitting at the back of every class, and seemingly sleeping through everything, she'd passed lots of Highers with good grades. Within her diminutive skull lurked a brain and, despite her preposterous ancestry, she was no fool.

As the new university year approached, I met up with her in a wine bar in Leith. We got very drunk.

'You should become a free spirit,' Patsy told me as we started in on another bottle of white wine.

'I suppose.' I had no idea what she was saying.

'Suppose nothing. Do something.'

'Like what?' I asked.

'Free spirits need air and space. To be nearer to God, to touch the stars.'

'Sounds fun,' I replied, bemused.

Patsy was scribbling on a scrap of paper. 'Go to your

crummy hovel, get your things together, grab a cab and come … *here*.' An address, in Patsy's sloping writing, was thrust at me. 'Trouble at mill, alas. One of the free spirits has gone walkabout. Anyway, the lift rarely works, there's lots of stairs, but low rent.'

'You're asking me to move in?'

'Why not? The room's empty, and it'll be fun having someone else from the ol' home town. You don't watch *Neighbours*, do you?'

'God, no! Is that important?'

'Not really. See, you've passed the test. Well, will you, won't you?'

I laughed and, sight unseen, moved in the next day, heaving my suitcase and rucksack up six flights of stairs – the lift was broken – to the dockland eyrie with its vistas of ships, cranes, rooftops, and of sky. I marvelled at the view – and the *light*. Up there, above the noise and exhaust fumes, the light had a different quality, almost a luminescence. It was drizzling, although a weak sun beamed down. The sunshine was catching in the beads of rain and transforming them into a galaxy of falling stars.

'You'll be happy here,' said Patsy.

I had accepted Patsy's offer with some trepidation; I wasn't really the free spirit type, whatever that was. But, standing in the mess of my new living room, I also felt liberated, in control. I looked down on the rooftops, slate-black and gleaming in the rain, as if surveying a new royal domain.

'I'll show you your room,' said Patsy, leading the way down a long passage, round a corner, and along another passage. Framed sepia prints, mostly scenes from Victorian London, hung on the walls under naked light bulbs. I saw other passages linking to the furthest reaches of the flat and, behind an open door, a bedroom with a garish quilt on a double bed, a golliwog perched on a nest of cushions, a whiff of perfume.

'Constance,' said Patsy, 'Mad cow. Likes Barry Manilow. You'll meet her later.'

Behind another door with a frosted pane, a bathroom with an ornate cast-iron bath with lion's feet. Dust, like gun smoke, rose about us in shafts of light. Patsy chattered all the way, turning her head to make sure that I was following in her wake. As we traversed the flat's great length, I now felt a sense of journey.

'It's big,' I remarked.

'The term I prefer is "spacious",' corrected Patsy with a backward smile.

'"Big" does for me.'

The bedroom, after our long and winding journey, was small and narrow, with a high ceiling. A low-wattage light was encased in a paper globe. A single bed occupied one wall, a wardrobe another. But again, arranged below like an unfolding map, were the rooftops of Leith. Diamond raindrops fell past my window. I breathed in the room's musty scent, searching for clues.

'Not spacious,' I said.

'Not big either,' she agreed.

'But perfect.' I pronounced it *purr*fect, throwing my rucksack onto the bed and dumping my suitcase on the floor. 'Whose room was it? Before me, I mean?' I was looking at a poster pinned over the bed; a girl playing tennis and scratching her bum.

'Name of Sammy. Very hetero and hunky. Gone to make his fortune in Canada, poor bastard. Upped and left, just like that.'

'Anyway, he's left his stereo.' I pulled it from underneath the bed and sat it on a small table by the window. 'Maybe Sammy hasn't left after all. Maybe he's still here, living in a distant cupboard.'

Patsy laughed. 'The flat's certainly spacious enough,' she agreed then, after a pause, 'I hope the sod doesn't expect me to post the bloody thing to him.'

'There's just one thing, Pats …' I bit my lip, feeling foolish. 'I don't want anybody to know about … well, you know.'

'Still doing the "incognito" thing?'

I nodded.

'You do know that you're being stupid, don't you?'

'I just don't want anyone to know that he's my father.'

I stared her down until Patsy tapped the side of her nose with one finger. 'OK, OK. Our secret, Maria.'

'My father died years ago.'

'Yeah, yeah. Whatever.'

'Tell anyone, and I'll kill you. Actually, Patsy, I kind of mean that.'

We then traversed the flat's great length to a cavernous kitchen made for giants and which was furnished in a strange mixture of the modern – cooker – and the decrepit: everything else. The uneven floor, covered in floral linoleum had probably seen better days at the time of the Queen's coronation. A very large black cat regarded me balefully from a high shelf, its tail swishing like a bad-tempered metronome.

'That's Knox,' said Patsy. 'Don't go near it, don't pet it, and don't try to be nice to it.'

'Knox?'

'After the father of Scottish Presbyterianism. A rather apt name for a cat which disapproves of everyone and everything. Sammy found it on the landing, and it followed him in. Now it won't bloody leave.'

'But it must belong to someone.' Knox seemed an appropriate name for a cat cloaked in black furry robes.

'It believes that we belong to him, although he doesn't like any of us. If you get too close, he'll hiss and spit. Try to stroke him and he'll either bite or scratch, or both. All we do is feed the brute and hope he'll bugger off.'

The cat's tail was still swishing, and its yellow eyes were fixed on me, perhaps searching my soul for impure thoughts.

Growing up, I'd always wanted a pet. A dog, preferably, but a cat would have done. 'Does it have a litter tray somewhere?'

'Not exactly,' said Patsy, spooning instant coffee into two chipped and very dirty mugs. 'Sammy's great triumph was to teach it to use the loo.'

I laughed, then realised that Patsy was being serious. 'Don't be ridiculous! Cats can't do that.'

'Strange but true.' Patsy had rummaged in the fridge, pulled out a carton of milk, sniffed it, and tipped the contents into the sink. 'Hope black coffee is OK. Tough if it isn't OK. Sammy searched on the Internet and found a training device.'

'A training device,' I echoed. 'Does Knox flush afterwards?'

'Alas, no.'

'And does he sit in the loo and read a newspaper?'

'Don't be silly, Maria. He's a cat.'

Patsy attracted the rootless, her 'free spirits', who soared around her candle, drawn by her bonhomie and the cheap champagne of the Leith eyrie. To make ends meet, she worked several evenings a week at a tawdry club off the Grassmarket, a nocturnal place for visiting businessmen to meet up with avaricious escorts – some of whom, I learned, were impoverished medical students.

Patsy seemed to have free rein to the wine cellar and empty magnums of *Champagne Methodoise Club de Luxe* littered the arteries of the huge flat, piling up in corners, turning up in odd places. In the evenings, if Patsy wasn't working, she was rarely without a glass in hand, and the corridors outside my bedroom echoed to a daily gunfire of popping corks.

The free spirits made me welcome, regaling me with tales of riotous parties. I was introduced to the others. Patsy made it a kind of ceremony, an initiation, inviting each of the free spirits to kiss or shake my hand, whilst the others sat in distant corners of the living room clapping and laughing. I, of course, had to stand in the middle of the room, searching the dimmer corners for new faces. Knox sat on top of a bookcase and looked suitably appalled.

'You are one of us now,' said Patsy, gripping my arm and leading me around the room for closer inspection. 'A free spirit.' Then, in her best Margaret Thatcher voice, added, 'One of us.'

First, Antoine: a student from Paris on an exchange placement at the Scottish parliament, then Philip, a jobless roofer from Glasgow with a rare talent for mimicry and whose imitation of Cliff Richard was much in demand at the *Duck and Bill* just down the road, the flat's favoured pub. There was also Constance, research assistant to a well-known Labour MP; Ted, an administrator with a children's charity, Amanda, an Irish air-hostess, and Juniper – commonly referred to as 'Berry' – another student on Patsy's business studies course, and who also sometimes worked at the *Club de Luxe*.

'What do you do exactly?' asked Constance when the formalities were over and Patsy had gone to fetch the bubbly. She called it 'shampoo', dragging out the second syllable through pouted lips.

'I'm at Queen Margaret University.'

'Good gracious!' shouted Ted, returning from the kitchen with Patsy. They were laden with bottles and glasses on silver trays. 'How can a technical college suddenly become a university?' Ted was tall and his ponytail was held together by an elastic band. His John Lennon glasses sparkled from across the room.

'It just is, I suppose.'

'Who the hell was Queen Margaret anyway?' he now asked, pulling the wire cage from a bottle.

This I did know. 'Eleventh century Scottish queen who was also a saint.'

'I myself am Hungarian,' said Patsy, putting on a heavy

mid-European accent. 'Of aristocratic lineage, actually.'

'Up the workers!' shouted Constance, popping the first of many corks.

A toast was drunk in my honour, glasses were refilled, and the Leith eyrie echoed to a drumbeat of opening bottles, the corks fired from the window at those less fortunate who were excluded from our circle. Knox looked on, seemingly shaking his head.

In the weeks that followed I became aware of alliances among the spirits; of Ted's eyes always seeking Constance, of Amanda's ample shadow at Antoine's door. But by unspoken agreement, hanky-panky went unremarked. It would have been divisive, I supposed, to admit to partiality. In the night I heard soft footfalls pass my door; I wondered if one night they would stop by mine, and whose feet they would belong to.

I'd lie awake, staring upwards through the darkness, snug in my small bed, but lonely also. So I listened to the footsteps and pieced together the dalliances, the stifled giggles behind closed doors, thinking myself part of the complex equation that was the Leith eyrie.

In daylight, the flat had no real centre, no common meeting ground; we'd rattle round, meeting at unexpected corners, saying things like *I didn't know you'd got back* to one other. I preferred the kitchen, all faded lino and Formica, a relic of 1950s chic. It was the one room that was always hot, the boiler in the corner burning all day long.

The kitchen, like the rest of the flat, was built for large ogres, a long refectory table in its centre at which I would sit and contemplate my good fortune. The kitchen table told the history of the flat, its pitted surface scored with dents and burns. Antoine, who I fancied like mad but whose footfalls ended at Berry's door, sat with me sometimes, smoking his Gauloises, and telling tales of the other occupants.

'But it's Patsy we all love,' he remarked to me one late

morning, sitting in sunshine at the long table, with mugs of strong tea. 'Isn't that right, Phil?'

Philip, looking the worse for wear, grunted as he passed through the kitchen en route to a distant bathroom, hopefully free of feline occupation. 'An inspiration to us all,' he said, pausing long enough to steal Antoine's cigarette for a quick puff. 'God, these things are awful. Only the French could smoke something so revolting.'

Antoine shrugged. 'You see what I have to put up with?'

Between school and university, Patsy had been transformed. When she smiled, she was beautiful; she lit up. Her personality transformed her; she was charged like a battery; she fizzed with energy. Her spirits flew around her, given wings by her infectious good humour. She was my best friend, but I was a pale imitation – the rich girl masquerading as a poor girl; the university student living a lie, while everyone else lived in the real world.

My father's not really dead, by the way, or not yet, striding energetically across the golf course, with talk of yet another leading role in a new blockbuster, and of a high-end TV series.

But then came the visit from Sarah that changed everything, arriving from Edinburgh airport with a larger suitcase than she normally came with. It was my first year at university, and I was still flitting between my student hovel and home. His misfortune was that I had chosen to flit to North Berwick that weekend.

Mr Perkins, who also doubles as guest porter, lugs the suitcase up to her room. I still can't imagine him ballroom dancing with his wife; I can only imagine him weeding, and that doesn't take much imagination as it's what he does most days. The reason for its weight becomes apparent the next day. Sarah appears in the kitchen wearing a bright green golfing outfit – Pringle sweater, windcheater, and matching trousers.

In one hand she is carrying brand-new golf shoes. She lays them down on the worktop by the sink. Mum didn't tolerate shoes on kitchen worktops. I look at her sullenly. I may now be an adult, if only just, but am still very good at looking sullen.

'Your father's invited me to play a round of golf,' she says unnecessarily.

My father is rummaging in a downstairs cupboard. We have several downstairs cupboards, but because many of them are locked, I have no idea what they contain. Mum never knew either and would sometimes look through their keyholes as if there might be brightly-lit rooms on the other side. I hear the sound of golf bags being heaved out and dumped in the porch.

'We can get breakfast at the club,' I hear him shout. Then he comes into the kitchen. If Sarah is dressed brightly, my father is positively luminous in blues and reds. It seems to me to signify that his period of mourning has well and truly passed, that he can now finally dispose of Mum's memory and, in lurid clothing, introduce a new woman to the golf club membership.

'Damned strange though,' he says to nobody in particular. He is looking out the window, gauging the likelihood of rain. 'One of the clubs is missing.'

Dad has his own set of finely wrought golf clubs, lovingly hand-carved, I presume, from precious metals by Buddhist monks. But he also has another set, just in case visitors to our house have forgotten theirs, and it's this set that's missing a club.

It's something in Sarah's expression that decides me, something in her demeanour: the way she's been looking at paintings, at our furnishings, always looking around, sizing the house up, already making changes to colour schemes.

I know that their relationship must have stalled with Mum's death, but I also now see a gleam of possession in her eye: this wasn't just a golf game – can she actually *play*

189

golf? Has she *ever* played golf? – it signified that normal service has been resumed, and that she would shortly and finally take her rightful place by Dad's side. In that moment, I want to hurt her; to put a stop to her scheming. I also want to hurt him.

'I know where it is,' I say.

I go to my room and retrieve the club from the back of the wardrobe. When I go back downstairs they're both standing in the hallway. Dad is looking predatory, and I wonder if golf is uppermost in his mind. His foot is tapping impatiently.

'Excellent, old girl!' he says, taking the proffered 5-iron. He looks at it closely. 'What the hell?' he now says. 'What the hell have you done to it?' His eyes flash angrily. The club's head is black; the rubber handle melted.

'It's how I found it,' I tell him.

'Found it? Found it where?'

'It was in her hand. When I found Mum, she was holding it. I threw it down the hillside so that nobody would find it. Then I went and found it again.' The words have just gushed out.

Sarah goes and stands by Dad and takes the club from his hand. She runs her fingers down its length, feels the jagged molten rubber handle. 'I don't understand,' she says.

I am surprised by my voice. It seems to echo my father's; I too have found a controlled baritone. 'Then tell me this, Sarah. Why would anybody stand on the top of a hillside in a thunderstorm with a golf club in their hand?'

Sarah looks blank then laughs. 'That's just crazy,' she says.

Dad takes the club from Sarah and walks into the kitchen. He places the club on the table and stands looking at it for a few moments. 'No,' he says finally, 'that's exactly what she'd do. Christ almighty!'

His shoulders seem to have slumped, his clothes less luminous. 'You can't be serious,' says Sarah from the doorway. She is ashen; her new golf clothes now look

190

ridiculous.

'She wanted to kill herself,' I tell her.

Sarah gestures to the club. 'But not like that,' she says. 'The chances of being struck by lightning would have been astronomical.'

'In probability theory, nothing is impossible,' I tell her.

'Then you're mad as well! You *and* your bloody mother!' Sarah is looking flushed now; too much colour has come into her face. She senses danger; that things aren't going according to plan. This is something that she absolutely hasn't seen coming, like my mother, Sarah hates surprises. 'Paul, you really don't believe any of this codswallop, do you?' He doesn't reply. 'Well, *do* you?' she demands in a louder voice.

It has started to rain; their golf game now seems completely ruined. 'She'd seen your picture in the *Express*,' I tell her. 'She'd even cut it out and put the cutting on the table. This table.' I give it a tap with my knuckles.

'Christ!' Sarah pulls out a kitchen chair and sits down heavily. 'Most people just cut their wrists or hang themselves.'

I see my father's eyes flash. She catches the expression and holds up a hand. 'I'm sorry, Paul. That came out completely wrong. Emma, I'm sorry. I just don't know what to think.'

'She wouldn't have wanted to bother anyone,' I say. 'She never liked bothering people. This way, whoever found her, it could still be seen as an accident.' I'd been back to the Law months and months before and retrieved the club. I knew that it might offer ammunition.

Sarah momentarily looks more cheerful. She places her hands on the table, palms upward. Her fingers wriggle like upturned sea animals. 'Then maybe it was just an accident. Look, none of this changes anything.'

'No, it changes everything,' says Dad. There is a shaken conviction in his voice. Sarah looks at him sharply, biting

191

her lip. Her hands are now palm downwards. 'Emma, why didn't you say something before now?'

'Because I found her,' I blurt out, feeling tears well in my eyes. 'And because I didn't want anybody thinking bad things about Mum.'

Nobody says anything for a while, then Sarah takes a deep breath and exhales slowly. 'OK, then we need to keep this among ourselves. Emma, have you told anybody else?'

'No.' I am standing at the window, watching rain course down the glass. Pinpricks of water turning into small rivulets. I put my hand to the glass, feeling the rhythm of the rain.

'Emma, this must stay our secret. God, Paul, I dread to think what the papers would say!' Sarah has come up behind me to place a hand on my shoulder. 'Emma, you must promise.'

I turn to face her. 'I already have promised,' I tell Sarah. 'I don't need to promise anything to you.'

'Emma, please!' my father says. He is still looking intently at the golf club.

'Don't call me Emma!' I shout back at him. 'From now on, call me Maria!'

'For God's sake, Emma!'

'You changed your name. Now I'm changing mine!'

'Emma, please!'

'I hate you!' I scream at him. 'Both of you!'

It changes everything, my father had said. And it did. Until that morning, he had once again become the great movie star – perhaps more glittering than before, if that was possible, with actual tragedy in his resumé.

Afterwards, nothing was the same. He waved Sarah off, her car leaving scrunch marks in the gravel. There was a desperation to her, a realisation that something was coming to an end. She alternately looked puzzled, then tearful. She didn't bother packing her new golf clothes. Mrs Perkins found them in a pile in her bedroom when she went to do the cleaning. I put them in the bin.

It completely changed my father. He'd felt guilty about my mother; now he had the proof of his crime. Mum, betrayed and depressed, had every right to have gone a little bit mad. She could put up with his infidelity with Sarah Parker, and all the others, no doubt strung out across the film-making globe, but not with the shame of exposure.

She had come to accept what her husband was, and to blinding her disappointment with vodka when she thought I wasn't looking, but she couldn't face the public scrutiny that the *Express* article invited. She was terrified of crowds and hated being the centre of attention. This was her way of making a dignified, if eccentric, exit.

$$\frac{R}{\ddot{R}}\left[\frac{13\Lambda c^2}{3} - \frac{52\pi G}{3}\left(\rho + \frac{3\rho}{c^2}\right)\right] = 13$$

Acceleration equation for the universe

By common consent – mostly Patsy's – we're going to have a flat-warming party for my benefit, which is a nice thought, but I don't really know many people. Not now that I have adopted my middle name. There are a few leftover friends from North Berwick who have stayed on in Edinburgh but, really, I don't see much of them. They still think of me as Emma, the film star's daughter, and I no longer answer to Emma.

I haven't made many new friends. The only people I come into contact with on a daily basis are the inmates of the Leith flat – who are invited anyway – and the assorted losers of the media and communications department. It's a bit like my first birthday party in North Berwick, but with added complications. Back then, I was the daughter of someone famous; now, I'm the daughter of a father who has maybe died, or abandoned his family, perhaps for another man, or simply disappeared. If anyone asks and, this being Edinburgh, they often do ask to in order to more clearly pigeonhole my class and background, I prefer variations of 'I never knew my father' or 'I'd rather not talk about it.'

This does at least confer on me a little bit of mystery although, after a few drinks, I am apt to over-egg the pudding – as in, to a toothy nursing student with a phobia of blood, 'Dad was eaten by sharks, or maybe just the one shark, it was hard to tell.'

Or, to a Russian exchange student, 'Dad joined the American space programme. We don't know where he is.' The general consensus at university is that Dad died of natural causes – which, strangely, is a cause of death I haven't mentioned. I also can't tell anyone that Mum was killed by lightning; as far as I know, Mum is the only person to have died in that way for many years. It would be asking people to put two and two together and even the dullards in media and communications might make the connection.

I simply don't want my new flatmates or fellow Queen Margaret students to know who I am. I no longer want to be Paul Ross's daughter; I want to be myself, someone standing on their own feet, without having my name bracketed with someone else's. I want to be my own little planet, bustling quietly around the universe. I don't want to be in someone else's orbit, especially the same someone who drove my mother to kill herself, her veins full of alcohol and depression.

I can't therefore invite anyone from North Berwick to the party and am reduced instead to inviting the crème de la crème of Queen Margaret University. Patsy is also under strict instructions not to invite anybody from North Berwick. I am consequently not looking forward to the party.

I do, however, offer to pay for everything, a suggestion that meets with no resistance whatsoever. The paradox – which I'm not comfortable with – is that while I'm slightly wary about telling people that Dad was the victim of a fish incident, or is living with a South Seas tribal chieftain, or secretly manning a US base on the Moon, I'm more than happy to be the beneficiary of a trust fund in my name. Every month I receive a letter from a firm of London financiers telling me how much I'm worth, which is quite a lot. Dad set it up for me after Mum died, but I'm not grateful. He's filthy rich, so doesn't need the money.

I see it as blood money, as a way of atoning for his sins, but I do look at all the noughts on the bank statements and wonder whether I need ever again attend a lecture from the increasingly fragile Professor MacBeth. Last week she broke down in tears while giving a lecture on media theory and the complexity of socio-political philosophy principles; hardly an emotionally-charged subject area. Reluctantly, despite the noughts, I always decide to stick it out: as useless as I am at most things, I simply don't want to be the rich kid with nothing in life except money.

The only person who doesn't seem to agree with my pay-for-everything suggestion is Knox, and he's not really a person, although he does use the human loo nearest the kitchen. We have several other loos, some en suite, but Knox doesn't use those. Unlike everyone else in the flat, Knox seems to like me, perhaps because I've made an effort to get to know him. I've fussed over him, spoken to him in a squeaky voice – everyone else just ignores him or shouts at him – and bought him cat treats, which he greedily devours.

He even allows me to stroke him, although only in moderation. When his eyes open wide and he starts to growl, I remove my hand quickly. I like Knox because he reminds me of Mum: a prickly, no-nonsense character that you really don't want to get on the wrong side of.

I also wonder if Knox has a sixth sense, and if he sees something in me that's missing from everyone else. Are we, somehow, kindred spirits, separated by sex and species? Is he a little bit damaged, as I suppose I am?

However, Knox, it appears, doesn't much like parties, which must be hard for him because the flat is constantly having variations of parties, with strange faces – and bodies – forever littering the living room carpet. And I've only been here a week. The carpet is also a Victorian relic and it's now difficult to tell if the carpet was originally green or blue, or some other colour entirely. The high traffic areas, mostly from the doorway to the sofas, are virtually bare and a trip hazard for the unwary.

Knox doesn't approve, I sense, because he knows better than me that my charade can't go on forever. Edinburgh is a very small city and people know one another. They get to talking and say things like 'I met a girl the other day whose father was eaten by a shark, although it might have been several sharks,' and the other person will say, 'Oh, that's Emma Ross whose father is the famous actor. She's nice, but delusional. Don't go anywhere near her.'

Knox watches with wary interest while I unpack shopping bags onto the kitchen table. He shakes his head sadly at the many party-size bags of crisps and looks sternly at me when I unpack a large assortment of oven-ready pizza. (Culinary tip from an Italian-Scot: buy cheap pizzas and then add more toppings, but not pineapple. Pineapple on pizza makes no sense to Italians, and is considered barbaric),

Then, over several trips to the supermarket, I unload boxes of beer, cider, and wine bottles onto the table. Thankfully, the lift is working again. Knox climbs to the top of the box mountain, licks his tail, and looks disappointed. He runs his tongue around his mouth and then resumes staring at me, once more looking into my soul and reminding me that this amount of alcohol can only lead to trouble. I should really listen to cats more often.

By the end of the day I've – sort of – cleaned the kitchen floor, and – sort of – cleared away a great many *Club de Luxe* champagne bottles from various extremities of the flat. I have been to the recycling centre several times, watched with increasing fascination by Council staff who have probably never seen so many champagne bottles in their life and certainly never coming out of a Citröen 2CV. And yes, the car is another way of getting back at Dad, because it's the very opposite of a fancy Bentley.

By the time that the rest of my flatmates arrive back – except Amanda who's somewhere over the Irish Sea serving drinks to drunks – the flat is looking almost tidy and festive. The food has been laid out, I've lit a great many candles, and in one particularly dark corner of the kitchen all I can see are two reproachful yellow eyes.

The only person not in a party mood is jobless Phil who spends most days in the *Duck and Bill*, and who now tells everyone that he's not well. 'Dicky tummy,' he explains, patting his abdomen and wincing.

'Nothing that a few beers won't cure,' suggests Juniper, although Phil has probably had several of those already.

'It's not funny,' says Phil.

'Well, it should be,' I tell him. 'After all, laughter is the best medicine.'

'Not when you have diarrhoea,' says Phil.

I down a couple of glasses of white wine and then, as the first guests arrive, drift into the living room to find Patsy in deep conversation with two earnest young men. Patsy is wearing very un-Patsy-like dungarees and a red T-shirt; one of the men is large and black with long dreadlocks, the other is very pale with shaggy black hair. They stop talking when I come in, neatly avoiding the death-trap bit of carpet, and sit opposite.

'This is Carlo,' says Patsy, indicating the black boy, who looks both large and muscular, 'and this is Dave.'

'Hello,' I say, holding up my glass.

'And this is Maria, my best friend and flatmate.'

The two boys look at one another. I am aware that their animated conversation has entirely stilled. 'Am I interrupting something?' I ask.

'Absolutely nothing,' says Carlo, in a deep and attractively rumbling voice.

'Nothing at all,' echoes Dave, rather too quickly.

'Look, Maria,' says Patsy, 'we were just having a political discussion.'

I get up. 'In which case, I'll leave you to it.'

Dave also gets up. He's wearing a black leather jacket and blue jeans. He smells of testosterone and motorcycles, both of which I like. He looks – and smells – as if he's just driven down Route 66 on his Harley-Davidson and straight into our flat. 'You don't have to leave, not if you don't want to. I assume that Comrade Patsy will vouch for you.'

'Vouch for me?' I snort into my white wine. 'Comrade

Patsy!'

'I'm sort of into political activism,' says Patsy. In her dungarees and big boots, I can somehow believe it, although I can't understand how it could have happened so quickly.

'You've become a Trotskyite revolutionary! Christ, when did that happen?' Without waiting for an answer, I turn and head for the door. 'Sorry, guys, but it's a party, remember?'

'So are we,' I hear Dave say, almost plaintively.

Back in the kitchen, a gaggle from media and communications has arrived, and are now standing around the table but not really communicating, as most of them are a bit dim and socially inept. One of them is also called Maria and I say to her, rather unnecessarily, 'So you made it!'

Maria is very small and round, like a beach ball and with as much personality, and I've always wondered whether, if I turned her on one side, she could roll down corridors. It would save her the effort of walking and make her more interesting.

'We were discussing Professor MacBeth,' says Maria, the not-me Maria, although everybody in the MedComms group – yes, we really do call it that – just seems to be staring at different corners of the kitchen, perhaps wondering where the family of huge goblins which live here has gone. 'We all feel very sorry for her. Particularly when she cried last week.'

'Well, discovering her husband in bed with someone else must have been a bit of a shock.'

'What?'

'Their au pair.'

I'm aware that everybody has forgotten about the goblins and are now looking at me. 'We didn't know that,' says Maria. 'How do *you* know that?'

I know that because I'd been passing her office and heard her, through the open door, on the telephone. It had been an animated conversation, and she'd been speaking rather loudly. I now realise that, having drunk several glasses of wine, the cat is definitely right about alcohol. I should not repeat casually overheard conversations that don't concern me.

The au pair's name was Gabrielle, by the way, and she's a Spanish trollop – apparently – and has 'buggered off back to Madrid with a rocket from my lawyer up her arse.' I'd charitably hoped that it wasn't a real rocket, which would have been uncomfortable and difficult to squeeze past airport security.

'I just heard it,' I say.

'You just *heard* it.'

'Somebody told me. Look, it might not be true. Sorry, shouldn't repeat gossip. Anyway, must mingle.'

There's dancing now in the living room, and a stick-thin girl in a blue dress is sitting against the wall rubbing her leg. A bloke with a shaved head and a tattoo of a skull on his arm is standing beside her and rubbing her head. It turned out that she tripped over the carpet. Patsy is dancing slowly and sensually with Carlo, which looks odd because up-tempo rock is blaring from the speakers.

She's changed out of her dungarees and is wearing a clingy red dress that matches her hair. Carlo is many inches taller than Patsy and she should really be standing on his feet like a small child being guided around by her father.

'Are you enjoying your party?' says a voice behind me.

I turn to find Juniper with one arm draped over a raven-haired beauty that I don't recognise. Berry is very tall and sporty and, when sober, often goes jogging and plays squash every Saturday morning.

'Well, it's not really my party,' I reply, looking around the room and recognising nobody. The MedComms must presumably still be in the kitchen, now probably discussing the importance of viable two-way communications in modern marriage.

'This is Laura, by the way,' says Berry and, for Laura's benefit, adds, 'Maria is our new flatmate. This is her flat-warming party.'

'Nice to meet you.'

Berry is also quite drunk – more drunk than me – and leans down to kiss Laura on the mouth. This takes some time. 'We're an item,' Berry tells me, and gives Laura a squeeze.

'Well, good for you.'

'Laura's a medical student.'

'Then perhaps she could take a look at Phil's bottom.'

'I rather doubt it,' says Berry, relieving Laura of the need to say anything. 'She doesn't really like bottoms. We met at the *Club de Luxe*. Laura also works there. Don't you, you naughty girl?'

'Oh,' I say, rather too brightly. 'That sort of explains it.'

Later, on my way back from the loo, I find Patsy in a hallway, smoking a cigarette. More precisely, I find Patsy lying on the floor, staring at the ceiling and smoking a cigarette. I sit beside her and take a puff. I don't really smoke, only when I'm drunk.

'You've become a loony Leftie,' I tell her.

'Well, not really.'

'So, what's the name of this mad organisation you've joined?'

Patsy plumes smoke at the ceiling. 'The Workers' Democratic Socialist Party of Scotland.'

'Wow! It's certainly got a snappy ring to it.'

'I didn't come up with the bloody name!'

'Patsy, you've been my best friend for years and years. Now I discover that you've suddenly become an enemy of the people.'

'I only met Carlo last week,' concedes Patsy, and stubs her cigarette out on the carpet which, in this flat, is as good a place as any. She shifts up beside me and we both sit against the wall. 'I don't actually give a shit about politics.'

'Oh.'

This is my second 'oh' in five minutes, which is unusual. I don't often say 'oh'.

201

'It's just that I'm utterly and completely in love with him.'

'A bit sudden, wouldn't you say?'

'Like a bolt of lightning,' she agrees, then apologises. 'Anyway, you know what I mean.'

'And what else do you know about him?'

'He's a physics student.'

I resist saying 'oh' again. 'And that's all you know about him? Christ, Patsy! Does he know that you're in love with him?'

'Physics and politics are all he cares about.'

'So, he doesn't know, despite you knowing him for, let's see … several days.'

'Nor does he trust anyone who's not a Party member because he's terrified about infiltrators and being followed by Special Branch. That's the only reason I joined. He thinks his phone's being tapped.'

'Maybe it is.'

'He'd be disappointed if it wasn't,' says Patsy. 'However, in my quest to find true love, joining the Party seemed like a good idea.'

'Oh.'

'Emma … Maria …whatever you're called … all I want is to have his babies and live happily ever after. Does that sound weird?'

'Well, yes … a bit weird.'

Patsy smiles and lights another cigarette. 'I daren't tell him that I'm not really a committed socialist.' She slides down the wall and lies horizontal once again.

'So, what you're really saying is that you fancy him like mad and would like to shag his brains out.' I can hear raucous laughter from down the corridor and around several corners. We're in a distant extremity of the flat, close to my bedroom. 'I just don't see why two people can't hold different political beliefs but still be together.'

Patsy snorts. 'You don't know Carlo.'

202

'He's mad, isn't he?'

'Completely bonkers,' agrees Patsy, 'and the reason I know this is that your grandfather's Theorem is his favourite book.'

I leave Patsy on the floor, staring dreamily at the ceiling, having ascertained that she's told Carlo absolutely nothing about me being remotely related to the great Alberto, although one of Carlo's ambitions – apart from world revolution – is to shake Granddad's hand and I suspect that, at some point, I may be asked to introduce them. I find this rather touching because I've never thought of Gramps as an icon of radical socialism.

The dancing in the living room has become louder and more manic, malevolently presided over by Knox from his high shelf. Dancing can now be added to the long list of human activities that Knox doesn't approve of. In the kitchen, the MedComms are still grouped around the table, but do seem to be talking to one another, and the not-me Maria has an impressive variety of crumbs and stains down her jumper. 'You're a bit Italian, aren't you, Maria?' she asks me. 'Rossini, and all that.'

'Born 1792 and composed *The Barber of Seville*. Did you know he was obese, depressive and sadomasochistic?'

'Um, no.'

I turn to offer her my profile and point to my nose. 'I can test the depth of swimming pools with this.' Maria is looking blank. 'It's a Roman nose so, yes, I am a little bit Italian,' I tell her, feeling rather stupid. I resist the temptation to pick her up, turn her on her side, and roll her across the room. There's a gaggle of people over by the cooker I could use as skittles.

'By the way, the pizzas were yummy. Someone said that you made them.'

'Only the toppings. The rest of them came from Tesco.'

'But a word of advice,' says not-me Maria, 'make some

with pineapple next time.'

I look at my watch and realise that the party has been going on for hours, which is strange because I could have sworn that it had only just started. What have I been doing? Who have I talked to? Who have I offended this time? But that's the trouble with being drunk at parties: normal time is either speeds up or slows down, according to a complex equation involving the amount of alcohol consumed and the ambient level of boredom or enjoyment.

Granddad's Theorem quotes Einstein's remark that the distinction between past, present and future is only an illusion, however persistent. Einstein also said in his theory of general relativity that space and time are essentially the same thing. One theory is that, while I've been drinking glass after glass of wine, some bits of our local galactic cluster have been zooming away, so reducing gravitational strength – and therefore, according to the Rossini Theorem, speeding up time itself.

At the same time, the likes of the Andromeda galaxy are zooming towards us, and maybe slowing down time. In other words, has the known universe suddenly sped up so that hours on Earth have become minutes, or vice versa, and have I really been trying to explain all this to the other Maria, who is looking at me as if I'm completely insane? I rather think I have.

'I'm sorry,' I tell her, 'I'd better get some fresh air.'

Now that my brain has turned to mush, I'm also thinking about quantum nonlocality, which even Einstein described as 'spooky'. It's a strange phenomenon used to describe how some particles can act in a coordinated way despite being distant from one another and are therefore unable to gravitationally interact. One explanation, according to Granddad, is that the particles belong in a different kind of reality where distance has no meaning. In my befuddled state I simply know that, if I go onto our roof terrace, I will find something really interesting.

Actually, calling it a 'roof terrace' is a little misleading. For a start, it's not a terrace so, more precisely, it's simply the roof. But it's big and flat and can be accessed by a rusty spiral staircase that leads upwards from what is now our dining room, although a dining room without furniture for that purpose. We call it the 'dining room' because we can't think of anything else to call it. If someone were to leave a chessboard or Xbox in it, we'd probably immediately rename it the 'games room.' The room is empty except for the stick-thin girl in the blue dress and the man with the tattooed arm.

They are lying entwined in a corner and, while her leg seems to be better, it's draped over his back, her dress now looks injured and has slipped down around her waist. A pink bra is lying in a sad little heap beside her, looking like a lump of discarded flesh.

Quite why there is a wrought-iron spiral staircase leading from the flat to the roof is anybody's guess, although the building was once a warehouse of some sort and there are strange metal fixings on the roof that might have belonged to a winch.

The view from our roof terrace is spectacular and looks out over Leith docks to the darkness of the Forth. I can sit up there for hours – and I've barely moved in! – watching the very slow motion of ships coming and going, although most of them are quite small. There are strange-shaped ships with helicopter landing pads that I suppose are something to do with North Sea oil and naval patrol boats with little guns at the front that don't look as if they could threaten a Li-Lo. Battleships dock at the naval base across the river and gas tankers and container ships head further upstream.

But it's fun watching the dock's comings and goings and I've already seen a couple of cruise ships arrive and disgorge thousands of tourists onto the quayside – who then, not used to dry land, all looked a bit lost and frightened. Each time, the docking manoeuvre seems an impossibility; inching the vast hulls through the small opening between the sea and the port, and then, pushed and prodded by tugs, to their moorings. It looks almost as difficult as parking a Bentley, but without audible swearing.

Strangely, a couple of the MedComms have made it to the roof and, a safe distance from the edge, are admiring the view. That's the only real trouble with the roof terrace: because it's *not* a terrace, it doesn't have any kind of balustrade. Walk off the edge, accidentally or on purpose, and you'll be at street level in a few seconds. Patsy rarely goes up there: she says that she's frightened of heights but is somehow drawn to the danger of the edge.

I talk rubbish with the MedComms for a few minutes, mainly discussing our course, the mental state of Trish MacBeth – I wish I hadn't opened my mouth – and how much we're all enjoying the University of South Musselburgh. I keep expecting the other Maria to appear, perhaps waving a can of pineapple, but I don't suppose the narrow staircase can accommodate her girth.

Then, deciding that quantum nonlocality must be complete bollocks, I see a figure with his back to me standing perilously close to the edge of the roof. I go over to investigate.

It's Dave, the other revolutionary, and he's standing very still, with one hand in his trouser pocket and a can of beer in the other. 'You can jump if you want,' I tell him. 'I won't try to talk you out of it.'

To my relief, he takes a step back from the edge. 'Today would not be a good day to die,' he says. I now see that his shaggy black hair is actually a complex mat of endearing ringlets, like a big woolly dog's. I like dogs.

'Is any day a good day to die?'

'Well, no, I suppose not.' He gestures around him with the beer can. 'It's some place you've got here.'

'Well, we like it.'

We go and sit on a wooden bench that someone long ago must have manoeuvred up the spiral staircase. It's quite rotten now, and in daylight is mostly green, and was probably once a church pew. Handily, I find a half full bottle of white wine on the ground beside the bench and fill my glass which I then chink against his beer can.

'So, you're a friend of Carlo?' I offer. He has very blue eyes and his pale face is almost luminous. Like me, he has a Roman nose above thin lips, which are cracked wide in a smile. He looks like a Greek warrior, the kind of warrior that gets carved naked in marble. I look at him more closely, wondering what Dave would look like naked, and find the thought of finding out strangely attractive.

'He's a mate of mine,' he says, and I detect an east London accent. He still smells manly and his leather jacket creaks every time he lifts his beer can to his mouth. 'We grew up together. Hackney. It's in London,' he adds, just in case my geography isn't up to much.

We're quiet for a few moments. Neither of us seems to know what to say to the other, but it's a companionable silence compared to the raucous shouting and loud music eddying up the spiral staircase. I point upwards. 'That group of stars is The Plough. If you follow a line from the end two stars, that's the North Star. Sailors steered by it.' He looks at me but doesn't say anything.

'Also, even more interesting, wherever you are in the northern hemisphere, the North Star will always be the same angle above the horizon as your latitude.' He's still looking at me, still not saying anything. 'Did you know that there are more stars in the universe than grains of sand on Earth?'

'No.' His leather jacket creaks as he puts his can down on the ground. 'Would you mind if I kissed you?'

This takes me by surprise. I know he's called Dave, comes from either Hackney or Olympus, and is a revolutionary, but that's all. I then decide that's all I need to know.

Sometime later and we're lying naked in a heap of bedcovers. My small bed isn't designed for communal living, so we have to cling to one another to avoid one of us falling off the sides of the bed. The space between my legs feels warm and tender, and I can't quite believe what I've just done. I'm not quite as drunk as I was, and have the beginnings of a headache, and am thirsty. But I don't fancy the thought of creeping to the kitchen, treading carefully around prone bodies, and filling a glass of water.

In any case, the other Maria will probably still be there, searching for uneaten pizza. Even undressed, Dave still smells of engine oil, which isn't as unpleasant as it sounds. In the immediate aftermath of sex, in that interlude between passion and sleep, when it's customary to say something nice, Dave asked me if I'm going on the Day of Rage, and when I said that I don't know what it is, told me that it's a leftist solidarity march to highlight a variety of social issues.

Despite my headache and thirst, I am almost asleep, and snuggle into him, breathing in the smell of freedom and the open road. 'I'm not very good with days of rage,' I murmur. 'Couldn't it just be a morning of mild irritation?'

'It's a march along Princes Street and then a protest outside the Saudi Arabian consulate. We wanted to protest outside the Scottish parliament but were outvoted by the feminist collectives.'

'Good for them,' I say, wondering if he has a Harley-Davidson or a scooter, and fervently hope for the former.

'When you butted in on us earlier, we were trying to think up a chant … something to chant on the march.'

'I didn't butt in. It's my bloody living room.'

'Well, yes, if course it is. But we can't think of anything to rhyme with Saudi Arabia.'

'Labia,' I suggest.

'I'll put it to the committee,' he says, and falls asleep.

In the morning, or maybe afternoon – I have no way of telling without looking at my watch, which is presumably lying somewhere in the heap of discarded clothes on the floor –

I feel a hand creep up from my hip and latch itself to my breast. It's a nice feeling, being wanted, and being touched in unusual places – well, unusual for me. He's kissing the nape of my neck and I can feel his erection against my bottom, which is also a nice feeling, even if my head is throbbing and my mouth feels unpleasantly matted with fur.

'Can I make love to you again?' he asks in such a politically-correct way that I half expect him to whip out a sexual consent form and ask me to sign it in front of witnesses.

I shuffle round to face him, running my tongue round my mouth. In the morning light – if it is morning – he no longer looks luminous. He just looks pasty-white, and his hair is no longer woven from endearing ringlets, but an uncut mess. He also has an angry spot on his nose, and no longer smells of Route 66, although his breath probably smells no worse than mine.

'You have beautiful eyes,' he says, kissing my ear. 'They're like …'

At that moment, just as I'm about to dutifully spread my legs to his exploring fingers, we both hear a low growl from the end of the bed. It's Knox who, having had to put up with drinking and dancing, doesn't look happy at the prospect of fornication.

'Don't touch him,' I advise Dave. 'He doesn't like people.' Dave unwisely isn't listening and reaches down to scratch Knox who, deftly, in a blur of black fur draws blood from one of Dave's fingers. 'I did warn you,' I say, as Dave subsides down beside me. I feel his erection droop down my thigh.

Dave sucks his finger, and I have an immediate picture of him as baby. 'Does it hurt?' I ask.

He removes his finger from his mouth and looks at it. 'You have a psychotic cat.'

'Tell me something I don't know,' I reply and lean in to kiss him, but he says, 'Sorry, but I can't do it when I'm being

209

watched.'

I momentarily wonder how he's managed to find *that* out, but then remind him that Knox is only a cat and therefore doesn't really count.

'I still can't,' he says, as if Knox might turn into a boa constrictor or a lion, and I take a peek down the bed to make sure that he hasn't. Knox is sitting very prim and upright, with his ears slightly flattened.

'How the hell did it get in here anyway?'

'Through the door, I expect.'

'But you locked it.'

Strangely, despite much of the previous night being a bit hazy, I do remember locking the door, just before finding myself being undressed and spread-eagled on my bed. The only explanation is that Knox, using one of his God-given powers, dematerialised in the corridor and rematerialised in my bedroom. 'Then I have no idea, Dave.'

'Maybe I should go,' he now says.

'You were going to say something about my eyes,' I remind him.

'Was I? Oh yes. They're very big and brown.'

'So are grizzly bears.'

'Yours are more … like a cow's eyes.'

I prop myself up on one elbow. 'What?'

'A nice cow. A Fresian cow.'

'And that's supposed to be a compliment, is it?'

'Sorry, it kind of came out sort of wrong.'

I lie down on my back. 'You'd better go,' I tell him.

'I'll give you a call.'

'Actually, Dave, don't bother.' Bruised and hung-over, he really isn't a Greek warrior, and must therefore be from Hackney, and I've made a ghastly mistake. I also need to pee and to drink a glass of water and go back to sleep, because the flat will be trashed and, because it was my party, I'll be expected to do most of the clearing up.

'Please, Maria …'

But a red mist has descended. 'Just fuck off, Dave!'

Having prevented fornication, Knox now seems pleased with himself, and is curled up at the end of the bed and purring softly, believing perhaps that he has saved my mortal soul, although he should have been giving me moral guidance several hours earlier before I lost my virginity.

$$\frac{56\pi}{f(v)}\left(\frac{m}{2\pi kT}\right)^{3/2} v^2 e^{-\frac{mv^2}{2kT}} = 14$$

Maxwell-Boltzmann distribution density

I did go on the Day of Rage, which was incredibly stupid of me, because it ended in my arrest, utterly falsely in my view, simply for standing up for the rights of oppressed women everywhere, and specifically in the Middle East – apparently – and, before being arrested, being beaten unconscious by a policeman in riot gear, a protective shield in front of him, and a large truncheon in one hand.

Sitting in the police station afterwards, I couldn't quite believe how all this could have come about, because I've never given much thought to the rights of women and have no intention – ever – of visiting Saudi Arabia. With bloodstains on my fleece and another raging headache – truncheon not alcohol – I couldn't help but feel that there must be a logical explanation. Nobody else had been arrested, so that I was the only pinko Bolshevik in Gayfield police station.

Gramps would have written an equation. Meeting Dave + shagging Dave + not having anything better to do on Saturday afternoon + getting a bit carried away = an unavoidable mess. It would be an equation of certainty; an equation to absolve me of all responsibility because the universe is mysterious, despite lots of clever people toiling away with slide rules, telescopes and computers to demystify it.

Take, for example, the standard model of particle physics, which has been described as the 'theory of almost everything.'

Physicists have taken decades to come up with it and they are understandably rather pleased with themselves, because it does sort of explain electromagnetic fields and subatomic particles. Unfortunately, it doesn't precisely explain gravity or the acceleration of the universe. It also doesn't explain neutrino oscillations, but I haven't a clue what those are.

In other words, physicists are still to come up a 'theory of everything' that provides the theoretical framework for the whole universe, although general relativity and quantum field theory are – of course – very much in their thinking. However, despite every prediction made by these two theories being scientifically verified, they are mutually incompatible: both can't be right or, conversely, both might be right, except that we can't yet figure out the bit of physics to join them together and, in the meantime, the ultimate mystery of the universe goes on being depressingly mysterious.

Gramps simply stated that, beyond the known universe, there must be other dimensions of space and time, bending and rewriting the laws of physics, and that not everything can be predicted in our dimension alone.

I suppose that sums it up, with a large dollop of chaos theory thrown in: every small thing has consequences, although those can be difficult to predict and, in terms of my head, rather painful.

It was Patsy, of course, who talked me into it, reminding me that I wasn't doing anything on Saturday and that it was my chance to stand up for the rights of the less privileged. She emphasised those last two words, as a coy reminder that not everyone is the daughter of a multi-millionaire. It was a subtle blackmail, but Patsy does persuasion rather well and will probably, in some capacity, do it for a living.

The Day of Rage was supposed to make the world a better place and, to my genuine astonishment, thousands turned out for the demo. Towards the front of the march were the stalwarts of the Left; the agitators who could be counted upon to be angry about anything, and who the police were keeping a close eye on, knowing their capacity for mayhem.

Further back was a contingent from MUMS AGAINST

ABORTION, rubbing shoulders with BAN FOX HUNTING, and next to them, NO NUKES. There were environmentalists and feminists, Christians and Muslims, young people and pensioners, anti-war protestors and more than a few of the simply curious with nothing better to do, including me.

It started at a leisurely pace and, despite being the middle of winter and not really the marching season, unusually warm, with a bright clear sky and only the faintest breeze, which gave the event a carnival atmosphere. Our route took us first along Princes Street, the side streets littered with police vans filled with officers in riot gear, which I thought a little over-the-top considering how dignified and restrained everyone was being.

I looked back at the long column of people behind me, exhilarated by their numbers; ordinary people who wanted to make a difference, to make their voices heard, to make the government sit up and listen. They held their placards up proudly, proclaiming their opposition to nuclear weapons, nuclear power, gays in the church, genetically modified crops, gays not in the church, the war on terror … and while nobody could say that the people were speaking in one voice, they were certainly saying something.

The demo was to end outside the Saudi Arabian consulate; a regime that seemed to encapsulate everyone's angers, a country that killed and tortured, that oppressed its people, particularly women, and didn't allow gays of any sort to exist.

Patsy and Carlo were at the front of the march, Carlo helping to carry the main banner. Apparently, there had been several spirited debates in the days following my party about the banner's wording.

The shortlist was: SCOTLAND AGAINST INEQUALITY (the feminist collectives), A RAINBOW NATION (gay, lesbian, bisexual and transgender), FUCK CAPITALISM (Carlo), and DON'T EAT QUINOA OR KALE (me, but I don't think Patsy put my suggestion forward.)

The organisers had settled on SCOTLAND'S DAY OF RAG. The sign-maker had mistakenly omitted the 'E' – making it seem like an advertisement for a craft fair. Carlo himself had conjured up a can of black spray paint and added the final letter, although the banner wasn't paint-friendly and it had swiftly become a large and fuzzy full stop.

Carlo had been to the flat a couple of times since the party, his eyes full of excitement, but without Dave. This I was grateful for, as was Knox, who has since taken to sleeping on my bed, presumably to guard the privacy and chastity of someone he now considers a fallen woman. But it's nice sleeping with someone who purrs and doesn't want to have sex because, being my first time, it hurt a bit, I didn't much enjoy it, and I didn't really know what to do.

It's like driving a car: you can do all the theory you like, but when you have a man – or, gender equality, a woman – on top of you, it's difficult to change gear and switch the windscreen wipers on at the same time. On the roof terrace, with Leith spread below us, I'd decided that I'd done enough theory, and that everything I'd learned from TV and from behind the bike sheds should be put to the test, which I may or may not have passed.

It was a noisy parade down Princes Street, what with everybody chanting something, although not the same somethings, and I was beginning to get a bit carried away by it all – WHY *should* gays be allowed into the church, WHY *shouldn't* gays be allowed in the church, WHY women *should* have a right to choose, WHY abortion *should* be illegal. I could hear schoolchildren chanting, and the quavering voices of old people, a rising crescendo of people power that wasn't really a march of single-minded rage, but more a lively discussion between people of wildly differing opinions. However, I was enjoying the walk and listening to democracy speaking when Dave turned up at my shoulder and affectionately patted my bottom.

'You haven't been answering your phone,' he told me, speaking loudly over the cacophony of noise. I was pleased to see that the spot on his nose had cleared up, although I didn't much like my bum being groped. I tried to speed up and squeeze between two MUMS FOR BETTER CRÈCHE FACILITIES but he was soon back at my side again.

'I've missed you,' he said.

'I haven't missed you, Dave. Leave me alone.'

Now that he was beside me, in daylight, I couldn't immediately see what had attracted me to him in the first place. Over the previous days, I'd concluded that Dave had simply been in the right place at the right time. I would probably have gone to bed with anybody; in my mind, the party had become the date for my driving test and Dave, with his leather jacket and endearing ringlets, was the person chosen by fate as my examiner. I'd also been very drunk.

'Look, if I did anything stupid, I'm sorry.'

'You said I looked like a cow!'

'Only your eyes. Maria, it was a compliment.'

'A compliment I could have done without,' I told him, quickening my pace, and joining the ranks of MEAT MEANS MURDER.

To no avail. 'What exactly have you got against cows?' demanded Dave, seemingly unaware of the company we were now keeping. A large woman with a florid face who was having trouble keeping pace with our slow amble gave him a steely glance.

'I just don't like being called a cow,' I said. The fat woman, presumably more familiar with being called a cow, gave me a sympathetic smile. 'He probably eats them,' she said, as we turned off Princes Street and headed into the Georgian New Town.

'Maria, look … I'm sorry. It's just that I can't stop thinking about you.'

'You just want to fuck me again!' I said, more loudly than I'd intended, drawing further glances from two middle-aged women carrying a NO MEANS NO banner.

'That's not true,' protested Dave, who had also spotted the banner, 'although it would have to be mutually consensual sex.'

'The answer's "no", Dave.'

'But ...'

'She said "no".' This from one of the middle-aged women.

We had now come to a ragged stop outside a plush neo-classical building. A flagpole jutted out from a balcony, from which was fluttering a green flag emblazoned with Arabic writing and a sword. I presumed this was the Saudi Arabian flag and, if so, that this was their consulate. The march had fanned out around the impressive door – firmly closed – while the Saudi oppressors were drinking tea inside, or whatever Saudis drink, and ignoring us.

'Then I'll prove it to you,' said Dave and, delving into a small knapsack that had been over his shoulder, produced a brick.

'What the hell does that prove?'

'My love!' said Dave, threw the brick, and disappeared into the crowd. The brick soared majestically over the police line, and then landed with a disappointing thud on the pavement, nowhere near the consulate's front door, and broke into several pieces. It hadn't even bounced angrily.

It was then that I saw that one of the riot policemen had broken ranks and was advancing towards me, presumably thinking that I was the culprit. In a vague moment of *déjà vu*, I thought I recognised him, and even made to smile at him, before his truncheon made contact with my skull, and I found myself being dragged towards a police van, dazed and confused, not quite certain what had just happened, or what I'd done, or where I was.

At the police station, one eye already blue and puffy, a police doctor examined me and said I'd be fine. After several hours in police custody, and once it was established how I had sustained my injury, and that I was entirely innocent, I was released without charge. Carlo was at the flat when I arrived back, with Patsy simpering around him, and said that I was a 'heroine of the people' and that he wanted to shake my hand which, given that his other hero is my grandfather, I thought quite touching.

The episode in the police station wasn't entirely straightforward. When I was marched in, bloodied and handcuffed, everyone naturally assumed that I was guilty of something, if only of grievous bodily harm to a brick. But even the arresting officer couldn't be certain that it was me who had thrown the brick. I again had a sense of *déjà vu* and realised that it was like being back in hospital in Italy. First, I was put in a cell with the door locked. Then I was taken out of the cell, put into a nicer room, and examined by a doctor.

The doctor was female and didn't look much older than me. She also looked like the other Maria, and I wondered if they were sisters, and did ask, and was told I was probably suffering a mild concussion from being beaten up by 'the fascist oppressors.' I then wondered out loud how, if that's what she thought, she could hold down a job as a police doctor, and was told that she'd been joking.

I didn't know that doctors were allowed to make jokes, and said that as well, and was given two codeine tablets and told to keep quiet because I was talking gibberish and must also be in shock.

On my arrival, the custody sergeant asked for my name and address, and then asked if I had any proof. I told him that I knew who I was and had always known who I was ever since I'd been a small child and that, if he didn't believe me, I had friends who knew who I was, and maybe I should call them and they could come to the police station and tell him who I was, which would be the same someone as I've just told him. He then asked if I had a driving licence, and I handed it over and he looked at the picture, then at me, then at his computer, and then called for the doctor.

After a while, after the codeine had begun to work I'd stopped babbling nonsense, I was moved to an even nicer room and offered a cup of tea. A smiling police officer who looked a bit like Dave brought it to me, but I was recovering by then and didn't ask him if he had a brother.

The tea was very sweet and came with a chocolate biscuit. Through the open door, I could see the custody sergeant on the phone, and then in hushed conversation with a more senior fascist oppressor who had silver epaulettes. They then went into a small glass room with the arresting officer who, it appeared, was being shouted at by the other two.

Then the senior fascist came to see me and asked if I was feeling a bit better. I said that I had a headache which might be a sign of internal bleeding, and that I could collapse and die at any moment.

'The doctor thinks otherwise,' he said. 'Nevertheless, I have to ask if you would like to lodge an official complaint?'

'The chocolate biscuit was a bit stale.'

'Sorry, we don't usually offer biscuits to prisoners.'

'Is that what I am?' I asked.

'No, you are free to go. I'm simply here to ask if you wish to formally register a complaint regarding the circumstances of your arrest and subsequent treatment.'

'I didn't throw the brick,' I said. I hadn't had any opportunity to deny it before now. I'd been asked my name, address and whether I wanted a cup of tea, but not whether I'd thrown the brick. It also seemed important to underline my innocence with a bit of indignation. 'I was merely exercising my right to peaceful protest when I was assaulted by one of your police officers.'

'We now entirely accept that, Miss Rossini. But do you know who did throw the brick? It could have hurt someone.'

'He was standing beside me, but that's all I know,' I told him, and looked at the scuffed lino floor. 'I've no idea who he was.'

'Could you describe him?'

I could have said that he's called Dave, comes from either Hackney or Olympus – but probably Hackney – has unkempt black hair, is possibly related to one of your officers and smells of engine oil. Did I really lose my virginity to that? I suppose clever police computers could then have tracked him to his criminal lair, which would probably be a run-down squat somewhere.

'No, I didn't really notice what he looked like. However,' I added, 'my decision not to lodge a formal complaint is dependent on one thing.'

Ten minutes later, when I stepped out the police car – opened for me by a police officer who almost saluted – a bandage over one eye, and a packet of chocolate biscuits in one hand, Carlo and Patsy were at the living room window and Carlo was punching the air and whooping – even from street level I could hear him.

But all I could think of was the inspector's unctuous smile and the way that the whole police station seemed to have gathered to see me leave, as if I was a much-loved relative being waved off on a long journey. It was like Mum's death all over again. She'd been lifted by helicopter from the Law; anyone else would have been carried down.

I was chauffeur-driven back to the flat; anyone else would have been told to sod off and take the bus. I'd been made aware that the membrane between my different dimensions was thin and porous.

$$\frac{4\pi G \mu m_{\mathrm{K}} R_{\mathrm{M}}^2}{kT} = 15$$

Jeans' length

Precisely 423 days later, Gramps officially became a spherical bastard.

The Hubble space telescope was partially to blame. You see, as best I understand it, there are three theories as to how the universe will end. Despite the universe still expanding, the *closed* theory, speculates that gravity will eventually pull everything back into the centre, back into one blob again.

Or the universe could be *open*, meaning that it will expand forever, redshifted galaxies spinning their way further and further to infinity. Or it might be *flat*, meaning that the force of Big Bang and the forces of gravity will eventually cancel themselves out.

It's back to dark energy and dark matter because one is the accelerator, and the other is the brake. But if there is just the right amount of dark matter, and it's a big 'if', then our universe could just conceivably last forever. A possible immortality, born not of gods or preachers, but of stuff we can't see or touch or prove exists. That was Gramp's brilliance, to suggest that our immortality was all down to invisible particles in every corner of the universe, passing from our dimension to other dimensions and back again.

New scientific data was making particle physicists and astronomers reassess their ridicule and reread the Rossini Theorem. All that dark matter and dark energy and multiple dimensions talk might actually explain the mysteries of mass and gravity. Gramps, always a legend in our small family, was now achieving wider acclaim.

His moustache was also happy, despite now being grey and attached to a spherical bastard. Alberto was being fêted by Edinburgh University, his old stomping ground, and was due to give a lecture the next day at the Usher Hall, an accolade reserved for the very few. Granny and Gramps had flown from Italy, and I'd picked them up at the airport. Granny didn't like the 2CV as much as the Bentley and sat hunched in the back alongside their luggage, asking me why I couldn't buy a proper car, and wouldn't believe me when I said that the 2CV *was* a proper car.

That evening we ate in an outrageously expensive restaurant, with a discreet fountain and a small pond with circling carp. I checked that they weren't on the menu. Gramps, fresh from a festival reception at which he'd been guest of honour, and radio and TV interviews, was tired but ecstatic. It was one of Dad's favourite restaurants, but without Dad, who was again somewhere else. I sometimes wish there was a country called just that, which people could go to, and legitimately say that they'd been Somewhere Else.

We'd tried phoning him, sending texts, emailing him, but the elusive film star hadn't replied. I could have phoned Sarah but didn't bother. Whenever Dad wants to be invisible, it's Sarah's job to keep him that way. No tugging back the curtain to reveal him in the wings. In any case, I didn't much care. Granny and Gramps were disappointed by Dad's absence but used to it. 'Well, he's a busy man,' said Gramps, which is what he always says when Dad fails to show up. 'But you'll come and hear my lecture?' he asked me.

'Wild horses, Gramps. Of course I'll be there.'

His moustache looked happy, extending upwards almost to his ears. I laid a hand on his. 'Vindication,' I said. 'Pawns and bishops, Gramps.'

He laughed. My father, who doesn't play chess, would have looked baffled.

His great moment at the Usher Hall had been orchestrated

by former colleagues who, no doubt, felt some guilt at the way he'd been treated academically and the alacrity with which they had accepted his resignation. Now that science had moved on, and might possibly prove him correct, it was time to repay a debt; my grandfather was giving the keynote address at the Edinburgh International Festival of Natural Philosophy. A new generation of astrophysicists had emerged, new theories were being published and old theories re-examined. My grandfather's theorem had been dusted down and set against mathematical models run through supercomputers. It was concluded that, possibly, his theories might have been right all along, or at least a little bit right, or that some of them might be a little bit more right than wrong. Lots of maybes and possibilities; but not ridicule.

His address had originally been scheduled to take place in a much smaller lecture theatre, until the newspapers got to hear of his homecoming and, of course, who he was father to. Until then, the media hadn't paid Gramps much attention. He was just an Italian who happened to be Paul Ross's father, and who had taught physics.

Suddenly, out of nowhere, Gramps was being described as a genius, a great Scottish philosopher who straddled the worlds of philosophy, mathematics and physics, as someone who had challenged the scientific community to think in new ways – and allowed other scientists to break free, to look in new directions.

The newspapers' unexpected acclamation of his Scottish heritage amused him; in the years of vilification he had only ever been described as an Italian academic, with typically lunatic ideas – well, what can you expect from an Italian? – but inexplicably married to a Scottish wife. He and Granny had flown into a phalanx of professors all keen to meet him or renew their acquaintance – or apologise – before they'd been allowed to escape to their hotel.

From my spot at the front of the balcony I can look down on the plush velvet of the seats below. To my astonishment, the Usher Hall is soon packed. I had expected a few scholarly dons and a scattering of nerdy science students. Instead, he has attracted all colours and all ages – old, young and everyone in between. Some are wearing jeans, others, business suits. On stage is a simple lectern picked out by a single spotlight.

Granddad has even managed to generate a demonstration outside the Usher Hall. It's not a big demo or rowdy and doesn't need police in riot gear and big dogs patrolling its margins. It mainly consists of serious-looking people in drab clothing, some wearing dog collars, with a banner that says JESUS DIED FOR OUR SINS. They've even printed up leaflets, a sure sign of religious wrath, and equally drab women are handing them to anyone who approaches the Usher Hall. I don't bother even reading mine and crumple it up and throw it in a bin which is already overflowing with other crumpled-up leaflets.

I see Patsy and Carlo take their seats. Carlo is well over six feet tall but, with his dreadlocks, looks ogre-size, and therefore perfect for our kitchen. He's holding Patsy's hand and is looking excited. He's also wearing a suit and tie, which I've never seen him wear before. I didn't know that suits came in super-massive West Indian size.

Although I still see Gramps several times a year – I go to Italy every Easter, without Dad, and they regularly come to Scotland – he looks smaller and frail under the bright spotlight. He still radiates exuberance, but it seems muted, and he walks on stage leaning on a stick, which he then waves to acknowledge the raucous reception. It's like being at a sedate rock concert, with the kind of audience that the Rolling Stones perhaps now attract.

There isn't an empty seat anywhere. His steel-grey hair is almost shining, and his moustache is wreathed in smiles, bristling in evident pleasure. He takes some notes from the breast pocket of his jacket and lays them down on the lectern. He then runs his fingers along his moustache, like a pantomime villain, making some of the audience laugh. It's a gesture that has always made me laugh.

Members of the press in the front row take photographs. There are also two TV crews, and I must remember to watch the Scottish news later. Although I know that Gramps is now spherical, I hadn't realised quite how famously spherical. Then he conjures glasses from his top pocket and puts them on. I have never seen him wear glasses before.

He speaks for over an hour, although it seems like five minutes. He begins by paying tribute to all those who have come before, from the mathematicians of ancient China and India, the great thinkers of the Arab world, to Isaac Newton, Blaise Pascal and Fermat. The list is long and eloquent; an unassuming old man merely placing himself in a centuries-old line of superior intellects.

He mentions Zwicky, Einstein, and many others in the same vein, setting out a scientific continuum in which nobody has pre-eminence. His moustache twitches and curls; he is enjoying himself. He then pays fulsome tribute to a grey-haired man in the front row, whom he introduces as Peter Higgs, whose work on sub-atomic particles will undoubtedly win him the Nobel Prize. The grey-haired man half stands and bows to the audience.

'The Higgs boson, the particle he formulated, has been dubbed "the God particle",' says my grandfather. 'But it's a term that neither I nor Peter like very much. It suggests that a creator was at work; that a god decided the shape of our universe and made everything that it contains.' He spreads out his hands, gripping the edges of the lectern. 'Well, maybe,' he concedes. 'But all we really know is that well over ninety per cent of the universe is made up of stuff that we can't see.'

'Finding the Higgs boson is a huge step forwards. It proves that there is an energy field that fills the vacuum of the observable universe. It will be the missing link in the Standard Model of particle physics. But proving the Higgs will only be the start, because dark matter has never been seen, and maybe never will. It neither produces nor reflects light.

'But it is dark matter, the stuff we can't yet see, that holds galaxies together and makes up much of the mass of the cosmos. But what it is,' he shrugs, 'is anybody's guess.' It is an address in plain English, just as he'd written much of his book: a thesis to appeal to the widest audience, to connect with people with no interest in science.

Towards the end of his address he finally tries to describe dark matter. He could have talked about electromagnetic fields, the redshift of galaxies, the strange orbits of cluster galaxies. He could have talked about relativity or string theory or gravitational lensing, all the mumbo-jumbo he's so familiar with. Instead, he says, 'It's like a famous actor walking into a room.'

I can see him scanning the rows of faces, perhaps looking for a famous actor. 'Immediately, everyone starts to group around this famous somebody. But if the actor keeps moving, he is able to continue unimpeded through the room. The other people simply stream around in his wake. If, however, he stops, it then becomes difficult for him to start off again. All those people will have clustered around him.'

The allusion is lost on nobody; everybody knows who his son is. Faces in the audience turn and scan the filled rows of seats. Cameras turn, searching.

'And that, my friends, is what dark matter is all about. The famous actor has attracted all those people – all those particles of dark matter. They have given him additional mass. But without that mass, the actor is nothing. Without dark matter, *we* are nothing.' He puts both hands to his chest for emphasis, then produces a handkerchief from an inside pocket and wipes his forehead. He takes a deep breath and then folds it away.

'When I was a young scientist, I wanted to know why gravity made no sense. I wanted to find out why the universe was composed of material that we can't see. I wanted to know why we're made up of matter rather than anti-matter. My journey has taken me from mathematics to astrophysics, and from quantum mechanics to particle physics. If I am remembered,' he says, both hands now firm on the lectern, 'it will be as someone who tried to make sense of lots of other people's theories.'

He pauses, seemingly out of breath. 'I doubt that I'll live long enough for others to find answers to all the questions I have asked. However,' he now says, pointing around the vast auditorium, 'Many of you are young enough. The greatest scientific discoveries of all time will be realised in your lifetimes. We will understand what the universe is made of. We will understand what happened at the very moment of Big Bang. We will understand the secrets of dark matter and dark energy. We will understand how time and space and gravity fit together and, perhaps, learn how to travel through dimensions beyond our own. To travel beyond our solar system and visit distant galaxies.' His voice has risen and now he pauses.

He finishes almost in a whisper. 'Then we will finally and with absolute certainty know who or what created the universe.'

Once the applause has died away and my grandfather has left the stage, and as we are all rising to leave, I catch sight of someone who could be Dad, in a middle row of seats below me. He is wearing a dark blue overcoat with the collar turned up. On his head is a nondescript rain hat. I try to push through the crowd to reach the stairs, but there are just too many people.

But why should I be trying to catch up with him? To say what? I have nothing to say to him. In any case, the crowd around me is impenetrable. Dad, if it is Dad, is almost at the door to the auditorium, people are milling about, but they don't recognise him and, having no mass, he is able to slip out and away.

When I do eventually make it outside, most of the demonstrators have melted away, although a few stragglers in shapeless anoraks and bad haircuts are still handing out leaflets denouncing Satan – Granddad – and all his works – the theorem. The ultra-Christians don't look very happy, or healthy, and for a moment I almost feel sorry for them, standing in the drizzle, when they could be at home reading the Bible and eating gruel – whatever 'gruel' is – or something healthier to help with their complexions.

I then realise that, despite feeling sorry for them, this isn't a very charitable thought, so I take another of their leaflets and put it in my pocket, and smile at the leaflet-person who doesn't smile back, and hope that it was a friend who cut his hair rather than a professional barber, because it doesn't look like something you would pay money for.

There is also a whiff of thunder in the air, a crackle in my lungs when I take breath, and immediately I am looking upwards, searching the sky for faces that might be searching for me. It happens like that, but only sometimes, because thunder and lightning are rare in Edinburgh.

Changing my name was mostly to hurt my father, but it was also to confuse my demon: the one without a face, whose static power I can now feel with every breath and whose knowing eyes are forever seeking out the motherless child. I know it makes no sense and it's never made sense to me either.

In no particular order, the six major anxiety disorders are: generalised anxiety disorder, agoraphobia, specific phobia, social phobia, obsessive compulsive disorder, and post-traumatic stress disorder. Depending on the GP I could be suffering from several. In terms of diagnosis, it's been a matter of take my pick, and not put myself in situations that may make me cranky. One GP told me that agoraphobia, from the ancient Greek, meaning 'fear of an open market place', can cover a multitude of sins. Medically, it means being in a situation that causes anxiety and from which escape might be difficult. That can mean a fear of being alone or, conversely, the panic of being in a crowded place.

Or it can be a generalised fear of being outside the home, or the specific anxiety of, for example, travelling in a car. Like an amoeba, it can change from individual to individual. The rational part of me knows that my overwhelming fear of thunderstorms is irrational. But I also know that my mother is dead and that the sky, when provoked, can kill without compassion.

I hide in a nearby cafe and wear my sunglasses but can't drink the coffee because my hands are shaking. I can't look out the window in case the cloud-faces see me. *But you're OK*, I keep telling myself over and over, *you're inside*. Nobody else seems worried by the thunderstorm, although there are a few grumbles about the rain, and nobody seems to think it odd that I'm wearing sunglasses, or that I haven't drunk my coffee which has now grown a protective skin. The thunder grumbles into the distance and stops.

I get back to an empty flat and make a cup of coffee which, this time, I do drink, although my hands are still trembling with all the stress hormones washing around my innards. It takes me a while to get over thunderstorms and, if I'm honest, it's taking me longer and longer. Only when my hands have stopped shaking do I open my laptop. I have an essay that's due – well, it was due last Monday, but nobody at South Musselburgh seems to mind – on "*The news agenda: but what is news?*"

I've already written:

"A busker starts playing his violin in a Washington DC metro station at the height of the morning rush hour, and in the course of 40 minutes makes just over $30 – not a bad return. Of the 1,097 people who passed by, only seven stopped to listen. Most were late for work or thinking about the day ahead. A busker with a violin they could do without. When he finished playing, there was no applause. Except that it was a stunt dreamed up by the *Washington Post*. The busker was Joshua Bell, one of the finest classical musicians in the world, and he was playing a 1713 Stradivarius worth $3.5 million. Many of those who passed by would have paid huge sums to hear him play, but in a familiar context at a familiar time of day. In a busy morning metro station, he was therefore someone to be ignored. Which underlines one aspect of news, that context is...."

I drum my fingers on the kitchen table. The thunderstorm has unsettled me – made me feel again that I'm a little bit mad, which I'm not – and reminded me *again* about Mum and the small indignities Dad inflicted on her. Her *and* me. I'm not in the mood for media and communications, and think instead about Gramps and his grey hair, and Granny's thin arms, of applause in the Usher Hall and disapproving Christians outside it.

"How did the adjective 'new' become a noun ('news')? Well, there's one interesting (and most probably false) suggestion that in the 16th to 18th centuries some periodicals of the day printed the points of the compass on the front page, to signify that they were covering national and international events – and the points of the compass spell out NEWS...."

My grandparents will be on their way back to the airport now – fancy limousine for the return trip – and then to Alpine forests and Carla's cackle. I remember the leaflet in my pocket and unfold it. '*The Lord God created the Heavens and the Earth in six days.*' I tear up the leaflet without reading anything more, because everybody except Christians knows that the world wasn't created in six days.

"King Boabdil, the 15th century king of Grenada, didn't much like the news that a city had fallen to his enemies. So he had the messenger killed. It wasn't the first time that the bearer of bad news had got the blame, or the last. The origins of the phrase 'shooting the messenger', goes back to Sophocles and Plutarch. Nowadays, we're a bit more civilised and, of course, the media is today's messenger...."

It's no use. My mind is fused somewhere between the Usher Hall and Lake Como, between eloquence and succulence, with an aftertaste of thunderstorm. I can taste grappa and smell cheroots, and my phone is making the irritating buzzing noise that tells me a text is coming through, and which I should look at in case the limousine has broken down and my sturdy 2CV is required.

But it's from Dad, no doubt feeling contrite and remorseful at missing his father's lecture, or for rushing out at the end of it, and making typically outlandish excuses; no doubt composed from a hotel bedroom in Somewhere Else, with whatever sultry beauty is spreadeagled over him, the selfish bastard. He'll have had a leisurely lunch and a woozy fuck with someone who's not Mum. I sometimes have to remind myself that he's not dead, although, since it's a while since I last saw him, he could indeed have been eaten by sharks or be living on the Moon.

I close my computer and pour myself a large glass of white wine and take it up to the roof terrace. The dining room has a dead mouse at its centre which has either crawled from behind the skirting board and died peacefully of old age, or been murdered by Knox for being a Catholic mouse. The storm has long passed and the sky is uniformly blue and I watch an aeroplane rise over the Forth and turn south, wondering if my grandparents are on it.

A cruise ship has also docked and there is a line of coaches on the dockside to transport everyone into Edinburgh. I sit on the green-mildew bench and look out over the bustle of

231

the port to the flat surface of the river, which is where Patsy finds me a short while later.

She's brought the last *Club de Luxe* wine bottle with her – she's left the job, to concentrate on her finals – which is nice because my glass is empty. We fire the cork over the roof and down onto the street, talk about Granddad's lecture, how much Carlo enjoyed it – the suit was out of respect, apparently – and how she had only understood every tenth word. Carlo isn't as radical anymore, which suits Patsy because that means he has more time for her.

Carlo still believes in a socialist utopia, but no longer wants to smash capitalism to pieces, and seems to now prefer Patsy, soft drugs and physics, possibly in that order. I don't think that Carlo knows that I'm Alberto's granddaughter, despite Patsy calling me Emma every other day, and having introduced him to several mutual friends from North Berwick, and I wonder if the charade is worth it. The dull edges of my anger have worn smooth.

'He's doing a dissertation on Einstein-Rosen bridges,' says Patsy.

'Good for Carlo.'

'Yes, but what are they? I did ask him but didn't understand the answer.'

'They're portals to other parts of the universe.'

'I see,' says Patsy and sips at her glass, which is nearly empty, so she refills it. 'Are there many of these portal things?'

'Granddad doesn't believe in them,' I say, also refilling my glass.

'Well, maybe Carlo will discover that they're as common as muck. Incidentally, was your Dad there?' she asks.

The essay on the news agenda will have to be postponed, as I've drunk too much wine and can't now be bothered. It's a common excuse from Queen Margaret students.

'No.'

'Where was he?'

'In hospital,' I say, looking out at cranes and wharfs and moored ships. 'I got a text from him. He has terminal cancer.'

$$\frac{8B_\lambda \lambda^4}{ck_B T} = 16$$

Rayleigh-Jeans law

'Mrs Macgregor? Hello, I'm Maria. From the newspaper.'

Mrs Macgregor is sitting in one of those big high-backed chairs that old people like to sit in, or maybe don't like to sit in, but have to because they're told to sit in them. Mrs Macgregor looks too frail to be sitting in anything; she's bird-like – a baby sparrow, maybe – and very thin. If she was to lie down and die in a desert, the vultures would go away hungry. She's looking at me with mild curiosity, as if I might be someone she knows well but whose name she has temporarily forgotten.

I take out my notebook and hold it up to her. 'I'm here to ask you a few questions. Would that be OK, Mrs Macgregor?'

She's now looking a little alarmed, but still doesn't say anything. Her room is painted in pastel shades of pink like the inside of her mouth, which I can see into because her mouth is hanging open.

'Your. Daughter. Said. It. Would. Be. OK. For. Me. To. Talk. To. You.'

I have the impression that Mrs Macgregor is in there somewhere, because she's still looking me and I see that her lips are moving. I move my chair closer and lean in to her. 'Have you come to take me home?' she's saying in a thin, tired voice.

'No, Mrs Macgregor. I think you live here now.'

'But I don't know where here is. Am I in Sweden?'

'No, Mrs Macgregor. You're in Edinburgh.'

'It's just that they give me Swedish food for breakfast.'

'That's probably muesli, Mrs Macgregor.'

'Who did you say you were?'

'I'm Maria, from the newspaper.'

She's trying to say something else. Again, I have to bend my head close to her mouth. 'They're trying to kill me, you know.'

'Who?' I'm not very good with old people, and Mrs Macgregor is becoming very irritating. Granny and Gramps don't count and I've never encountered dementia before.

'Them.' She seems clear about this, nodding and winking.

'I'm sure they're not, Mrs Macgregor.'

'Who did you say you were?' But she seems to be perking up, speaking almost audibly, moving slightly in her big chair, making herself more comfortable. Her eyes seem more alert, less glassy. She's now closed her mouth but is dribbling like a very old Labrador.

'Maria, Mrs Macgregor.'

'You're not from the TV?'

'No, I'm from the newspaper. Your daughter Vikki told you I was coming, didn't she? Do you remember?'

'I was on TV once,' she says, looking momentarily wistful. My pen is still poised hopefully over my notepad, although I've yet to write anything about Britain's oldest woman. 'The Queen sent me a letter, which was nice of her, don't you think?'

'It was very nice of her, Mrs Macgregor! Do you still have the letter? Could I see it?'

'Goodness gracious, no! It's private,' she says. 'It was addressed to me personally. She wouldn't want me showing it to just anybody. That would be treason.'

'I'm sure she wouldn't mind.'

Mrs Macgregor turns blurred eyes to mine. 'She has very bad handwriting, the Queen. Full of squiggles and smudges and crossed-out words.' She laughs suddenly, or I think she's laughing; a small wheeze, like a distant set of bagpipes being tuned. 'I'll tell you this though. The Queen told me things that would make you blush! They made *me* blush, and I wasn't born yesterday!'

'Which is really why I'm here, Mrs Macgregor.'

'She told me everything about her holiday in Ibiza. Goodness me, can that girl dance! And the drinking! I only hope that Greek fellow she's married to doesn't mind.'

'Prince Phillip.'

'Are they still together? Anyway, I didn't know what a tequila slammer was and had to ask one of the nurses.' She subsides back into her chair and seems to deflate, becoming even smaller, like a creature in Alice in Wonderland. I wonder if she'll disappear entirely, except for her smile, which wouldn't be very nice as Mrs Macgregor doesn't have her teeth in.

'Maybe the TV will be along later,' I tell her.

'What?'

'MAYBE THE TV WILL BE HERE LATER!'

'What?'

'MAYBE THE QUEEN WILL COME AND VISIT LATER!'

She looks pleased and nods quietly for some moments. 'When?' she asks.

'I really don't know. Look, Mrs Macgregor, could I ask you some questions?' She's back to looking at me with friendly suspicion, as if I might be her closest friend or one of the people sent to kill her. 'For a start, do you remember the Blitz?' Maisie Anne Macgregor grew up in Clydebank and survived Hitler's bombers. A stalwart of the Maybole Bowling Club, she is now a national celebrity, simply for being old and is probably unaware that the previous holder of that accolade – Mrs Dorothy Frimpton from Ealing – died yesterday. But the Blitz she might remember.

'It was different when I was young,' she tells me, twining the twigs of her fingers together, and suddenly smiling. 'I used to dance; you know.'

'Just like the Queen,' I prompt. 'Was that before the war?'

'Which war, dear?'

'The war when Clydebank was bombed. Do you remember?'

With an effort of memory, she does seem to remember. 'They bombed the dance hall. I didn't go dancing after that.'

'I'm sorry about that, Mrs Macgregor.'

'Bastards!' she said suddenly. 'They killed him.'

'Who, Mrs Macgregor?'

'Reggie. We were going to be married.'

'What happened?'

'I don't know. I saw it on the TV.'

'Saw what?'

'Dinosaurs,' says Mrs Macgregor, smiling happily at nothing in particular, and by the time I've pocketed my pen and notebook, she's fast asleep.

'She has her good days and bad days,' says the care home manager, who's called Jackie and is wearing a lime-green trouser suit. She has very red cheeks, the colour of apples, although probably not as tasty. I try to think what kind of an apple. Royal Gala? Granny Smith? Golden Delicious? I'm not very good at apples. 'This, I'm afraid, is one of her good days.'

We're walking down a corridor. On either side are open doors and I can see old people sitting in other high-backed chairs, either fast asleep or watching TV. It must be quite nice to be very old, I think, and to spend every day watching TV, not having to cook, and having someone else wipe your bottom. 'We were hoping to do a story on her,' I say lamely, although Jackie knows who I am and why I'm here. 'But I think Maisie was hoping for a TV interview.'

'The BBC came here a few years ago when she became Scotland's oldest person. She loved that, seeing herself on the news. Fifteen minutes of fame, and all that. She was a lot more capable then, of course, despite telling the BBC that her long life was all down to cigarettes and whisky.'

We turn a corner and find ourselves in another featureless

corridor, with more old people watching TV. 'She's never smoked in her life,' says Jackie, 'and they didn't broadcast that bit. Said it wasn't the best kind of advice to be giving young people. But that's when we began to suspect that Maisie's brain functions were beginning to deteriorate.'

I try to remember the last time I smoked a cigarette by trying to remember the last time I was drunk. I can't remember that either, although it was possibly last weekend, and I have an urge to turn off the corridor into one of the little rooms and curl up on a bed and spend the rest of the day watching black and white Westerns, or whatever passes for entertainment on daytime TV, and I do almost go into one of the bedrooms, if only to find out what they're all watching.

'Her family didn't want any more TV interviews. She's not really up to it these days. So it's just you, I'm afraid.'

'The trouble is, she didn't really tell me anything.'

'Nothing at all?'

'Only that she liked dancing.'

'She did indeed!' Jackie confirms, 'Although she got a bit unsteady on her legs. Broke her hip tripping over a coffee table. Thought we'd lost her, to be honest. Broken hips in the elderly aren't a good thing. Anyway, she's not danced in a while.'

'Who was Reggie?' I ask.

'Her husband. Both of them were residents here. Come to think of it, she was dancing with him when they tripped over the coffee table.'

'What happened to him?'

She sighs. 'The same as happens to us all. Like I said, coffee tables and broken hips are not a good combination. Look, I've got some old newspaper cuttings if that would help? From her hundredth birthday. She was lucid then.'

I still feel myself to be a newcomer at *The Scotsman* and occupy a corner desk on the main news floor, close to the gents' toilet, and therefore know my male co-workers' personal habits quite well, or at least I like to think I do, but mostly it's just guesswork. The ladies' toilet is at the other end of the newsroom close to the water-fountain, photocopier and features desk, so that the features writers know a great deal about my toilet habits, or think they do. Or is it just me who thinks like this?

The other Maria has the desk next to mine and is the only other graduate in the year to have found work on a newspaper. Her Dad is the editor-in-chief, which is probably a coincidence. Unlike me, she takes everything very seriously and is forever having whispered phone conversations with her 'contacts', as she likes to describe them, although I don't ask who they are because she wouldn't tell me, and because she's never come up with an original story of her own.

Everything she's ever written has come down from the news editor, who hands out assignments based on length of service. The older hacks who've survived their probationary period get the good stories; the Marias get the dross – the colourful local stories to prove that the newspaper doesn't get all its news from news agencies – we mostly do – and which can be carried with a large photograph to save the expense of buying in other stories to fill the page.

In my first few weeks I have covered the opening of the Science Festival, a tram crash near Haymarket – nobody hurt, tram only slightly dented – and the grand unveiling of a JK Rowling statue – which will go somewhere eventually, when Edinburgh finally creates its long-planned 'literary quarter'.

I also spent a fruitless afternoon shouting through a letter box in west Edinburgh at a woman who owns about a million cats, and who I knew was inside because she'd barricaded herself in to stop the authorities gaining entry. Her neighbours had had enough of the smell, the cats probably needed veterinary attention, and the woman was probably mad. She didn't come to the door or speak to me through the letter box, although I could hear a multitude of cats trying to tell me something, perhaps knowing that the newspaper was going to feature her under the headline THE CAT WOMAN OF CORSTORPHINE. I must have covered other stuff but, in the torpor of a long Friday afternoon, I simply can't remember what.

My phone buzzes. It's John, from high up in his goldfish box.

'Thank you for sending me garbage,' he informs me politely, once I've been to the ladies' loo, and climbed the stairs to his domain. You can hear the loo's hand-dryer on the features desk outside, so everyone there now knows that I wash my hands. Or that I don't wash my hands but, perversely, still press the ON button on the hand-dryer. Or maybe they have better things to think about and don't care.

He reads aloud what I've just sent him:

'"Maisie Tulloch was born in Clydebank and worked in local government for over forty years, which was where she met her husband Reginald Macgregor to whom she was married for a very long time. They had two daughters, liked dancing and bowls, and Maisie is now the oldest person in Britain. Reginald was eaten by dinosaurs ten years ago.".'

'Dinosaurs,' says John, who still looks like a man-child who should be riding around his office on a tricycle.

'It's what she thinks happened to him.'

'And what did happen to him?'

'He fell over a coffee table and broke his hip. Actually, I do have a different version of the story all written up,' I tell him.

'A proper version? A version we can print?'

'Probably. We also got some good snaps.' The paper's photographer had come in later, and Maisie was woken up, and had her teeth put in, and even smiled at the camera.

'Look, Maria, I know you hate writing this stuff, but please don't make it so bloody obvious!'

I gesture towards his computer screen. 'I thought it summed up her life quite well because she hasn't actually *done* anything. All she's done is live for a very long time.'

'Which makes it a story.'

'But not a very good story.'

'Maria, please try to be a little less mad. In a while, we'll give you more interesting stuff. It's called pecking order, and you are the smallest bird on the news desk.'

Given the size of the other Maria, this is factually correct, if borderline sexist. 'And when do the newer, littler birds arrive?'

'Just send me the other version, OK?' says John who I think actually quite likes me, despite my palpable frustrations, partly because I don't keep sending him story suggestions from dubious sources, such as: 'I hear that Police Scotland are buying water cannon' (other Maria) or 'I have it on good authority that a puma is on the loose in East Lothian' (the same).

But mainly it's because of the series of stories we ran over a full week under the splash headline "DORIS GLIMPTON: HER SHOCK REVELATIONS". It took a while for the stories to appear because all sorts of affidavits had to be signed, with a small army of lawyers poring over every word. Is there a noun for an army of lawyers? If so, would it be printable? There were endless phone calls and emails with Doris and her lawyers, and more bits of paper for her to sign, but appear they did, to a collective intake of breath across the country – apparently – and a spike in newspaper sales that even won me a handshake from the editor-in-chief – who occupies a bigger glass box than John.

Buckingham Palace and political parties were drawn into the maelstrom, angry rebuttals were made that were swiftly and easily swatted away by Doris – you can't argue with a national treasure – and, for one heady week, it was all very entertaining. For that week I was a celebrity journalist, the toast of the news desk.

The other Maria was also grudgingly impressed and even offered me one of her cream cakes, but I know she doesn't wash her hands after going to the loo – no hand-dryer noises, I was doing some photocopying, so I declined, telling her instead that I didn't want to get fat, which she took badly and hasn't been so friendly since.

But after the euphoria of the Doris revelations it was back to the crumbs, studying other people's toilet habits – which is actually more interesting than it sounds – and trying not to listen to the other Maria's hushed telephone conversations. Unlike me, she's also kept in touch with some of the other MedComms and will say things like 'Janie sends love' or 'Max says "hi"' – presumably trying to make me feel guilty for leaving them all behind.

Most of them, according to the other Maria, are still looking for work, although several of the least competent are now in PR, which is the best place for them as they can't do much harm there.

I suppose I could have contacted some of Dad's other cronies and written more showbiz stuff. Tom Cruise would, I'm sure, be more than happy to talk about Scientology. But I don't want to blow my cover by being too obviously connected to celebrity and, in any case, I don't want to be part of that world anymore. I have cut myself free from tinsel.

I send John the more fulsome version of the Maisie Macgregor story and then stare at my computer screen. The other Maria appears to have vanished into thin air, because her handbag is still by her chair and a half-eaten bar of chocolate is beside her keyboard. I resist the temptation to eat it, and conclude that she may inadvertently have stepped into an Einstein-Rosen bridge and now be standing, rather surprised, on one of the moons of Jupiter. If so, I will definitely eat her bar of chocolate, except for the bits she may have touched, because I'm not sure if it's possible for her to make the return journey.

Gramps doesn't really think they can exist, although Einstein's equations suggest otherwise, because the cosmos is made up of mysteries that even the cleverest people around – including Gramps – are still scratching their heads about, and because, at the fringes of our understanding, the normal rules of physics don't work, and because space and time and gravity don't add up.

It was M87 that provoked the initial head-scratching. M87 is not a motorway but an elliptical galaxy in the Virgo constellation that astronomers quite like because it's only about fifty million light years away which, in cosmic terms, is just a short stroll to the shops. You can therefore observe it quite easily, even through a cheap and shoddy telescope. If you're interested, it has a diameter of one hundred and twenty thousand light years, contains nearly three trillion solar masses, and is roughly the same size as our own galaxy.

Over the years, M87 has swallowed up to a hundred other galaxies, which has had the same effect as eating too many cream cakes or pineapple pizzas. The super-massive black hole at the centre of M87 has a mass of more than three and a half billion Suns and, by some estimates, is eating the equivalent of ninety-one Earths every day, which is quite greedy.

The problem is that, in this kind of cosmic feeding frenzy, Einstein's equations – on the really big stuff – break down, as do theories of quantum mechanics, the sub-atomic little stuff. Until someone comes up with a clever idea that combines both of them, scientists have concluded, looking at M87, that it's mathematically possible to fly into a black hole and, instead of being squashed, find yourself in a tunnel.

Think of it like this: draw two dots at either end of a sheet of paper, then fold the sheet of paper in half. The two dots, which were quite far apart, are now on top of one another. Space and time have effectively been short-circuited, and the small gap between the two dots has become a tunnel.

This tunnel, or Einstein-Rosen bridge, would then shoot

243

you out into a distant part of the galaxy, or into a different dimension or a parallel universe or somewhere else in time. It's a branch of physics that makes *Star Wars* seem oddly unimaginative.

Instead of popping to the shops for a loaf of bread, you might find yourself on one of Jupiter's moons trying to make friends with the other Maria, who has suddenly reappeared at her desk with a large supermarket bag. I resist the temptation to ask whether she's enjoyed her stay on Ganymede or Europa – there are 67 Jovian moons – and instead, looking at her shopping bag, ask if she's having people over for supper.

'Just my sister and her boyfriend,' she replies, covertly looking at her bar of chocolate and, no doubt, estimating if any of it has been eaten. I may have had a small piece, but only one or two squares, probably. 'I'm cooking spaghetti,' she adds, because she still thinks I'm more Italian than Scottish and therefore that I will be pleased about her choice of supper. 'You got any plans?'

'Seeing my father,' I say stupidly, then bite my tongue.

'I thought your father was dead?'

Distracted, I've allowed my worlds to collide. 'Not completely,' I tell her.

$$\frac{34G(M + m)P^2}{8a^3\pi^2} = 17$$

Orbital radius from Kepler's third law

I haven't seen much of Dad since the episode in our kitchen: the retrieved golf club proving his guilt, even to him. I'd seen it in his eyes, in his voice: the realisation of what he'd done, to all of us. I suppose I have made my anger into a part of me, like an arm or a leg.

I haven't much visited him since he became ill because he couldn't be bothered to see much of us when he was well and Mum was alive. I'm just repaying the debt of desertion that he visited upon us, and I don't feel guilty about it, and he knows that. As his life has entered its final countdown, maybe he does wish that he could wind back the clock and do things differently. Divorce Mum? Marry Sarah or one of his other starlets? Or just try to fit into our world a little more. It's where Mum wanted him, until we realised that the constraints of marriage and family life were pretty flimsy, and that fame and destiny lay elsewhere.

I also slightly hate myself when I do visit him. We don't discuss the past, or Mum, because these subjects are off-limits; instead we talk inconsequentials, and I don't stay long. Why do I do this? He knows what I feel, and my visits only remind him of his crimes against Mum. But he's never admitted to remorse. I don't suppose it's in his nature. He can't admit to being wrong.

My father had been so many people, some recognisably still him, others less so, so that I would sometimes have to look twice to be sure it was him. Now he is just himself, stripped of his chameleon's skin. With his stick-on moustache, hair gelled back and chest puffed out, he could be anybody he fancied: hero or villain, lover or killer, clutching roses or a gun with equal dexterity, treading the boards with quick sure steps, his face lifted to the gods, precise words falling on our ears with perfect intonation. Now he is diminished, a smaller version of the father I've always known, and it gives me a small frisson of pleasure to know that I am still living, and he is only clinging on. Maybe that is why I still see him: I am winning, and he isn't.

But this visit shocks me. In the course of the few weeks since I last saw him, he has become gaunt and frail. It takes me a moment to realise that this man had once been Number Eighteen, although mischievous life still burns in his eyes as he asks why I'm still driving 'that clapped-out piece of shit.' It's the kind of inconsequential stuff that we talk about now.

I'm barely in the door, with my clapped-out piece of shit making the immaculate driveway look untidy. I kiss Mrs Perkins on the cheek, because we're old friends really, and then kiss Dad on the cheek because I'm expected to and because, I have to admit, I do feel sorry for him. 'It's a classic, Dad. Utilitarian transport for the masses.'

'It's still shit.'

'But it's *my* shit, Dad.'

It's early evening and the sky is blue. I'd checked the weather forecasts, and everything is set fair, so it was OK for me to drive down.

'It's brown,' he says.

'It's always been brown, Dad.' His cars were always whiter-than-white, buffed to perfection by Mr Perkins, weeding duties permitting. Mrs Perkins then says her goodbyes and closes the front door.

Dad is now at a stage in his illness where he resembles Schrödinger's Cat, the hypothetical cat in the quantum mechanics theory that states that a particle exists in all states at once until observed. Erwin Schrödinger said that this was daft, put a cat in a box, and said that it was either alive or dead, whether or not anyone was looking at it. But it's how Dad looks now: neither alive nor dead. His eyes are piercing, but the rest of him seems as clapped out as my car, which, incidentally, still works perfectly well, despite bits falling off it, although none of the bits seem terribly important.

He'd texted me about a year beforehand with the news. He'd been in a hospital bed in London, but then flew up to an equally posh hospital in Edinburgh. Reluctantly, I had visited him. His room overlooked Murrayfield rugby stadium, where Dad has the most expensive debentures, but has rarely gone to watch Scotland play. I somehow doubt that he'll go again, as I have to help him down the steps from the front door and into the piece of shit. He has a baseball cap on, and his face is unshaven. He doesn't look like Paul Ross anymore: just someone who looks a bit like how Paul Ross would have looked like in advanced old age, but on a bad day.

'Look,' I tell him. 'It's even got air-conditioning.' I crank open the flap under the dashboard, although the 2CV doesn't really have a dashboard. Just a speedometer, and a couple of knobs.

'But no radio.'

'Who needs synthetic entertainment? It's a car made for singing in.'

'And is that what you do?' Dad asks.

'No, I can't sing.'

'Well, it can't be very reliable,' he says as we go round a sharp corner and the car leans over alarmingly. I can't remember if Dad has ever been in my car and am momentarily saddened by the expanse of things we haven't done.

'2CVs are kind and gentle, Dad. It's not in their nature to break down.'

We're booked into an Italian restaurant on the High Street – my choice – and, again, I have to help him from the car and to our table, and then move the car from double-yellow lines and find a parking space. When I get back, he's still wearing the baseball cap, and is nursing a glass of white wine. A menu is open on the table in front of him, although he tells me that he's not hungry and that he'll just have a starter, if that's all right with me.

'No, it isn't all right,' I reply. 'You have to eat.'

'Why?' he asks.

Despite myself, I find that I'm giving him good advice. 'Because it's what you're supposed to do. Eat, drink, go to the loo and sleep. Nothing else matters. Have some pasta, Dad. Slow-release carbohydrate. Good for you.'

'You should be your paper's medical correspondent.'

I don't bother telling him that the other Maria has her eyes on that job, although the current health and beauty editor is young and beautiful – Maria only ticks one of those boxes – and knows what she's talking about, as she's a failed medical student who, as far as I know, didn't work at the *Club de Luxe*.

'Anyway,' I say lamely, 'you have to eat.' I gesture to a waiter who glides over and takes our order.

I look around the restaurant, which is quite small. It has Italian scenes painted on the walls that make me think of Como. A jumbled village perched on a hill, a dusty town square dotted with cafes. There's only a handful of other diners, mostly middle-aged couples who aren't saying much to one another, having exhausted all avenues of conversation years beforehand. Looking at them, and their sad silences, I think that they should be knocking back Chianti and babbling nonsense to one another. That's what Italians do, even if they know that the other person isn't listening. It's what I hope to be doing a few decades from now, although it's what I'm sometimes accused of doing now.

'You haven't been down for a while,' says Dad, and when he raises his glass, he has to use both hands, as if it's become heavy.

'No, sorry. You know. Work.'

He nods, but doesn't look convinced, probably because

I don't sound convincing. He knows as well as I do that a metaphorical golf club still lies on the table between us. He's careful not to call me Emma but has never once called me Maria. The other diners don't pay any attention to him. Not long ago, he would have been sitting grandly, immaculately clothed, hair gelled, burning brightly like a 1,000-watt light bulb. The other diners would have had their heads together, whispering, surreptitiously taking photos with their phones, or apologetically asking for an autograph, then bowing their gratitude.

I suppose he misses the attention, but I can also see that he doesn't now want to be recognised. If someone comes into the restaurant, he tips his head forward, the visor hiding his face, a hint of nervousness in his eyes. The great actor, reduced to this.

'In which case, they're working you too hard,' he says. 'Are you still enjoying it?'

'Yes, mostly.'

He looks wistful for a moment. 'Other little girls played with their toys. You had your head in a book. Always reading, always by yourself. Such a solitary child.' I wonder if my dolls are still safe in the panic room, or if he's chopped them up and burned them. 'You're still in that gargantuan flat of yours?'

'Still there, Dad. But by myself now.'

'By yourself! It's bigger than my house!'

I can't recall him ever having been to the flat, and I certainly wouldn't have invited him. I notice that he didn't say *our house*. 'Maybe, but it doesn't have a cinema room, although I'm thinking of having one put in.'

'Don't bother,' he advises. 'We never used ours. An architectural vanity that turned out to be a mistake. Anyway, it's nice to see you. Thank you.'

'For what?' I ask.

A waiter has appeared with a plate of langoustines – me – and a plate of salad – him.

249

'For making the time to see me,' he says. 'These days, not many people do.'

I suppose he must be a bit lonely, with only Mrs Perkins to talk to, not forgetting the army of nurses who come in to sit with him, make sure that he's taking his medication, and basically doing fuck all. 'After all, it's a long drive from Edinburgh in a clapped-out piece of shit.'

'It's not that far, 'I remind him, remembering all his departures for Edinburgh airport, scattering gravel in his wake, desperate to be away from us. 'It also gives me time to practice my singing.'

He doesn't smile but pushes salad leaves around his plate with a fork that also seems too heavy. 'You have to eat, Dad,' I remind him and nearly put my hand on his.

There are things I would like to ask him, but which I daren't ask because I don't want to know the answers. I want to know if he really did love Mum. I want to know why he married her – and vice versa. I want to know why the church mouse ended up with the cathedral cat. But I'd also like to know if any of the endless rumours were true – for example, if he really did have a fling with Sandra Bullock. Their on-screen love scenes were very convincing, and far too convincing for Mum.

He still hasn't eaten anything by the time the waiter comes back for our plates and doesn't know whether to take Dad's untouched plate away, and therefore if Dad has hated his starter and whether that will affect his tip. The waiter gives Dad a closer look, but without apparent recognition.

'Anyway,' says Dad, 'I've made a decision.' Dad was always a decisive person, although not always right. I still remember trips out to country parks where we'd end up somewhere else entirely because he wouldn't listen to Mum's map-reading – which would probably have taken us to somewhere else completely wrong. They didn't happen often, those family trips, and we rarely ended up where we were supposed to be going. I have a clear memory of standing in an empty field and wondering where the fun fair had gone. 'I'm going to move into a place in Edinburgh. Getting up stairs is a bit of a bugger.'

'You could move downstairs,' I tell him. 'Convert the study into a bedroom.' Or move into the basement and convert the swimming pool, although I don't suggest this. 'So what is this place you want to move to?'

'It's a hospice,' says Dad. 'Very comfortable, apparently, although I've only seen a brochure. It has lots of smiling people living there, so it must be simply wonderful. I just don't want to be by myself. You know, in case anything happens.'

'There's always Mrs Perkins,' I suggest.

'Precisely!' says Dad, and resumes pushing food around his plate with his heavy fork. His bits of salad have been replaced with bits of vegetable. I'm eating seafood spaghetti, because I'm hungry. 'She's not exactly a medic, is she? She wouldn't know what to do.'

'But you've got nurses who stay over at night, don't you?'

'It's not that simple,' says Dad. 'Well, I don't suppose that it's ever that simple. Fact is, I'd rather be somewhere that can provide proper care.' He looks up, suddenly smiles. His teeth look brown and fuzzy. 'But it means I'll be nearby and you can come and see me more often. You will come, won't you?' He's looking like a small boy when he says this, just in case Mummy says 'no'. I realise that he's frightened.

'Of course, Dad.' Well, what I am meant to say?

He smiles again, but a distant smile at the edges of his lips. 'It's called palliative care. Anyway, I'm sorry.'

'For what?'

Dad has lowered his head, so that I can't see his eyes. 'For everything,' he says and, despite myself, I do put a hand over his. I can't help it. It's the closest thing to an apology he's ever given.

But if Dad could step into a celestial time machine, would he want to go back and do things differently?

I think about this on the drive back to Edinburgh, and about how Einstein's theory of gravity and quantum theory are seemingly incompatible. So, while we know an awful lot about the universe, we still don't have a theory of everything.

Well, maybe we do, and it's called superstring theory. It says that sub-atomic particles are just the vibrations of a very small string which, as it moves through time, warps the fabric of space. You don't actually have to understand that last sentence, because I've simply copied it from the Rossini Theorem, and don't understand it myself. But it means that the universe is really a vast symphony orchestra playing a kind of celestial music – a music of the spheres – and it makes Einstein's equations and quantum physics fit together.

There's just one problem with superstring theory. To work, it has to occupy ten dimensions, because you can't throw a huge party in a phone box.

Patsy and I did once try that on Edinburgh's Royal Mile, but it wasn't successful, and then someone turned up who actually wanted to *use* the phone box, which was odd because we didn't think that anyone used phone boxes any more, and he threatened to call the police if we didn't all get out of it.

There were four of us in the phone box, and it was very cramped, although one of us was Carlo, who probably equals at least three people. It was late at night, and we were all drunk. Incidentally, the world record for cramming adult people into a phone box is 12 and was actually set in Edinburgh. I don't know which city holds the world record for people being sick in a phone box.

Anyway, the basic four dimensions, which include time, are too small for a party the size of the universe. It also means, for example, that light may be nothing more than a vibration on the fifth dimension.

When Granddad lent his name to superstring theory – like dark matter, he didn't come up with the idea first – and placed it in a mathematically complex model to explain dark matter and dark energy, he was vilified. His theorem on everything had too many assumptions and, as anyone who's studied chaos theory knows, too many assumptions can only add up to bollocks.

Except that the Hubble telescope then started to throw out data that suggested that Granddad might only have written semi-bollocks. Then several scientists independently found that string theory completely solved the mysteries of a quantum black hole, which must be nice for the black hole, knowing that someone finally understands it.

But string theory also means that there may be wormholes through time, ways to revisit the dead before they've died, and tell them that you're sorry. Maybe that's what Dad is trying to do.

But there's also another reason why I don't see Dad so often, and it's all because I live in Scotland and the weather is often cloudy and unpredictable, and I therefore have to be careful because I don't want to be seen. It's an amoebic fear that's been forming, dissolving and reforming for years now, a fear I can almost forget about until the next thunderstorm reminds me of the cloud-faces that are still looking for me.

It doesn't bother me so much when I'm in Edinburgh – or any city – because there are pubs or cafes to hide in. But I feel vulnerable in the countryside, away from sanctuary, and have to be careful if the weather might be stormy.

I became acutely aware of it around the time that Patsy announced she was going to live with Carlo. All of us were in the kitchen drinking vodka martini – because Phil had perfected the recipe – and beer – because Phil didn't actually like vodka martini – and milk – Knox, because he's teetotal – and cheap champagne, because Berry was still working nights at the *Club de Luxe* and had inherited Patsy's light fingers and large handbag. It was an announcement that was met with good-natured ridicule because we all still thought of Carlo as a Trotskyite leftie who would dump her the moment a proper revolutionary came along, despite Patsy repeatedly telling everyone that he'd mellowed and wasn't like that at all.

But it marked the beginning of an end, that's for sure. Patsy was our little star and, without her gravity, everyone else soon announced other plans and floated off. Berry to Manchester – without Laura – Antoine and his French cigarettes back to Paris, Ted to work for another charity in Liverpool, Constance to London, Phil back to Glasgow to be unemployed somewhere else, and Amanda to Gatwick, although I think she's actually living somewhere *near* Gatwick, not in the departures lounge.

'But what about you?' asked Patsy. We were on the roof terrace and watching another cruise ship inch its way to the dockside.

'I'm going to stay.'

'Then you'll have to advertise. If you want, I could help you vet people? You don't want to end up with another bunch of lunatics.'

I thought about it. 'Who owns this place?'

'No idea. Probably some rich bastard. I suppose the letting agency will tell you.'

It wasn't quite dark and the outline of Fife was clear across the water, and I momentarily wanted to be over there, walking on the beach I thought I could see, listening to the sea, feeling melded to something greater than me, when there was a flicker of lightning away to the east, the merest flicker, and immediately I didn't want to be in Fife, or anywhere without a roof over my head and a lightning conductor on the roof – *Christ, do we have one*?

Patsy found me later, back in the kitchen, still drinking Phil's vodka martini. He'd made a bucketful – literally – and I'd made it my mission to finish it. The others were crashed

254

out in the living room, watching a film. Knox was on a high shelf and fast asleep. I think he's given up trying to reform me, although he does still visit me at night.

'What's wrong with you, Maria?' she asked. 'You're getting odder every bloody day.'

'Not odd, just drunk.'

'Odd and drunk,' said Patsy. 'You're going to buy this place, aren't you?'

'Maybe.' Knox and the room were beginning to spin, but I was inside and the thunderstorm had petered out somewhere over the North Sea, so I was safe, although I was still wearing sunglasses just in case.

'But there again,' said Patsy, 'what can you expect from a rich bitch.'

'Thank you,' I said, enunciating very clearly, because it was getting difficult to speak. 'I've always wondered whether I was a rich bitch or a rich cow.'

'Both,' said Patsy.

I've never really thought of myself that way. My clothes all come from ordinary shops and I mostly wear jeans. The only expensive jewellery I own all came from Mum after her death – mostly guilt offerings from Dad, I expect – and I keep it in the bank. I still have the two posh watches I was given for my birthday, and I do wear those, although everyone at university probably thought they were cheap Chinese fakes. Over the years I have simply tried to fit in: going to cheap pubs, eating in the crap places that only students inhabit, and pretending that I don't have a Swiss bank account.

I only have one expensive dress, a black Dior that belonged to Mum, and she wore it only once on a catwalk in London. I can still feel the press of her hand in mine, and how I wanted to grow up and be just like her, because I was so proud of the way she looked and how she could smile, despite her hand shaking in mine and having had an underwear meltdown. I keep her dress in my wardrobe, and every time I open the wardrobe door, I smell her scent.

The next afternoon once I'd recovered from too many vodka martinis – how *does* James Bond do it? Does he ever suffer from hangovers? Does he ever shoot the wrong people and blame it on the wrong brand of vodka? – I drove round the city bypass to the other side of Edinburgh. I was going to buy something-or-other and thought that the big shopping centre there would stock it. But it was the first time I also checked, double-checked, and triple-checked the weather forecast before setting off. I told myself that I just didn't want to get wet, and that repeatedly checking the weather forecast was quite normal.

Then, once I got to the shopping centre, I'd completely forgotten why I was there or what I was intending to buy. Instead, I walked to the end of the shopping centre car park and looked at the city bypass, where all the traffic has to slow down to go round a big roundabout. On the other side of the dual carriageway is countryside, Edinburgh's green belt, on my side of the bypass are shopping centres and office blocks. The road marks a boundary between city and country and, I realised, between where I felt safe and where it was threatening. There's nowhere to hide in open spaces, because the countryside is part of the natural world, and the natural world would like to kill me if it ever finds out that I'm now Maria Rossini.

$$-\frac{6\dot{\rho}a}{\dot{a}\left(\rho + \frac{P}{c^2}\right)} = 18$$

Fluid equation

Dad stayed on in North Berwick for a few months, but became confined to his bedroom. Getting downstairs – and back up again – was too much of a strain. He could have had a stairlift installed, and stayed on for longer, but he didn't like the thought of someone butchering our grand staircase, or the ignominy of having to use it. Mrs Perkins did the cleaning, ironing and cooking, although much of the food she cooked was thrown away. Dad's appetite had diminished from human to hamster to nothing. I know that Sarah came up from time to time, no doubt bringing gossip, but probably nothing else.

The bevy of nurses did try to chivvy him along and take him on exciting excursions in a wheelchair which, for Dad, must have been ghastly. His normal means of propulsion was striding purposefully, not being pushed by a bimbo with big boobs, who may or may not have had any medical qualifications. I suspect that the prettier nurses at the agency fought to the death for the chance to minister to Dad.

These excursions were made worse by the reactions of everyone they met because, by then, word had got around town that Dad was only a shadow of his former self. Women who once would have dreamed of meeting him, and of wearing only their best knickers if they were invited to our house, now smiled at him sadly, or pretended not to recognise him, and only wore their fourth-best knickers. Dad, with his bright eyes, would have seen all this and grown tired of it, and decided that the time had come to retire from the world.

I come down by train for his final journey into Edinburgh. Mr Perkins picks me up at the station. In the hallway is a Gucci suitcase that Mr Perkins deposits in the Bentley's boot. The boot closes with a small sigh of pleasure. It must have taken Bentley millions of pounds to perfect that muted sigh. The 2CV doesn't really have a boot, or one that's useful, and you have to slam the boot door very hard, otherwise it won't close. My car boot doesn't sigh. Dad stands in the hallway for a few minutes, leaning on a stick, just looking around, thinking about something.

Mrs Perkins is also just standing around, but she's in floods of tears and twisting a handkerchief in her fingers. She too knows that this is an ending, although Dad's told her that they can stay until the house is sold and that, maybe, the new owners will also need a housekeeper and gardener.

He's said that he'll put in a good word for them, but Mrs Perkins knows that the old order is changing; the prince is about to leave his castle for the last time. She kisses him on the cheek and even tells him to be a 'good boy.' Dad raises an eyebrow; he's never been a good boy in his life, but has no option now.

I sit in the back seats with Dad. Mr Perkins is a careful driver and considerate to other road users and I know that Dad is willing him to put his foot down and do a bit of screeching round corners, just as he would have done, one hand somewhere near the steering wheel and the other on a terrified Mum's knee. We leave the smaller roads for the dual carriageway into Edinburgh, and with all opportunities for screeching at an end, Dad goes to sleep. He's wearing his baseball cap, the one he wore to the restaurant, and I take it off because he looks uncomfortable wearing it, and realise that he's mostly bald, so put his cap back on. Mr Perkins smiles sadly at me in the rear-view mirror and I smile sadly back.

We arrive at The Swallows and a small welcoming party is already assembled on the steps. One of the staff – blonde, big boobs – guides a wheelchair to the car, while another heaves Dad's suitcase from the boot, and places it on the kind of trolley you see in posh hotels. Bimbo pushes Dad up the disabled access ramp, followed by his suitcase, while I have a quick look upwards. It's still a fine day, and promises to get hotter and, anyway, The Swallows is inside the city boundary, so I'm safe.

Dad's new home does resemble the pictures in the brochure, with its Georgian exterior covered over with ivy, and the wood-panelled entrance with its lustrous oak flooring. But I don't see any of the smiling faces that adorned every picture in the brochure. The people that I do see, presumably all staff, just look either bored or vaguely pissed off, except for one middle-aged man with grey hair and matching suit who is advancing across the floor, his shoes making small squeaking noises.

'Miss Rossini,' he says with a quiet confidence. Mr Perkins is back outside and guarding the Bentley from vandalism by the terminally ill. 'How very nice to meet you.' He leads me to a small office and I sign a few papers on behalf of Dad who, now he's in a hospice, is presumably deemed incapable of using a pen.

Dad's room is on the first floor, but there's a lift to transport him to communal areas on the ground floor. He's leaning on his stick when I enter and doesn't turn around. He's looking north, towards the Forth. 'It's like your room in North Berwick,' he says.

I look around the room but can see no similarity whatsoever. For a start, my room was filled with familiar things. This room doesn't have anything in it that either of us would recognise.

He gestures to the window. 'The estuary,' he says. 'You could stare at it for hours.'

I stand beside him, the young princess by the dying king, remembering when Vikings might just be about to invade, or dragons might swoop down, but that it was OK because my toys were in the panic room, and surface-to-surface missiles would simply bounce off our windows, but I don't reply because I have nothing to say, and I close my eyes and stand beside my father, and listen to the sea although it's a long way away, and it could simply be the sound of my father's laboured breathing.

I did buy the Leith flat, paying an exorbitant amount for it, but reasoning that it was an investment and was also Knox's home. In any case, would he recognise a new toilet? Would he reluctantly move to my new place only to escape back here? He didn't seem to mind the others moving out and took a swing at Patsy when she inadvisably tried to pat his head goodbye. The flat's old owner was an investment company in Panama and seemed surprised that they actually owned an apartment in Edinburgh because it didn't seem to be in their database or fit their normal investment criteria, which suggested that they owned quite a lot of other places.

My solicitor, a thin and dapper man who looked round the flat, but pointedly didn't touch anything, couldn't understand why I wanted the place to myself, a view shared by my surveyor, who spent the best part of a day poking around cupboards and who was utterly horrified by the roof terrace, which he said wasn't really a roof terrace and that the current owners – I hadn't yet bought it – should be taken to court for 'providing accommodation in a most dangerous and unlawful condition.'

I tried to tell him that the roof terrace was only dangerous if you stepped over the edge, and was therefore a kind of Darwinian selection test, but he said that wasn't the point and that landlords have 'a duty of responsibility to their tenants,' He continued on in much the same vein as he went from room to room checking for damp or alien life forms, or whatever surveyors check for, and which is probably why Knox hissed at him and scratched at his leg when he went to inspect one of the flat's toilets. He was wearing boring surveyor trousers, baggy and sensible, so no damage done, except to Knox's dignity. Nobody likes it when someone barges in when they're on the loo.

The first task was to throw everything away, which simply took a phone call, and then burly men came and lifted everything down to a lorry. Beds, mattresses, carpets – everything went into the lorry, which then had to come back several times, to also carry away the remains of the kitchen, living room shelving, bathroom fittings, and the dead mouse in the dining room.

As this was going on, I phoned the interior decorator who had worked on our North Berwick house, and she came round with a clipboard – which, to me, indicated her professionalism – and marvelled at the flat's size, and measured up rooms, asked lots and lots of questions – some of which I answered sensibly and some, regrettably, which I didn't – then went away and came back with concept drawings that I flicked through on her computer and said 'yes' to.

The interior decorator seemed both very surprised and very happy – mostly surprised – but also looked on the verge of tears, and told me how bold and adventurous I was, which made me think that I should have looked at her concept drawings more carefully.

At the height of the renovations, I moved out to a hotel. I could have moved back to North Berwick but didn't want to share our old family home with Dad. I left everything in the hands of the interior decorator, although I did give the builders precise instructions on how to feed Knox, when to feed Knox, and how they must never try to be friendly. One did try but the other builders soon learned not to go anywhere near him.

Floors were sanded down, a new kitchen – with pizza oven – and bathrooms fitted, wall coverings were scraped off and new coverings stuck on, beds, bedside tables, wardrobes and light shades arrived. A dining table also arrived, a bespoke creation from Ogilvies of Haddington, who I can thoroughly recommend, along with twelve dining chairs, and new bookcases, sofas, chairs and carpets.

It was like stepping into a parallel universe when I saw it for the first time: a place that I thought I knew well but that was utterly different. Each room had been themed. There was an Oriental bedroom with damask drapes and black walls, an African bedroom with ethnically patterned curtains and bamboo furniture – which should really have been in the Oriental room, and an Incan bedroom with strange patterns on the walls and tribal heads on heavy oak furniture, which should really have been in the African room.

The kitchen was now all chrome and marble and discreet down lighters, there were ensuite bathrooms, and other bathrooms with no discernible purpose, and the spiral staircase to the roof had been stripped back and painted black. Best of all, the roof terrace had real chairs and a proper table, with a BBQ built into the stonework, and a parapet with thick wires to prevent drunks taking a shortcut to the road below.

On my first evening back in the old/new flat, I sat in one of my comfortable new roof terrace chairs, drinking a glass of wine, and staring out at the ocean. Knox came and sat on my knee, the first time he'd done that, and purred loudly. Perhaps he'd been lonely, with only daytime builders and without his dead mouse. He even allowed me to tickle him behind his ears, which he'd never allowed before. I don't think he could have much liked the previous inhabitants, or the sound of popping corks, which always made him jump. We sat for a long time looking at the sea; me, thinking about nothing in particular, the same kind of nothing that Knox probably thinks about all the time.

Next morning, I can't make myself a cup of coffee because, despite now owning a coffee machine the size of a tumble dryer, I can't figure out how to use it. Its instruction 'leaflet' is the length of *War and Peace,* but probably less entertaining, and I don't have the time or inclination to start reading it. I also don't seem to own a kettle and, once I've located a shiny new saucepan to boil some water and worked out how to turn the hob on, I realise that I don't have any instant coffee either. Did I actually order a coffee machine? What else have I ordered? I must have a proper look around. No wonder the interior decorator looked happy, and actually cried when she left.

By the time I arrive at work, I'm late, and I don't like being late. It's a trait I've inherited from Mum who hated being late for anything, The hearse carrying her body to the funeral service was held up for some time by the crowds outside, which would have *really* pissed her off. I usually buy myself a large espresso from the shop across the road, but I haven't had time this morning, and heave off my jacket in a bad mood and switch my computer on.

Beside me, the other Maria isn't there, but a half-eaten chocolate bar is. Her first? Her twentieth? But just as I'm about to reach across and break off a piece, she rolls back to her desk looking flustered. 'It seems we're working together today,' she says.

'We are?' The paper is normally so short-staffed that world war, global starvation and everything else is usually covered by one reporter.

'A balloon's crashed,' she says, looking flushed and excited. I'm thinking child-size, and don't immediately see the point of all this. 'A hot air balloon with people on it,' says the other Maria, no doubt hoping for fireballs and charred bodies.

It turns out to have been a charity stunt gone wrong, a well-meaning attempt to recreate Scotland's first aerial voyage in 1785, which also went wrong. The story goes that Vincenzo Lunardi only wanted to fly his new-fangled balloon a short distance from a garden in Edinburgh but drifted so far north that he had no option but to overfly the

Forth and land in Fife, a distance of forty-six miles, a feat which earned him footnote in history.

However, and the reason why I'm now in a taxi with the other Maria, is that a bunch of amateur balloonists have just tried to recreate Vincenzo's dashing exploit and crashed in Leith, without even reaching the Forth. The irony is that, if I'd stayed at the flat a little longer, I would have had a ringside seat.

There's a sizeable crowd on the quayside when we arrive, and a police line beyond which the public is not allowed to pass. There are police cars, ambulances and several fire engines and, on the other side of a warehouse, we can see the flaccid canopy of a jaunty red and orange balloon. It seems to be deflating, which is possibly why it crashed. The other Maria has already rolled off as quickly as her little legs will carry her, and is pushing her way through the crowd, telling everyone she's a newspaper reporter and asking if anyone saw what happened.

She seems to be doing both our jobs admirably, and so I stand where I am, wondering if I have time to nip back to the flat and have the cup of coffee that I've so far failed to have. I could even figure out how to use the coffee machine.

I am distracted by a man and woman behind me who are talking about the crash. They're both wearing white aprons – and other clothes obviously – with "CHIP CHOP" emblazoned on their lapels. I recognise them from the Chinese carry-out and fish and chip shop beside my block of flats, and they recognise me, and tell me how they saw everything happen in slow motion, which, I suppose, is how hot air balloons generally crash. They'd been in the cafe and seen it pass overhead and gone out to look then heard one of the balloonists shout that there was something wrong with the propane burners and that he couldn't get any height. 'It's not something you see every day,' said Mick, as I took down his name and age. 'It was, like, 9/11 all over again,' said Marlene, with greater imagination. 'We took lots of pictures as it went over,' said Mick.

I then went to the police line, showed my press card, and was allowed through and spoke at length to a police inspector, someone from the Edinburgh Students Balloon Club – it just *had* to be students! – and a representative of the Lothian Dog Trust, which had hoped to benefit from the charity flight.

I can't now see the other Maria and am about to text her when she appears beside me, accusing me of being in the same spot as she'd left me, and of therefore doing fuck-all, and visibly panting with the effort of having walked a few dozen yards. She says that she's spoken to loads of people, some of whom nearly saw the balloon crash, and got good quotes from people who had arrived soon afterwards, and is visibly angry when I tell her that the balloon had developed a propane burner problem, that three people were slightly injured, that I have good quotes from eye-witnesses, the police, the organisers and the charity, and that I'm being sent moment-by-moment photographs of the crash on an exclusive basis.

The other Maria listens to this in miserable silence, deflating as visibly as the balloon we can still see on the other side of the warehouse, and then says that she's got to have a pee urgently and could we pop quickly to my flat, because she's remembered that I live just up the road.

The entrance lobby is more refined than on her last visit, with pot plants and leather sofas, and the lift has been cleaned and refurbished, and now usually works. I gesture down the hall to the nearest toilet, tell her I'll be on the roof terrace, take my camera up with me, and shoot some long-range shots of the balloon's basket being lifted onto a low-loader, while the nylon canopy is slowly rolled up.

'You've got a sauna,' says the other Maria who, despite her size, has an uncanny ability to move quietly.

'I do?' I reply, and ask her to show me, and we traverse a long corridor and arrive at a familiar doorway, which has

265

been replaced by a Scandinavian lacquered wood door with a small window in it. I open the door to find that my old bedroom – I've decided to sleep in all the other bedrooms before deciding which one I like the best – is now a sauna with a shimmering plunge pool.

The room is warm and smells of chlorine. Another instruction booklet is lying on a three-legged stool, beside a chrome towel rail on which have been draped thick white towels. 'Good heavens,' I say, realising that I now have a sort of indoor swimming pool.

'You didn't know that this was here?' asks the other Maria. I can almost hear cogs whirring in her brain. *How can she afford this*? she's thinking, because I've never given any outward indication of wealth before, and even joined in a student protest when prices went up in the university cafeteria.

'Not entirely, no,' I say.

It doesn't take long to transcribe my notes and for the bare facts to be loaded onto the paper's website – BALLOON DRAMA IN CAPITAL – and for me to write a longer version which I send to the other Maria, who is pulling the story together for tomorrow's editions. My photographs from the roof terrace and Mick's photographs of the crash are forwarded to the picture desk. All in all, we'll probably have the best coverage in tomorrow's newspapers.

My phone rings. It's John. 'My office, if you will, Maria.'

Now that the story is written – although the other Maria is still feverishly phoning her 'contacts' – I've nothing better to do, and he is my boss, so I ascend the staircase to his office. He's also on the phone and pages of my transcribed notes are spread across his desk. He motions me to the seat opposite, while I wonder if I'm ever going to get a cup of coffee.

He eventually puts the phone down. 'Good work this morning, Maria,' he says, indicating the pile of papers, with my words across them in Times New Roman. 'I particularly like the fact that the balloon was carrying a dog.'

'He was the charity's mascot, name of Hamish. He did, alas, break a leg in the crash and may have to be put down.'

'It's that kind of detail that sells newspapers,' says John.

'I've already sent a photo of Hamish to the picture desk. Cute little thing, taken just before they took off. Might not be quite so cute now, of course. However, I'll make it my life's mission to follow every moment of Hamish's progress.' I have an image of Doris Glimpton lingering for months at death's door, and wonder if we can pull the same kind of stunt for Hamish.

But John isn't looking very happy, and a touch of colour has crept up his neck. 'Actually, Maria, that's not what I want to talk to you about.'

'Oh. Then what do you want to talk to me about?'

John puffs out his cheeks. 'It's just that there have been some complaints about you.'

'Complaints? Look, if it's anything to do with that old bat, Mrs Macgregor …'

'It's not about her.'

I spread my hands in exasperation and, not to be outdone, also puff out my cheeks so that, for a few moments, we look like a couple of tropical fish.

'Members of staff have complained about you.'

'What? Who?'

'About your behaviour.'

'What? Behaviour? Who?'

'To be more precise, people have raised concerns.'

'Concerns? Who? What?'

'The thing is, Maria, I think it would be best if you took a few days off.'

'What?'

I hadn't been expecting this, what with doing the other Maria's job for her, and having to interview very old people and cat lunatics.

267

'Listen, you're a good reporter and, with a bit of diligence and application, you could be a very good reporter. I do actually mean that. But I think it would be better if you took some time away from your job here. Time to reflect, to get a good rest.'

'What?'

He's looking even more uncomfortable, and has picked up a pen, looked at it, and put it down again. 'It's just that people have been voicing some small concerns about you. Eating other people's food, listening outside the ladies' toilets … things like that.' John holds up a hand in mock surrender. 'It's all probably nothing, I agree, and this isn't any kind of formal warning or anything like that. I'm taking into consideration that you have already proved yourself a valuable member of staff, and that you're very good at your job. My advice is to go and see your GP.'

'I don't listen at toilet doors.'

He sighs. 'You accused the features editor of not washing her hands.'

'But she didn't wash her hands. I merely pointed out her omission.'

'To the entire features desk,' says John, whose whole face is now a rather jolly shade of red. 'And why do you wear sunglasses all the time?'

'Not all the time,' I point to my face, which is currently devoid of sunglasses. There again, the sky is blue, and a storm front isn't expected for at least another day. 'Well, OK, maybe I haven't been sleeping very well,' I concede. When *was* the last time I had a proper night's sleep, despite having a large number of bedrooms to choose from?

The interior decorator has also scented each bedroom to fit in with its theme, so that the Inca room smells of rainforest, although toilet cleaner springs to mind, the African room smells of open savannah, and the Asian room of incense. And that's not to mention the Russian room, with icons on the wall – real icons? – and gritty pictures of Soviet workers with their faces uplifted to a socialist dawn, and the American Dream room, with a large picture of a can of soup behind the bed.

I haven't yet been into the Norwegian, Roman or Classical Greek rooms, worried that I might find someone from Hackney or Olympus hiding inside. I really must have a better look around. Maybe I have an indoor tennis court or, God forbid, a cinema room. The only room that doesn't smell of anything is the kitchen, which should smell of coffee, but doesn't, because I don't have a post-doctoral qualification in mechanical engineering and have no idea what's happened to the kettle.

'In which case, I demand to see the union rep.'

'This isn't a disciplinary matter.'

'That's what it fucking sounds like to me!'

John holds up both hands in a gesture of surrender. 'Go and see your GP, Maria, and then let me know what you both decide. As far as anybody else needs know, you're taking time off to look after a sick relative. Do you perchance have a sick relative?'

'My father.'

'I thought your father was dead?'

'He soon will be,' I say.

Although my chat with John came as a complete surprise, I do admit that I may have been behaving a bit oddly. My new flat is the biggest and most extravagant example, with all its exotic trimmings. I've never even wanted to visit a sauna, let alone own one. I suppose also that the weather problem has been getting a bit worse, although I didn't think that anyone had noticed. The stealing food accusation I entirely refute because the other Maria shouldn't eat so much of it, and I'm doing her a favour by eating it for her, for which she should be grateful. And as for the features editor's catty complaint – well, she could then have touched a doorknob, which someone else might touch, who then shakes hands with a number of people, and pretty soon we've all got something nasty.

But come to think of it, this small and insignificant obsession with toilet hygiene is also quite new. Our old flat didn't much bother me, and that was a genuine health hazard.

The other Maria sees me approach and quickly hides things in her desk drawer, which normally only contains a pen and a copy of the newspaper's house rules on grammar and syntax, and which isn't very long. Not that I often look in her drawer but am occasionally overcome with curiosity. Is this another unspoken charge against me? Is this normal behaviour?

'I'm going home,' I tell her. She looks at her watch, which isn't a Rolex, although she's probably always assumed that my Rolex must be a fake. I make a show of looking at mine, which is real, and know that, having seen my old/new flat, the other Maria isn't so sure about my watch, or about anything. 'I have to look after my father.'

'The one who isn't completely dead?'

'That's the one,' I say and head for the office car park. I nose my 2CV into the traffic around the parliament building and suddenly feel very small.

Partly it's because there are about a hundred billion galaxies in the universe, with each of those galaxies having between ten million and a trillion stars. That's an awful lot of stars and planetary bodies. The universe is also over ninety billion light years in diameter, and that should make all of us feel small. Partly, also, it's that most of the universe is missing – well, you know that by now – and I feel that most of me has also gone missing.

My hands are shaking on the steering wheel, and I nearly knock down a cyclist – which is really *his* fault because he shouldn't be cycling on a road in daylight – and I have to pull over and stop the car because my head is hurting, and I can't think straight.

But it's also because I don't want to be alone and, now

that John and everyone else think I'm odd, I feel even more alone, despite owning a plunge pool and what might be a Warhol in one of my bedrooms.

I take no comfort from the fact that our own little world probably exists in a miasma of dimensions and that, across time and space, all of human existence may have been played out many times. Gramps, while not following the more absurd fringes of physics, even wrote down the precise equation that would mean that there is another Emma Maria Rossini in another part of the universe. I still have that equation somewhere, because I've kept all the equations he's ever written down for me.

Every year on my birthday, he sends me a card with a complex equation written inside, with each equation equalling my new age, even for my first birthday, when it was unlikely I would understand what actually meant.

The other Maria – my body double, not the fat one – is ten to the power of ten to the power of twenty-eight metres away. I thought it nice when Gramps wrote it down, because it meant that I had a sister somewhere in the cosmos and that, maybe, we could one day become pen pals, until Gramps explained that the distance between us was one followed by ten billion billion billion zeroes.

Then I realised that we couldn't be pen friends, and that maybe she didn't exist, and that I was only a tiny bit of nothingness, and that's how I'm feeling now when I eventually park my car, buy painkillers at the corner shop, then eat the bar of chocolate I found in the other Maria's drawer – who shouldn't be eating chocolate – and then cry over the kitchen table.

That night I dream about Mum, which I often do. We're on a film set and there are cameras on trolleys, and big lights, and microphones on sound booms, although there don't seem to be any people. We're on what appears to be an American street; there are yellow cabs parked at the curb, and there's a diner across the road. Discarded scripts are lying on the ground, pages flapping in the light breeze, and I pick one up and look at its cover. It's a film that Dad starred in.

I not only dream about her, I often see her. I can be walking down a street and through a crowd of shoppers recognise her hair or a fleeting glimpse of her face in profile and, instinctively, I quicken my step, barging into other shoppers, apologising, then realise my stupidity.

It happened when I last visited North Berwick and nearly became one of the many casualties of the town's narrow pavements. I thought I'd seen her through the glass front of a shop, counting change onto the shop's counter. I was crossing the road, and was momentarily distracted, and hesitated. The car was moving slowly, blared its horn, and stopped. I was saved.

Or I hear her voice in a busy room and turn to search for her. Once, at a party, I smelled her perfume and came close to tears. I still feel that she's close by, almost within touching distance, her hand not quite on my shoulder, her lips about to kiss the top of my head, not quite, and just out of sight. It's as if she's in another room, close by, her cremated particles reaching out, decaying on the breeze, becoming smaller, and smaller, and smaller.

Just the other day I went to the loo to splash water on my face and, fleetingly, had one of my *moments*. It sometimes happens; that I have no sense of self, I can look in mirrors and not recognise the face looking back. Only for a moment, and then it passes; a few quick blinks to clear my head, and normal service resumed. The face is again mine. But in that moment I am removed from myself, able to see myself as others must: big brown cow's eyes – Hackney Dave was right – Roman nose – long! – straight black hair – *God, it needs cutting*! – and a slightly startled look to my expression, as if spooked by a loud noise. A face with character rather than Mum's Hollywood good looks, with just a hint of doubt around the eyes, the beginnings of a puzzled frown. A face like any other, belonging to a someone you could pass by any day on a busy street, and not notice. An anybody's face. I welcome those moments of self-loss and rediscovery, the mirror turning back a stranger's face, a reminder of impermanence, my mother's death.

And then we see Sandra Bullock. She's standing beside one of the big cameras and is reading a script. Her lips are moving, she's memorising the words. She's wearing jeans, a T-shirt and a red lifejacket. We walk towards her, and she doesn't look up until we're quite close. She seems to recognise Mum and her smile of greeting freezes over a little. Sandra is looking a little wary, especially as Mum isn't smiling and we've increased our pace. Mum seems to be turning into a tiger, all taut sinew and muscle, and Sandra knows that she's the tethered goat, and is now looking around her for help.

'Emma!' says Mum, her voice slurred and imploring, 'there's something I have to tell you …'

… but the phone is ringing, and I open my eyes to darkness, and look at the clock beside my bed, and it's the middle of the night, and I immediately know who must be calling.

273

$$\frac{38GM}{r_{\vee}c^2} = 19$$

Schwarzschild radius

Of course, you know my father. Everybody knows my father, or thinks they do, plucked from celluloid and spread across cinema and TV. But it's all fluff, including the Oscar he didn't win; you shouldn't envy me, the rich daughter of an idol, because it wasn't like that.

When he died, there was only me there, standing at the window in the Edinburgh hospice, counting out the breaths. No paparazzi, no red carpets, no Hollywood starlets looking for seduction.

So many faces, so many people, but now in the room where he was dying, there was no fanfare, no curtain call, no applause, nothing to mark the moment. It was as if, in that room, we were in a theatre without an audience, my father and I, with things going on outside, but with nothing happening inside. That nothingness seemed odd, even inappropriate.

But what had I expected? It wasn't a situation I had been prepared for – no rehearsal time. On the other side of the closed door, a trolley was making its way along the corridor. I heard soft footfalls squeaking on the lino floor. It was mid-morning and teacups were rattling on the trolley. I licked my lips, suddenly thirsty, then felt guilty. I'd never been in this situation before, I didn't know if there was an etiquette to observe, or if it didn't matter. Nobody had thought to tell me of the niceties, or if there were any.

I had been shown to Dad's room by a tired-looking young nurse, who must have known who my father was, and what he had become. It was the same nurse who had phoned me earlier, so she explained. I'd been sleeping badly, worried for Sandra Bullock and about what Mum was going to tell me and hadn't wanted to be woken. My first waking thought was to feel irritated by the phone call, then guilty about feeling irritated. Then I'd dressed in yesterday's clothes. I'd arrived at the hospice as dawn cracked the sky.

The rise and fall of my father's chest under the thin cotton sheet had become ragged and uneven. Dad seemed to be frowning but, there again, he often seemed to be frowning. It was sometimes impossible to know if my father was happy or sad. His furrowed eyebrows could signal anything. His hair, such as it was, was neatly combed, and he was lying on his back. Someone had thoughtfully shaved him. His arms lay outside the cotton sheet, straight down by his side.

Dad seemed to be looking intently at the ceiling, as if offended by its gaudy mauve colour. But his eyes were closed and had been for some time. Sometimes a finger or thumb would move. His pyjamas were neatly buttoned to his chin, which also seemed incongruous. Dad never wore pyjamas, or so he said, although what Dad said and what was true were sometimes different things.

There was a last moment of life, my father's moving chest signifying that he was still here, then there was that other moment, the moment when his chest seemed to pause, finding it harder to suck down air, then gradually gave up. It wasn't much of a moment and, watching intently, I wasn't sure if it had really happened. I didn't know if I should hold Dad's hand or say something in his ear. But he'd never been one for sentimentality or family hugs, so I did neither, feeling guilty about *that* as well, wondering what it was I should do. All knew was that I didn't want to touch my father and, as we'd never kissed or hugged, I didn't think it right to start now. So why was I there? To share a private and irrevocable moment? And if so, then for which one of us?

Dad was still frowning, his eyes closed. His sparse grey

hair was still neatly parted. But his fingers and thumbs had become still, and the cotton sheet was no longer rising and falling. I now realised that the absence of movement signified that he had gone somewhere else. Or gone nowhere. Dad, like his father, wasn't a religious man. I was free, I now realised.

I crossed to the window and drew back the curtains. They were happy curtains, much like the room, in pastel shades of lilac, pink and mauve, with framed prints of green hills and blue seas on the walls that seemed to have been chosen solely for their cheerfulness. The room seemed designed for optimism but would only have depressed him. It was a room of clichés, and Dad hated clichés.

I phone Patsy from the telephone on Dad's bedside table. She answers on the second ring, sounding breathless. I look at my watch and find that it's still morning.

'Pats, it's me.'

She doesn't say anything, knowing what must have happened.

'Actually, it was all rather peaceful.'

I'd pulled on a cord above my father's bed and, moments later, a nurse had knocked and entered. She'd offered me a wan smile, felt for my father's pulse, and shaken her head. Dad could now officially be considered in the past tense.

'Maria, I'm sorry.'

'Don't be. Happens to the best of us.' I see the curtains move against a small breeze. I must have opened the window, but can't remember having done so. 'There wasn't any pain or anything.' I try to echo the room's good humour, trying to sound like the room would sound if it could talk. I'm standing by a watercolour print and it's hanging slightly squint, and I straighten it, then stand back to admire my handiwork.

The print is of a green hillside dotted with sheep. Looking more closely, I see that they are actually cows.

Dad would have laughed at the picture's poor brushstrokes. I can imagine the kind of things he would have said and his dismissive, booming laugh.

But I keep looking at the picture. My father is still in his bed, and I don't want to look at him.

'Do you want me to pick you up?'

I think about it for a few moments, hearing birdsong. 'No, but thanks. I suppose there are things I've got to do now.' I have no precise idea what these *things* are, or in what order they might have to be done, but I know that significant events require formalities. I suppose that the hospice will know about everything. 'Anyway, you've got better things to do,' I tell her.

I can hear Patsy clear her throat, a small rasping sound. In the background is a ringing telephone. She'll be at work. 'You are all right, aren't you?' she asks eventually.

'Everything's OK, really it is.'

'Then I'll drop by later.'

'Sure, thanks.'

'Is there anything you need? Anything I can bring?'

'I'm not an invalid, Patsy.'

'I'm just trying to be helpful.'

'I'm sorry,' I say. 'No, I don't need anything.'

All I really want is to be by myself, to gather my thoughts, but I don't know how to tell her this. I don't want the burden of other people's condolence, not just yet. I also feel a little numb, and don't want to speak. I had known it was coming, known for days, as my father had known. I'd wondered what the moment would be like, or whether it would be the same as other moments. Not knowing what to expect, I had expected to feel something, but it hadn't been like that and now, with nothing to mark the moment, I couldn't feel its sharp impact. In the blink of an eye, the moment had passed. I felt neither happy nor sad. The questions I could have asked him would now go unanswered. I could now forget his presences and absences: he was now permanently absent.

I resume my place by the window. My hands are in my pockets, and I'm standing like Dad would stand in the living room of our North Berwick home, quietly and still, his legs solid on the carpeted floor. I never knew what Dad was thinking when he stood there, hands in pockets, staring towards the small copse of trees on the hillside beyond the fields behind our home. I suspect, Mum. She often went walking on that hillside.

'I'm very sorry.'

A nurse has quietly entered, startling me, then leads me down a corridor full of bustling activity to a small quiet room at the other side of the building. It looks out onto a small courtyard, with lines of parked cars. Amongst them is my Citröen, looking jaunty and cheerful, just like Dad's room. Maybe I should offer to give lifts to the hospice's other residents. 2CVs always make people smile, usually in a nice way.

There is a plastic tray on a low wooden table on which has been placed a pot of tea, milk, sugar and digestive biscuits. Beside the tray is a bowl of wilting flowers. Mum, in her presidential heyday, might have known what they were. I don't. Arranged around the table are two small sofas, with plump cushions, and a high-backed chair. On the walls are vibrant prints of flamenco dancers. The nurse motions me to a sofa and indicates the tea.

'I'm sorry for your loss,' she says.

I nod, unsure how to reply.

'Is there anything I can get you?' she asks.

I shake my head, then run a hand through my hair, and my tongue around my mouth. I want to brush my teeth. The tea is hot and strong, the first thing I have tasted since last night, and even then it was only painkillers. I look again at my watch. It's still morning, if only just. A few minutes later I am joined by a young man with floppy brown hair. He is dressed in a blue suit and wearing a red tie. He sits on the high-backed chair opposite mine. He is carrying a clipboard and holds out a hand and shakes mine. 'On behalf of everyone here, let me extend our sympathies.' Although he must have said this many times before, he seems to mean it.

'Thank you for looking after him,' I reply, remembering his shaven face and Paisley-pattern pyjamas, neatly buttoned to his chin. Apart from Mum, he probably only wore bimbos with big boobs in bed, although I don't suppose they really count.

'It was our pleasure,' he says, which sounds odd to me. 'I was one of your father's doctors.'

I clear my throat but can't think of anything to say. I've been staring at my cup and saucer for some time. In the circumstances, I think, there will be a well-thumbed checklist to follow, from recommended funeral directors to obituary notices in the newspapers. I think about this: I don't even know what newspapers Dad read, or if he read anything beyond *The Stage* or the theatre reviews. I can't remember him ever reading a newspaper properly, starting at the front, making his way through news, features, business to sport. He only ever started and finished in the middle, where the culture pages were. Great or tragic events could be unfolding in the world but Dad could be blissfully unaware of them.

'He was a very nice man, your father,' he says. I have the oddest sense that I recognise that voice.

But *nice* wasn't an adjective Dad would have applied to himself. He was a strong man with large hands who latterly liked to paint. 'I'm sure he appreciated everything that was done for him,' I reply, not looking at the young doctor.

There is a short silence, through which I can hear footsteps in the corridor and the distant whine of a vacuum cleaner. 'Our task here is to offer our residents a place of solace. I think your father appreciated that.'

'As you say, a nice man.'

There, now I've said it as well. Well, maybe he had been a nice man. I frown, because *I* don't think of him as a 'nice'

279

man, but does that make him a bad man? But now he's dead, my view of him is already melding into something more nuanced. No, he hadn't been a bad man, I have to concede, and this charitable thought surprises me. He'd just been a bad father and a bad husband. In the end, he once told me, all roads lead back to the first person singular, and throughout his life he'd never been anywhere except the first person singular.

He is holding his clipboard in both hands. 'There are, I'm afraid, certain practicalities to go through, although we don't have to discuss them immediately. I'll fully understand if you'd prefer some time to yourself.'

'No, now is fine,' I say.

He is smiling, sunlight in his hair, which is why his face is out of focus. Now he leans over the table and appears to be examining my face in detail, which seems a little personal, unless a seagull has done a poo on my head on the way in and I haven't noticed. 'You really don't remember me, do you?' he finally asks.

Distracted by my father, I have barely noticed him. Now, looking more closely and peeling back years, I see a much younger person, who could have been a monster, but probably wasn't.

'Oz! My God!' I say, immediately remembering jumbled-up feelings and a time best forgotten. He's smiling, and his smile hasn't changed. A dimple has appeared on one cheek, just as I remember. 'You could have said something sooner,' I chide him.

'I wanted to see if you remembered me.'

'It's been years and years,' I remind him, then relent. 'Of course, I remember you.'

'Then please don't tell me that I haven't changed,' he says.

Before I can reply, the nurse who escorted me here knocks and enters. She is carrying a red plastic box which she lays on the table beside the cups and saucers and wilting flowers.

Inside the box are my father's possessions, the things that he chose to bring with him. On the top is a framed photograph.

My father is wearing a tuxedo and is smiling. My mother is holding tight to my hand. She is wearing a black Dior dress and is looking nervous. Over the years, I can feel the pressure of her trembling fingers. We are on a red carpet and in the background are smiling faces roped off from the red carpet. Beside my father is William Hurt, and Judi Dench is just out of camera shot. Without consciously meaning to, I have taken the picture from the box and am holding it in both hands. We'd stayed the night before in a fancy hotel on Park Lane and eaten in a restaurant where I'd tasted champagne for the first time. During the film, I kept expecting baddies with guns to rush in, but none did.

My father played a businessman who was also a CIA agent, but the film was mostly about the romantic choices we make, and the mistakes that can follow us across years. In the film, I could barely recognise him. He spoke with an Irish accent and walked with a limp. In real life, my father didn't limp. At the end of the film, everyone stood and applauded. Although it was an incredibly dull film, I realised that my father was now somebody, and had also made it through the entire film without being shot.

'It made him famous,' I say, 'at least for a while.'

Underneath the framed picture is a large book. I frown, knowing what the book is. Dad, as useless with numbers as I am, wouldn't have understood it. Nor did he much like my grandfather, as I too grew apart from Dad. On the book's cover, in silver on brown leather, is Granddad's name, Alberto Rossini.

'A really great man,' says Oz softly.

I nod. 'For an actor.'

'I didn't mean your father,' says Oz, looking flustered, and indicates my grandfather's theorem. I pick it up, surprised as always by its weight, and flick through pages.

I am surprised that Oz has even heard of him and tell him

this. Not many people have heard of the Rossini Theorem, and even fewer understand it. He might have written a great theory, but nobody is yet sure if his theorem is a work of genius or complete gibberish.

'I never had the slightest intention of reading it,' he says, 'but then I saw his name in the newspapers and thought that I'd better read it just in case I ever saw you again.'

The dimple has reappeared. I realise that the gawkish boy that I had once known is now quite handsome, in a nearly rugged sort of way. But he also now looks a little bookish and doesn't seem like someone who would still enjoy kicking shit out of other rugby players. He also seems to be frowning through his smile. 'His great triumph was to explain life, the universe and everything. Not even the Bible manages that, Emma.' I've never met anyone wax so complimentary about my grandfather except, of course, my grandmother.

'Actually, it's now Maria.' I shrug. 'I got bored with Emma and adopted my middle name. It's a long story.'

'Then it's good to meet you again, Maria.'

I realise that Oz has extracted a piece of paper from his clipboard and has laid it down beside the picture of my father. My father is still grinning. My mother is still gripping onto my hand. I am just about to be utterly bored by one of the worst films I have ever seen. It's my father's death certificate.

Oz comes down to reception and helps me load Dad's stuff into the back of my car. He is carrying the red plastic box in both hands. There are glass doors leading into the car park that swish open as we reach them. Only a few weeks ago, my father arrived through them, pushed by the obliging bimbo, grey and unrecognised. The receptionist, noticing the plastic box, smiles uncertainly at me.

'Didn't we have a teacher at North Berwick with one of those?' he asks, walking round my car.

'The very same car, Oz. I bought it from her.'

He laughs, but a kindly laugh, and the 2CV doesn't take offence, which it almost never does, being utilitarian and not given to self-importance. 'You will be all right, won't you?' he asks, one eyebrow raised. He's taller than I am now, and I don't remember him being as tall. 'You look a little shaky.'

I do feel shaky – and very tired, because I hardly slept last night, or the night before – and look upwards at the sky, although I've already checked the weather forecast on my iPhone and everything is going to be OK.

'You might get a few journalists poking their noses in,' I tell him and feel the start of a headache, a nagging pain behind one eye. 'But there's no need for the hospice to get involved,' I add quickly. 'Dad's people will sort everything out.'

In his world, dead people don't have people. He doesn't reply.

The plastic box with my father's few possessions feels insubstantial as I load it into the 2CV's boot, then have to slam the boot door several times before it closes, and which probably wakes even the most comatose of the hospice's residents. A photograph, a book, a watch, his wallet, some clothes. Things I would have expected, except for the book. My father didn't read books and wasn't scientific.

'Very few people at the hospice knew who he was,' says Oz. 'Your father was admitted under his real name. He didn't want a fuss, or so he said.' I can't decide whether the father I grew up with would have been saddened or amused by this.

'I also wondered if I'd ever see you again. You didn't visit him very often.'

'We kind of fell out.' Oz raises an eyebrow but doesn't say anything. 'You should have contacted me.'

'I was going to, but I only started here a month ago. I'm not a real doctor, by the way. Still training, all that shit. Right now, I'm attached to the GP practice that provides medical cover for this place.'

'You mean Dad could still be alive if he'd had a real

doctor?'

'You were always a bit mad, Emma.'

On impulse, I kiss him on the cheek, feeling years slip away, and the time he kissed me, and my compass rose was smashed. He was smaller then, and I have to stand on tiptoe to kiss him.

'Then why don't we have lunch on Sunday?' I suggest and feel suddenly nervous, my chest constricting. 'Patsy and her boyfriend are cooking. Remember her? Actually, *she's* cooking. Carlo just eats. She'd also like to see you again,' I finish lamely. I don't want him to think that I'm inviting him out. I don't want to give him a reason to say 'no'.

'I'd like that,' he says.

I place the plastic box on the kitchen table, realise that I still haven't bought coffee, and instead drink milk and feel other palpitations: my mother's hand on my shoulder, my father's absences, and Granny Mary sitting on the balcony, her sewing perched across her knee, her kindly eyes over half-moon spectacles.

I check for emails and, inevitably, there are several from Sarah Parker. I'd texted her from the hospice because, even after death, she is still Dad's portal to the outside world. I haven't seen her, or spoken to her, since their abortive golf game. She's sent a draft form of words for the press release we've been working on and suggested dates for a remembrance service. My father's death certificate is still in my pocket.

On the phone, she sounds tired and hesitant. 'I'm really sorry, Emma.' I don't bother reminding her that I changed my name years ago. She's always known me as Emma, her laughter filling our house and my mother's narrowed eyes following her every move. 'Such a wonderful, wonderful man,' she says, almost reverentially. 'Such a huge talent. Such a waste,' she whispers, then becomes business-like. 'I'll see you tomorrow, Emma. The Balmoral. Nine o'clock.'

It's probably how she spoke to Dad, firm and authoritative, leaving no room for manoeuvre or evasion.

'Of course, Sarah. Nine o'clock.'

Then I phone Granny and Gramps in Italy. They'd been over a couple of weeks before, and had sat by Dad's bed for several days, but he was never awake or responsive, and nobody knew if he would stay like that for a week or several months. Granny found it too upsetting, and they went back to Como.

After that I phone Fran and then realise that I have no one else to phone. Telling the world of my father's death, one of the most famous and recognizable people in the world, has only taken three phone calls.

The one person who I feel I should tell in person is Mrs Perkins, who is nearly family, and has devoted years to the Ross/Rossini household without once, as far as we know, blabbing anything to the *Daily Mail*. I still have all the magic buttons in the car, and the driveway gates swing open, and Mrs Perkins is on the doorstep before I come to a stop outside the house.

As always, she's wiping her hands on a dishcloth and the hallway, as always, smells of cleaning fluid, although I'm too late with the news of Dad's death. A bunch of flowers is already lying on the kitchen table, delivered in the last few minutes by a 'sturdy bloke in a colourful van and a moustache,' according to Mrs Perkins. He'd congratulated her on the birth of a daughter, which seemed a little optimistic, and then consulted his list, apologised, and driven off. I look at the flowers, delivered from *Tulipa* – an exceptionally good flower shop in North Berwick, despite its delivery driver. The flowers are from Sarah Parker who, as always, thinks of everything.

We sit at the kitchen table and drink tea, and Mrs Perkins has a dignified cry before fetching her husband in from the garden, and the three of us sit rather awkwardly, with Mrs

Perkins saying what a gentleman Dad was and how losing a close someone is always a shock, even though you know it's coming.

Mr Perkins doesn't say much because, over the years, he's delegated all talking to his wife. But he pats my shoulder and makes appropriate noises, although not actual words, like a gruff but friendly forest animal. Both of them visited Dad in the hospice, even bringing him flowers from the garden.

It feels funny being in the house again because it now feels eerily empty and unfamiliar. An energy has left it, and I try hard to remember the good times, walking slowly from room to room. I stand for a long while in my old bedroom looking out at the sea, mesmerised as always by the golden expanse of beach and the tensile colours of the water.

Eventually I end up outside Dad's old study, remembering Mum's ear pressed against the door. Inside, his desk is still where it was, although the Persian rugs have been removed. The bare wooden floor is now covered in paint blobs. An easel is propped up by the window with a half-finished painting of the view outside: green grass, then beach, then sea.

He'd painted in the sky and sea, the one becoming the other, and started on the beach and dunes. The bottom of the canvas is blank, and the composition feels forced, the brushstrokes indecisive. This half-finished canvas seems mute and dispirited, unlike the bright paintings that he'd exhibited a couple of times in Bond Street – Doris Glimpton did buy one – with all proceeds generously donated to charity. I'd been dismissive at the time, sensing Sarah's PR fingers all over the gesture, but now I'm not so sure. In his decline, Dad did seem to become a nicer person. I've now admitted that for the second time in one day.

In the corner of the room are a stack of canvases leaning against the wall and I pick one up and look at it, and then pick up another, and another and find that he has painted Mum over and over again.

In one painting, she's on a city street wearing a short blue dress. She's striking a pose, with one leg bent upwards and the tip of one finger on her chin. In another, she's walking away across an open meadow, with flowers around her feet, but looking over her shoulder. A white scarf is billowing behind her and she seems to be walking into a sunset.

In another, she's leaning against a wall, looking thoughtful, her eyes fixed on a distant point. Other paintings are just portraits; Mum sitting at a table – or standing at a window – or standing in front of our front door.

In another, Mum is wearing the black Dior dress that I have in my wardrobe in Edinburgh. She's standing on a red carpet and is holding the hand of a small girl next to her. I look carefully at the small girl, who has my eyes, and my hair, but don't recognise myself. Is it that Dad couldn't quite remember what I looked like? I can't answer that, although there's no mistaking Mum. He's even captured her hesitant smile and the way she's standing slightly awkwardly, teetering uncertainly on her high heels, willing herself not to fall over in front of the world's press.

But the picture is incomplete. Not only is Judi Dench's shoulder missing, but so too is Dad. He'd been standing next to us. But it's just Mum and me on the red carpet. It's as if he'd wanted to paint the picture as an onlooker, as one of the paparazzi on the other side of the roped-off red carpet, as an ordinary person marvelling at the exquisite beauty of the film star's wife.

I sit at Dad's desk for a long while, the picture on my lap, and then I take the picture back to Edinburgh with me, and hang it in the hallway where I can see it every day.

Patsy arrives later with a Chinese carry-out.

'Maria, I'm really sorry.'

'Don't be. I'm not sure I am.'

She doesn't know how to reply to this, shifting large plastic carrier bags from one hand to another, before plonking them down on the kitchen table. 'Thought you might want something to eat.'

'Expecting an army?' I ask.

'Didn't quite know what to get,' she explains, 'so I got most things.' Then she finally takes in the marble and chrome and discreet lighting, not to mention the pizza oven and coffee machine. 'For God's sake, Maria! What the hell have you done?'

I've forgotten that Patsy hasn't been to the flat since the builders and decorators left. She's been on holiday, then away on business, then on a corporate training course, then on another holiday. Her hair looks shorter, more stylish, more business-like. Between her freckles, she also looks tanned. Meanwhile, I've interviewed Britain's oldest person and been nowhere.

'I've merely made a few improvements.'

'Jesus! Improvements? Can I have a look round?' Patsy marches off and is gone for some time when I hear a scream from a distant part of the flat. I find her outside the Classical Greek room with a hand to her mouth. 'There's a Dalek in there,' she says.

I open the door and, sure enough, there is a Dalek inside, with its ray gun pointed in our direction. It's about my height and very scary and I can understand why it's given Patsy a fright. She seems to be hyperventilating, and still has a hand over her mouth. The room is dominated by a four-poster bed, with the posters shaped like Greek pillars.

Unlike much of the flat, which is lushly carpeted, the floor seems to be marble, and there are two classical figures framed under lighting by the corners by the bed. One is a naked woman holding out a small posy of flowers, maybe offering them to the other; male, also naked, and wearing a helmet with small wings. I look more closely, but he doesn't seem to be from Hackney.

There's a sheet of paper stuck to the Dalek, in my interior designer's flowery handwriting.

The name Dalek is actually a Slovakian boy's name, and Slovakia is quite near Greece, so I thought it would be appropriate for the Classical Greek bedroom. The name means 'to fight afar' which is quite a good meaning for a Dalek. Strangely, in numerology, 'people with this name have a deep inner desire for a stable, loving family or community, and a need to work with others and to be appreciated.'

So there you are: Daleks are actually friendly and, to be honest, I've always wanted to buy one for a client, but have never had a client who might appreciate one, until I met you!

I give the Dalek a little push and it moves backwards on little rubber wheels and bumps into the Greek god. The Dalek's sucker arm fits neatly over the god's genitalia, so that it looks like he's being given a blow-job. I quickly wheel the Dalek away, because at least one of them would probably find the experience undignified.

Patsy heads off back to the kitchen, having completed her tour of inspection. I follow her, pushing the Dalek in front of me. If it scared Patsy, I think, then it really should live in the front hall to scare off any burglar who has made it through my new steel-reinforced front door.

I hand Patsy a large glass of white wine.

'You are completely mad,' she says. 'All of this must have cost a fortune! And why, for God's sake, is your old bedroom now a sauna?'

'It's in case my Norwegian friends come to stay.'

'Do you actually have any Norwegian friends?'

'Not yet. But you must admit that the roof garden is quite cool.'

'I didn't go up there. I was afraid I'd find a tennis court. Incidentally, you look terrible,' she says.

'I haven't been sleeping,' I reply, trying to remember where the plates are, and which drawer holds the cutlery, and whether I have plates or cutlery. Eventually, I spread out food on the table.

'You're also shaking like a leaf.'

'Like I say, I've not been sleeping.'

Patsy helps herself to another glass of wine. 'Anyway, Carlo sends his sympathy,' she says, and spears a prawn ball.

'Thanks,' I tell her, 'But definitely not sympathy.'

Patsy chews and swallows. 'He wasn't a bad bloke, your dad.' She isn't really looking at me as she says this, having seen the Dalek's menacing shadow in the hallway.

I think back to earlier. 'At the hospice, they told me he was a *nice* man.' I can't help but make the word seem petty. 'How the hell would they know?'

Patsy says nothing for a few moments, her mouth full of food. 'Well, maybe they were right. Have you ever considered that?' She is scrutinising my face. 'Put it this way, he wasn't exactly ordinary, was he?'

'And what's that supposed to mean?' I ask. I can't help it; my voice has risen.

'Christ, Maria! What do you think I mean? Look, you might not have got on with him, but you can't deny what he was.'

I take a deep breath. 'I'm neither denying what he was or *who* he was.' According to one headline I remember, my father used to be the housewife's favourite, whoever *she* was. It was an epithet my mother would have snorted at, and probably did. 'Anyway, he wasn't your father,' I say, lamely.

'But he was yours,' Patsy reminds me.

'So?'

'So, he's dead, Maria. Christ, you've been pretending he was dead for years! Because of him, you changed your name! Maybe it's time to put away all the angst. Let it drop.'

I realise that I was probably sounding bitter or foolish or both. I refill our glasses. 'Let's just leave it, shall we?'

We then eat mostly in silence. More precisely, Patsy eats while I try to remember the last time I did eat, apart from the other Maria's chocolate. Intermittently, the phone rings. I don't bother answering. Patsy doesn't bother asking why.

Then we take our glasses into the living room and watch the news on my giant plasma TV. Knox is curled up on a sofa but doesn't seem to remember Patsy and ignores her. Towards the end of the programme comes a photograph of my father. He is wearing a tuxedo and his hair is slicked back. In front of him is a microphone and he is holding a statuette.

The newscaster, who had been smiling at the previous item, now looks solemn. 'The worlds of stage and film are this evening mourning the passing of Paul Ross who died earlier today. He was fifty-three and had been suffering from cancer. Paul Ross made his name in the 1980s and 1990s with a string of critically acclaimed performances, winning numerous awards, including two Oscar nominations. Fellow actors today paid tribute to a man regarded as one of the supreme talents of his generation ...'

I switch off the TV and take my glass to the window. It looks out onto a street that falls away to docklands and the North Sea, the same water in which I would paddle, my mother looking on indulgently.

'He never did win that Oscar,' I say to the glass, watching my words form and dissolve in steam. If my father regretted anything, it was being only a nominee. My hands have begun to tremble again, and I can feel miniscule particles on my skin. Until his death, there had always been someone else to blame. Now, I realise, I can only blame myself.

'Or get to play James Bond,' Patsy reminds me.

'Pierce Brosnan once wrote to Dad,' I say, remembering him in his glory years, when producers and directors were falling over themselves to secure Dad's signature on film contracts. 'He said that he hoped Dad would get the part after him. Dad tore the letter up.' He was superstitious that way. Well, actors often are. He saw the letter as a bad omen, as well he might; by the time Daniel Craig took over, even Dad admitted that he was too old and, as far as I know, never forgave Pierce Brosnan.

In the hospice that morning, my father had been grey and gaunt, exuding nothing. On the TV screen on the news, he had been a different person, fizzing energy. The same person, but different people; one instantly recognisable, the other less so. 'I also bumped into Oz Clarke today,' I now say, turning away from the window. 'Remember him?'

She's grinning. 'The wee boy, if I remember, who was the love of your little life.' She has both hands knotted behind her head and her feet are propped on top of my new coffee table. Cedar, or oak, or elm, or something. Another Ogilvies creation, sophisticated and chic. Her glass is balanced on the arm of the sofa.

'He's training to be a GP, practising his life-giving skills on the nearly dead. I met him at the hospice this morning.'

'How was he?'

'Taller,' I reply.

Patsy eventually leaves, warily keeping well clear of the guardian Dalek. He's absolutely realistic and I wonder where the interior designer bought him, and whether most Daleks really are friendly and community-minded, and why Dr Who only seems to chance on the bad ones. The phone has stopped ringing and my hands have stopped shaking.

The nurse who had earlier escorted me down the corridor to meet Oz had explained that the lock on Dad's suitcase had broken. It wouldn't now close, she explained. I told her that it wasn't a problem. It was old, I said. Throw it away. Gucci make terrible suitcases, I joked. It was the same suitcase that he would take with him to the airport. It seemed ironic, or fitting, that his favourite suitcase should have died on the same day as him.

Even stranger, having lived his life as Paul Ross, he had chosen to enter the hospice as Paul Rossini. Shrunken and grey, he had reverted to the person he'd once been. I think about this, from my roof garden eyrie, watching the last stragglers leave the Caledonia Bar opposite. A man is laughing. He has one hand on a woman's shoulder. She's trying to light a cigarette and shrug off his unwanted attentions. She twists away from him, and I see the spark of her lighter.

Was it simply that my father didn't want anybody's pity? The once-great actor, reduced to *this*? Maybe, or maybe something had happened to change his mind about himself. It was unlikely that I'd now find out. All I do know is that he'd donned a cloak of invisibility for his last journey, taking also a book on astrophysics that he didn't understand, and which was written by a man whose name he had forsaken.

For the first time since his death, like a charge of static electricity, I feel the tug and pull of dark matter and, sitting on my roof terrace, watching the banal world below, I unexpectedly feel tears on my face.

I am awake at dawn, although I'm not sure how much sleep I've had, and my mind is fogged with tiredness and a hangover. I lie and stare at the ceiling, weak sunlight shape-shifting through partially-drawn curtains and casting moving whorls of light and shade. My mouth is dry, and the sky is grey and leaden. It has rained overnight, and the pavements are slick.

I check emails and phone messages. Mostly old school friends offering their condolences, although there's one from Fran saying how sorry she is. She's in New York, but hopes to come back for the funeral, and asks me to give her the details, which I don't have, because I've never organised a funeral before and don't know where to start. Unexpectedly, there's an email from John Salmond, who also offers sympathies and then asks if I'd like to write a piece on my father. I write back asking how long he's known, and he replies almost immediately to say that he's always known, because nobody but nobody has ever interviewed Doris Glimpton, except me. I wonder at this, then realise that nothing is impregnable, and I send an email back to him saying that I may in time write a eulogy about Dad, but not now.

Although my flat is nominally owned by an investment company based in Zurich, of which I am the sole beneficiary, and my phone number is ex-directory, nobody can be completely invisible. Unlike my father, I haven't yet learned how to hide in plain sight although, as my father's star diminished to obscurity, I had hoped that the connection between Ross and Rossini would also have grown tenuous.

I finally make it to the corner shop and buy coffee and milk and boil up water on the hob. I must remember to buy a kettle or have a better look for the old one. By the time I've drunk a second cup, the city is also waking; car doors slamming, engines revving. The sky has brightened, and a small breeze has sprung up off the Forth. I put on a coat and old trainers and pause in the hallway, wondering if I should say 'goodbye' to the Dalek, and instead say 'goodbye' to Knox who is curled up on the kitchen table. He doesn't seem much bothered by the intergalactic alien, so I leave them together, then hesitate when I get outside, looking upwards at churning clouds.

I walk to the modernist buttress of the Scottish Executive, hemmed in by disused wharfs that have become trendy bars and restaurants. A cruise liner with cream superstructure is heading out to sea. Cars are lined up at the Executive's security barriers, exhaust smoke fogging the air. I look out over the Firth. The water is lustrous and coils ashore with a rhythmic strength. Along the river is North Berwick Law, from which Mum was lifted. Then, abruptly, I turn back to the shore road and flag down a taxi.

Sarah Parker is already at The Balmoral when I arrive, pacing the plush reception area with a briefcase under one arm. I haven't seen her for years and it takes me some moments to recognise her. There are grey streaks in her hair and craggy lines on her face. The beautiful and commanding woman I remember has become someone else. But she's also immaculate in cream blouse and blue knee-length skirt.

She kisses me hesitantly on the cheek. She doesn't know how I now feel about her.

We eat breakfast in a hushed dining room, although I mostly watch her eat. Sarah fusses with her napkin and her cutlery. She has flown up from London that morning and looks tired and drawn, although probably better than I do.

'I should have come up before now,' she offers, sipping orange juice.

'It all happened suddenly,' I remind her. Two days ago, there had been nothing to immediately worry about. I also know that Sarah had been to visit him in the hospice. Oz told me. 'You don't have anything to feel guilty about.'

'But I *do*,' she says, tapping her knife against her plate for emphasis. She is eating sausage and eggs and tomatoes. On my plate is a piece of brown toast. I finish my coffee and signal to the waiter for a refill.

Sarah is looking wistful. 'I can't actually believe he's not with us,' she says and for a moment I wonder if she's going to cry. 'In his prime, Emma, he was so ... so utterly elemental. He seemed, well ... immortal.' She looks down at her plate, looking faintly surprised. 'Stupid, I know,' she adds, still looking at her plate. 'None of us are.'

'He was certainly a character,' I reply. In her mind I am melded to a past in which my father was her bread-and-butter with lots of jam on top. I too look down. I don't really know the secrets of their shared past, and I don't want to know. I thank her for sending flowers to Mrs Perkins, which she appreciated, despite not having a new-born daughter.

She puts down her knife and fork with a small clatter. 'Emma, I know you have mixed feelings about me,' she begins, then drifts into silence.

'It hardly matters now,' I reply.

'I loved him,' she says abruptly. 'Utterly and completely.' She pauses. 'It wasn't reciprocated. He only ever loved your mother. So, please, you have no reason to hate me.'

I don't know whether to believe her, although I don't

suppose she has any reason to lie. Maybe, in her way, Sarah is also a victim; the trusting agent who didn't quite get her leading man.

I shrug. 'I'm not sure that I ever hated you, Sarah.'

'That morning when you produced the golf club. You hated me then.'

'Maybe, but you *were* fucking my father.'

'Emma, it wasn't like that.' Sarah has the good grace to look a little shocked but doesn't bother to deny it.

'Frankly, I no longer care,' I tell her and, reaching into my bag, produce my reporter's notebook and lay it on the table. 'Let's just get on with it.'

Between us, we agree on a church for the funeral service, the same North Berwick church that catered for Mum. I suppose that if the church is doing anything else that day, like hosting a marriage, everyone else will be told to bugger off. Sarah is checking the availability of the High Kirk of Scotland for a memorial service. It would be the most fitting place, she tells me. The actual funeral service will be for friends and family only. The memorial service will have a cast of thousands. Already, I learn, several luminaries of stage and screen have offered to say a few words. She tells me a few names, as if to impress me. Most of them I've met.

'It's just a pity that you two didn't get on,' she says.

'Shit happens, Sarah.'

'It shouldn't have been allowed to happen,' she says more forcibly. Her eyes are glittering. Then she relents. 'Anyway, how are you getting on?' she asks. She is looking at me intently. 'Your father worried about you. He was always worrying about you.' She has the good grace to look embarrassed and runs a hand through her hair.

I swallow a piece of toast and add milk to my coffee. 'I know that Sarah,' I say.

'Try to get some rest,' she advises. 'You look tired.'

She kisses me again when we're on the pavement. The

sky is still grey, and a light drizzle is falling. Shoppers hurry by with umbrellas raised. Outside the railway station, a piper is jauntily playing *Scotland the Brave*. I now have to see my father's accountant and then his lawyer. Sarah has other arrangements to make for the funeral. Among them, security, and a PR firm to handle the media. My father is centre stage again. 'Thank you,' I tell her, because whatever my feelings, I couldn't have begun to organise his funeral.

She looks pleased then flustered. 'I still can't believe it,' she says. She is smiling, but only just. 'God, they were heady days! Your father absolutely had it all. Well, I suppose that even good things come to an end.' She sighs. 'But it shouldn't have happened like that. Not in the way that it did. It was so … *unfair*.' She almost spits out this last word.

'It was a long time ago,' I remind her, knowing what she means.

She is looking distantly at the hurrying shoppers. After a few moments, she takes a deep breath, reaches into her briefcase, and extracts a manila envelope. She hands it to me, almost thrusting it into my hand. She is once again the forceful Sarah Parker that I remember.

'He wanted me to give you this,' she tells me, heavier rain now patterning her hair. 'After his death.' My name is written on the envelope in my father's handwriting.

I walk home quickly, because eyes are everywhere: the eyes of passers-by looking upwards at the sky, other eyes, crocodile eyes, looking down. I know I should take a taxi, but they all seem to have vanished. When it rains in Edinburgh, taxis disappear. I keep to the shadows, eyes cast down and collar turned up. I get home and place my father's unopened letter on the mantelpiece.

I know that I'll have to open it sometime, and I pick it off the mantelpiece and tap it against the palm of one hand. My name on the envelope is written boldly enough; it must therefore have been written some weeks ago, before Dad's final deterioration. In the last few weeks, he could barely do anything. I look at it, telling myself to open it, then replace it on the mantelpiece.

I don't know what my father's letter will contain. An apology perhaps, or a confession, perhaps a denial, a protestation of innocence. Perhaps all of those things, because truth is complicated, bound by threads that have been stitched by other fingers. Meeting Oz again has taken me back to the person I once was and, as thunder finally grumbles across the Forth, and beams of light illuminate my flat, to a past in which I don't steal other people's chocolate, listen at toilet doors or buy replica Daleks. I then have to go and make sure that the Dalek really is a replica and hasn't moved, perhaps to trundle back to the Classical Greek room and give the Olympic god another blow-job, but it's still where I left it, with its ray gun pointed at the front door, and Knox is looking at me in an almost concerned way.

$$\frac{4(m - M)}{\alpha j_{10}(d) - 1} = 20$$

The distance modulus

By the Sunday I am barely functioning, although I haven't bothered seeing my GP, who I hardly know and, anyway, my symptoms are too vague to bother him about. I suspect he'd just give me sleeping tablets or more brain pills. I don't feel in the mood for those because I'm not really mad, or so I tell myself. But I still haven't slept properly, just dozed off from time to time – sometimes over the kitchen table, sometimes on a sofa in the living room, and once in the plunge pool, because I'd never had a sauna before and didn't know what to expect. I keep my old bedroom door firmly closed, just in case Knox mistakes the plunge pool for a luxury toilet. It was nice to be in warm water that wasn't a bath, and to close my eyes and pretend I was somewhere hot like Greece, which I haven't actually been to. The next thing I knew I'm breathing in water, then coughing and retching, remembering a family outing to Portobello when I didn't know I couldn't swim and had to be rescued by Dad. I had almost forgotten that memory and how Dad may have saved my life.

I'm also a little bit nervous because I'll be seeing Oz again and I don't want him to feel that I'm looking to start off again where we finished. I know it's a stupid thing to think. For all I know he might be with someone saner than me. It's only lunch after all and do I really want to have a relationship with anyone? We're different people now, I tell myself, as I try on several outfits, discarding each one in a growing pile on my bed.

I'm now in the Classical Greek room because it's the

only bedroom with a four-poster bed, which makes me feel special, and because the Greek god is quite hunky. But it's difficult putting on make-up, as I'm not used to putting on make-up and my hands are shaking and it's distracting having a naked man standing in the corner of the room.

Of course, I've been thinking about him; of the people we'd been, and the people we've become. In that comparison, I am distinctly second best, a not-quite-journalist who has remained rooted in Edinburgh and never set out to achieve anything because I possess the intelligence of a gnat. My ambitions have always been modest; his seem large. He gets to put 'Doctor' before his name. I don't even have a proper name.

But that's not all I've been thinking, remembering racing hormones, because despite the added years, he seems much the same: his laugh hasn't changed, the dimples on his cheek are still there. He has simply grown to be a larger and more mature version of his smaller self, he still has the self-assurance and languid poise that attracted me to him in the first place.

I look at myself in the bathroom mirror – because the naked man was becoming too distracting, and I've moved from the bedroom – examining my face from different angles. I have the same brown eyes, long nose and dark wavy hair as I had back then, the same Mediterranean skin, inherited from my grandfather. On the surface, I too am much the same, except that I've smudged my lipstick and eyeshadow and, if I venture into the hallway, I'll probably frighten the sensitive and community-spirited Dalek.

I check for emails. There is only one I need to read, from Sarah Parker, informing me of further progress on Dad's funeral. Friends, colleagues and a few adversaries whom he hadn't seen for a decade or more have all declared their utmost respect for him, and how they'll absolutely be at the funeral, including Captain Marko Alexandrovich Ramius, commander of the *Red October*, who my father loathed with a particular vengeance. Sarah seems to have everything under control. I delete the other emails.

I decide to walk, because I'm early and I think the exercise will do me good, and because the sky is blue without a hint of precipitation, and none forecast. As I walk, the accents change. In Leith, apart from the arty people, the accents are broad and working-class, but as you ascend Leith Walk and into the New Town, the accents become more modulated; this is where financiers and lawyers live, insulated by wealth and fine architecture. On the other side of Princes Street is the Old Town, a melting pot; within its close confines is youthful exuberance, and the babble of a hundred languages. Continue on, through university faculties and student hangouts, and Edinburgh opens out into wide grassland on which lovers stroll and cricketers strut and dive.

On the south side of this open space are tall tenements, delineating grass from aspiring sophistication. This area too is a village, an eclectic place where people won't stay forever. Some will make good and move to the other side of Princes Street, others will move out of the city altogether; some, less fortunate, will trade downwards to more dubious suburbs.

It's a place where people are either on the up, or on the way down. Carlo, with his newly installed girlfriend, seems on the ascendant with a couple of research papers to his name. Their second-floor flat looks out over the Meadows to one side and a cobbled street on the other, in which is parked his vintage Jaguar.

As usual, to prevent him from being useful in the kitchen, Patsy has chased him to the Fox and Goblin round the corner. Carlo does try to be domestically helpful, but generally just gets in the way. Over a couple of drinks, I beat him four-two at pool, although beating Carlo at pool, as I never cease to remind him, is like taking sweeties from a baby. It's something to do with his size. The pool cue is a matchstick in his hands, and he's never mastered how to use it. He has to crouch, almost on all-fours, to get close to the table.

Carlo also knows how things work and can strip and rebuild car engines; he likes the smell of oil. On the day of my flat-warming party, Dave had been helping Carlo with his Jaguar. Dave, I now know, is driving socialist-coloured buses in London and engaged to someone called Wendy. When I asked Carlo what kind of a house she lived in, he didn't get the joke.

More than anything, apart from Patsy, his old Jaguar, drugs and physics, Carlo loves computers. He understands them and, with rapid keystrokes, can make them bend to his whim. His latest project, he's telling me, is to build an untraceable route round the Internet by making use of a server in Lesotho.

'I have no idea where Lesotho is,' I tell him, once we're sitting at a window seat overlooking the grass. Some men in white are limbering up and throwing a small ball to one another, which suggests a cricket match is about to start, or they're shooting an advertisement for washing powder. I conjure up a map of the world from which Lesotho is entirely missing.

Carlo produces a piece of paper from an inside pocket. Across it are scribbled notes in his appalling handwriting. He lays it flat on the table where it soaks up beer slops, ink spreading in swirls. 'It used to be called Basutoland,' he reads, struggling to read his own writing. 'Then it was renamed the Kingdom of Lesotho after achieving independence from you Brits in the mid-1960s.'

Carlo was born and brought up in Britain but doesn't seem to have registered this fact. 'It's a landlocked country entirely surrounded by South Africa. Maria, you *do* know where South Africa is, don't you?' I nod and drink some white wine. I have to hold the glass in two hands, because although it's not particularly big or heavy, my hands are shaking.

'Well, thank God for that. Lesotho's main resources

are diamonds and other minerals. I've no idea what those other minerals might be. The country boasts fewer than two million souls, mostly Christian, and the capital of Lesotho is Maseru, which is served by an international airport which is called Maseru-Moshoeshoe. Not boring you, am I, girl?

Carlo also likes to occasionally call people 'man' or 'girl' to reinforce his Jamaican roots, although he's never been to Jamaica in his life. 'On the road from the capital to the airport are, I now know, a number of industrial sites. Taken together, they represent one of the commercial hotspots of the country. In one such industrial site is a newly built warehouse in which sit some high-tech computer servers.

'Fascinating, Carlo.'

He folds away his sodden piece of paper. 'The thing is, these servers are off the grid, more dark than the dark web, utterly and completely untraceable. I could set up any kind of website I wanted, and nobody would ever know it was me.'

'To further the cause of world revolution?' I suggest.

'Well, no,' he says dismissively. 'I just wanted to find out if it was possible. 'I'm a scientist now, Maria. Not a social scientist.' He's looking awkwardly at the table, and I realise that there's something else on his mind. 'You should have told me, girl.'

'After the revolution, you'd have had me shot.' It's a joke that falls flat because we both know that he's right. 'Maybe I could have been a bit more honest.'

'So, was it just that you didn't like his films?'

'Something like that, Carlo. Look, we fell out years ago. I didn't want to have anything to do with him. I didn't want to be associated with him. I didn't want people to know he was my father. OK?' I end this slightly breathless.

Carlo looks at me for a few moments, then grins. 'And here's me thinking you were just poor white trash.'

Other people in the pub are now listening. It's not often you hear that kind of racism in Edinburgh. Carlo finishes his pint and twirls the empty glass on its paper coaster.

'Look, Carlo, to make it up, I'll give you my grandfather's address. You can write to him. Discuss whatever complete bollocks you're working on. He likes getting fan mail.'

He looks pleased. 'Actually, I would like his thoughts on some stuff I'm doing.'

I scribble down his address in Italy and hand it over.

'Doesn't he have email?'

Despite solving the mysteries of creation and the secrets of the universe, Granddad is surprising inept with much of the modern world, and has difficulty changing a plug, much to Granny's frustration. 'He does, but your chances of getting a reply are remote.'

Carlo looks at the address I've written down and folds it neatly into his wallet for safekeeping. He's looking thoughtful, or as thoughtful as a Giganotosaurus can look. 'Also, I don't usually ever win when we play pool,' he says eventually. 'Today I won twice.'

'Good for you, Carlo. Perhaps, finally, you're getting the hang of it. Actually, don't forget, I won four times. That still makes me the winner.'

'Even so,' he says.

I shake my head. 'I'm just a bit nervy, that's all. But I promise I'll also introduce you to my grandfather, OK? Patsy says that you'd like to shake his hand.'

He wipes one hand across his chin, his fat grin growing wider. 'Then make mine another pint,' he suggests.

Oz arrives carrying a plastic bag. I've been hovering, looking out of the living room window, Patsy has mostly been in the kitchen, Carlo has mostly been slumped in his favourite chair reading a Sunday newspaper. I hear kisses being exchanged and Patsy squealing as Oz lifts her bodily from the floor. After being introduced to Carlo, Oz announces that the lunch is also a reunion celebration and that he's brought champagne. Oz is looking at me as he says this, I am probably grinning inanely. Carlo takes the plastic bag, extracts the champagne bottle, crosses the room, and opens the window. 'In that case,' he says, 'we'll have to see what we can aim at.' Their living-cum-dining room overlooks the broad cobbled street.

'That ridiculous old Jaguar,' I suggest.

'It's a classic automobile. No way, sister.'

'OK, then that dog.'

Down below, on the pavement, is a black Labrador. It's just sitting, minding its own business, and is maybe lost, because we can't see its owner.

'Dog it is,' agrees Carlo.

'Don't you dare!' shouts Patsy from the kitchen door. Now that she's living in a nice part of town, in a nice flat, with nice neighbours, she no longer likes to fire corks out of windows. Carlo has no such inhibitions, although the champagne cork fizzes harmlessly onto the roof of a Fiat Uno and rolls into the gutter. 'For God's sake!' mutters Patsy, then retreats to a cupboard to fetch glasses.

'Anyway, it's good to see you both again,' says Oz, now folded into an armchair that's old and grimy and leaks stuffing, and which Patsy has been wanting to throw out from the moment she moved in.

'Maria's right. You are taller,' says Patsy.

'Taller! Is that all you can say? Well, I suppose I am,' he says, accepting a glass of champagne from Patsy. 'There again, I suppose we all are.'

'Taller and wiser,' I suggest.

'Well, maybe just taller.'

Carlo and Patsy met at a political gathering. Patsy, so the story goes, thought she'd been invited to a party, although everyone – apparently – quickly got tired of being radical and revolutionary and it turned into a party anyway. In those days, Carlo was the red revolutionary, Patsy the champagne methodoise socialist, which should have been a bit insipid for his taste. The story she tells is of seeing this large black man at the other side of the room and hoping fervently that he wouldn't come over and speak to her.

The story he tells is of nearly standing on this near-midget of a woman and then feeling obliged to talk to her. They are alike only in opposites. She is diminutive, he isn't. His voice carries across continents, hers usually doesn't. She is thin and almost bends in the breeze, he is an oak, solid and unyielding. She has short red hair and a gap between her top front teeth. It makes her appear elfin-like, fragile. Mutual friends call them Beauty and the Beast, although Patsy's no great beauty, and often says so, so shouldn't mind me saying so. But she has character, great dollops of it, and is usually right about most things.

Patsy now works in Human Resources for a retail chain and is therefore also used to getting things her own way. Since she moved in, Carlo's flat has been slowly transformed; a new picture over the mantelpiece, a new colour-scheme for the hall, a new settee nestling under the window. These are small, gradual and unthreatening changes that, in themselves, don't signify much but which, taken together, suggest that Patsy sees residence with Carlo to be a permanent arrangement.

This week I note, small tester daubs of paint have appeared on a wall in the living room; this is obviously next in line for rejuvenation. I suspect that Carlo hasn't noticed the paint, and perhaps only occasionally wonders where he bought the new settee from, or whether he ordered it from Amazon by mistake.

Oz fills in the intervening years. How he was whisked off to America, then back to Bristol to study medicine, now back to Scotland, the wanderer returning home. 'I didn't much like America,' he says. 'I didn't really make any friends. The boys all played American football and the girls just wanted to be prom queens.'

Oz says that he missed the wide Scottish spaces, the call

of birds, the expanse of sky. 'After a while, I realised that I wasn't just missing the countryside. I was missing the sea.'

I look at him sharply because I didn't know that he liked the sea. My glass is also empty, and Carlo rises reluctantly from his homely chair and pours more champagne. Carlo sits back down with a small sigh. Patsy, on the settee, has her feet on the coffee table, and an eye on Oz's chair which has leaked more stuffing, no doubt considering how to surreptitiously get rid of it as part of her grand scheme. 'Anyway,' says Oz. 'What's happened to everyone else?'

'I was wondering when you'd get around to that,' says Patsy.

'For starters, Mary Stewart?'

'Stripper,' says Patsy which, if you know Mary, is quite believable. Pretty, but unbelievably stupid.

Oz looks at her without expression. 'OK, Pete Davies?'

'Joined a circus.'

'Cath Rankin?'

'Ditto,' I say, because I haven't said anything in a long while, and have become aware of the others looking at me, but not saying anything, because my Dad's only just died and I have every right to be quiet. Nobody has mentioned Dad yet.

'Ditto circus or ditto stripper?'

'Both,' says Patsy.

'You don't really have a clue, do you?'

'Well, come on, they weren't really friends of mine. How the hell should I know what's happened to them?'

'Chris Henderson?'

'Got married and had a couple of kids.'

'Uh-huh.' Oz isn't convinced.

Patsy puts her glass down. 'Then he ran off to the circus.'

Oz sighs. 'Is there anybody from school you still keep up with?'

Patsy points over to me.

'Apart from her,' says Oz.

'Maria tells me you're a physicist,' says Oz to Carlo. By now, we're sitting in front of empty plates. Carlo is leaning back in his seat, having missed his cue to tidy them away.

'It's a living,' he replies, surveying the room for an ashtray. Much to Patsy's displeasure, Carlo likes to smoke, although not usually tobacco. He makes a big show of rolling a spliff while Patsy makes a big show of wafting her hands in the air and opening the window. Carlo blithely ignores her, puffing out smoke. 'I'm doing a doctorate and a bit of teaching.'

'A doctorate in what?'

'Quantum mechanics.'

'A load of bollocks, that's what,' says Patsy, who doesn't really know what quantum mechanics is, despite living with someone who's studying it.

'Specifically,' says Carlo, 'I'm trying to prove that Einstein-Rosen bridges and Einstein-Podolsky-Rosen entanglements are the same thing.'

It's been troubling me ever since his death. The photograph he took with him to the hospice I can understand; that night on the red carpet when he finally became somebody, and we were all together and holding hands and happily smiling like a proper family. The photograph marks a transition; a point of departure, and it had pride of place on the baby grand piano in our drawing room. After that premiere night, my father was famous, and his family had been witness to the transformation.

It was that picture he painted, and which I took back to Edinburgh and hung in my hall: the actor's wife and daughter standing on the red carpet, with the actor painting the scene from the other side of the security barrier. My father, the centre of attention, recasting himself as observer.

'What I'd like to know is why he took my grandfather's book with him,' I say, and wonder why my voice has now become shaky. We're still in the living room, but lounging on chairs, and Carlo's eyes are closing. I have a glass of red wine in one hand. 'I mean, why *that* book?'

'It's a very good book,' says Carlo, who is still probably stoned, but not yet entirely asleep.

'Yes, but you're a science nerd. My father was numerically dyslexic.'

'Maybe,' says Carlo in a deep grumble, 'he wanted to understand what his father's life's work had all been about.'

I shake my head. 'He wasn't interested in astrophysics and he took positively no interest in my granddad's research.'

Patsy has kicked off her shoes and is sitting with her legs tucked underneath her bottom. 'Maybe Carlo's right. Perhaps, since he knew his own time was coming, he wanted to connect with his own father.'

'Doesn't make sense.'

Carlo's eyes have momentarily opened. 'What doesn't make sense?'

'The universe,' I reply. 'Unless, of course, you happen to believe in my grandfather.' The sun is low over the rooftops and the room is filled with shadows. 'To you, he's a hero,' I say to Carlo. 'To me, he's mainly a moustache.'

He pulls a face. 'He'll be properly famous one day, sister, just you wait. You see, that's the whole point of theoretical science. Your grandfather's theories can't be proved because we don't yet have the technology.' He pauses, his face in profile, dying sunlight in his eye. His black skin looks carved from shadow.

'Darwin,' he continues, 'proved that life on Earth has evolved and that God couldn't have dreamed everything up in six days. However, that hasn't stopped people believing in God, has it?'

I pour more red wine into my glass, but not too much because my hands are shaking quite badly now, and I don't want to slop any. Oz is smiling at nobody in particular, and I'm aware of constantly looking at him, and of quickly looking away, just in case he notices. 'The simple fact of evolution is that, before mankind, there were dinosaurs and, before them, slimy creepy-crawlies. In all probability, therefore, we have come about as a result of random chaos and evolutionary luck.'

'OK,' says Patsy. 'So?'

'Until Maria's grandfather came along, religion was the preserve of theologians and priests. It was all about simple belief, or the lack of it. After all, if you can't prove the existence of God, you can't disprove His existence either.' Carlo turns from Patsy to me, his eyes sparking in candlelight. 'Your grandfather's theorem might finally prove that it was us who invented God, and not the other way around.'

'And is that so important?' asks Patsy. Her feet have returned to the coffee table.

'Maria's grandfather moved religion from the realms of theology to the realm of astrophysics. In other words, he shifted the focus of the argument. Darwin had proved, without really meaning to, that the Book of Genesis couldn't have happened. But the Rossini Theorem takes scientific scepticism several steps further. He says that, with modern scientific knowledge, we can finally debunk God Himself. In some circles, girl, your grandfather was regarded as a very dangerous man. Someone to be feared and therefore someone to be ridiculed.'

I know this, having listened to enough of my grandmother's anecdotes, and how Alberto was rewarded with snub after snub. Several publishers, no doubt leaned on from above, according to my grandmother, refused to publish his theorem. He'd eventually published it himself, at his own expense. He knew the controversy it would cause.

'Maybe your father had a very good reason to choose that book,' says Oz. 'Maybe he was trying to figure out what was going to happen to his own immortal soul.'

'Or if he had one,' I reply. His letter still lies unopened on my mantelpiece. I start to feel sick, and I can't stop shaking because I can hear the deep, distant, and unexpected, sound of thunder.

'Are you OK?' Oz asks.

'Of course, she's not OK,' snaps Patsy, and comes and sits on the arm on my chair. I try to say that I'm fine, but I'm not fine because, for some reason, I'm crying and the thunder is coming closer, and the curtains are open, and I can see faces in the clouds.

They know who I used to be but, like John Salmond, they now seem to have cleverly put two and two together, because I am still entangled with my other self, and can't completely hide from who I really am.

Oz has a hand on my forehead. 'She's burning up,' he says.

'I'll phone for a taxi,' says Patsy.

I can't remember the taxi ride home, or Oz beside me on the back seat. All I can remember is the thunderstorm and the rain beating on the taxi's window screen, and Oz holding my hand. I can't remember getting into the lift. I must have given Oz my front door keys because suddenly the front door was open and Oz was saying 'Christ!' in a very loud voice – because the Dalek was doing its job – and then him pushing me down onto a chair in the kitchen.

I do recall Knox sitting on a high shelf, and I remember wondering why he wasn't under a table somewhere because animals are supposed to be frightened of thunderstorms, and then wondering if Knox could teach me how to not be frightened of them. I then dimly remember Oz looking into my eyes in a professional way, taking my pulse and shaking his head in a way that could either have been professional or personal – or both – and saying that he was going to call an ambulance.

I can remember trying to suck in breath, but it was like being underwater, but without Dad there to rescue me, and each breath seemed filled with tiny particles that were jagged and sharp in my lungs. I remember being in pain, because dark matter had filled the room, and I couldn't breathe in

311

proper air.

I don't know what happened next because, when Oz came back into the room, he couldn't immediately see me, until he looked under the kitchen table and found that Knox had finally taken refuge there, and that I was beside him and lying in a large pool of blood.

Part Three: Synthesis

$$28\pi\rho\left[M_{\mathrm{M}}\left(\frac{5kT}{G\mu m_{\mathrm{K}}}\right)^{-3/2}\right]^2 = 21$$

Jeans' mass

Entanglement. That's all I could think about.

My obsession with the cloud-faces had been getting worse, but I didn't realise how bad it had become. I had chosen to be two people: Maria and my other self, Emma Rossini, who doesn't really exist anymore, but who still does exist because she's still me, and the cloud-faces had realised that we were the same person.

Entanglement is the quantum theory of nonlocality and describes the ability of objects to instantaneously know about each other's state, even though separated by large distances. It's as if the universe is constantly arranging all of its particles in anticipation of future events. It means that the cosmos may be connected in ways that we don't yet understand. Einstein didn't really understand either.

That's what the sky has been doing, finally realising that there must be a mirror-image Emma Rossini somewhere and tracking me across time and space, because it now knew where I lived, and what my new name was, and my head felt as if it was about to explode, and that's why I couldn't stop shaking and crying.

For the second time in my life, I was rushed to the Edinburgh Royal Infirmary by ambulance, but this time I had Oz beside me, and the noise of the sirens drowned out the noise of the storm.

At the hospital, doctors stitched my wrists and efficient nurses changed the dressings. I was given tranquillisers and put on a drip. Blood loss, I was told. But what I needed, they said, was proper assessment in a 'specialist unit' – it's called The Baltimore, I was told, a jewel in Edinburgh's psychiatric crown and very discreet. It's a private clinic, they said, but we're assured you have the necessary funds. Necessary funds? Oz, I supposed. Do you agree? I was asked, as if I had much choice in the matter.

'We all just want you to get better,' said Oz, who had stayed with me, sitting by my bed and looking tired. I was grateful that he didn't ask questions.

'I'm sorry,' I told him.

'For what?'

'For everything,' I replied.

The medication I was given not only blunted the sharp edges of my terrors but blunted everything else. I no longer had free choice. I couldn't make independent decisions.

A nurse gave me a leaflet. The Baltimore looked much like Dad's hospice and for a few moments I wondered if it was the same place and therefore if I was dying, and asked Oz who was still sitting by my bed and now looking very tired and he said 'no', so I went back to sleep.

In those first few days, I did a lot of sleeping. I didn't dream of anything.

On the back of the leaflet was an inspiring message from the clinical director, Dr Hermione Madison, about all the world-class treatments on offer – blah, blah, blah. I signed the proffered form without reading it, and two days later was transferred by private ambulance.

By then I was feeling foolish. I could hardly remember the episode in the flat and Oz phoning for an ambulance. I had caused pain to myself and to others. The brain pills were doing their stuff: I was beginning to regain some equilibrium but still couldn't stop shaking.

At first glance it looks like a country house hotel, with a long drive and climbing ivy. It doesn't seem to have bars

316

on the windows, although having been brought up in North Berwick, I know a thing or two about escape-proof glass. Hermione herself comes to the front steps to meet me. She is older, but much the same. 'Don't think of yourself as a patient,' she advises, steering me inside. On the inside, it doesn't seem much like a mental hospital either. There are polished wooden floors and an ornate cornice, nurses in blue tracksuits pad soundlessly on rubber shoes. 'You'll only be here for a few weeks.'

'Christ! Weeks!' I'd been expecting a stay measured in days, just like my incarceration by Lake Como. 'I really must be fucking bonkers,' I add in a quieter voice, but I don't think that Hermione heard.

She leads me down a corridor and into her office. We are still in the old part of the hospital (I can see that more modern buildings have sprouted up behind the ivy-encrusted façade). Her office is lined in dark wood and on the shelf behind her desk is the same photograph of her children that I remember from so many years ago. They will be grown up now, perhaps with their own children. In the photograph, they are caught in time: their hair frizzing in the sun, the bright sparkle of an ocean. She indicates the seat in front of her desk. She sits in a larger leather chair on the other side.

'I rather fancy that there's nothing much wrong with you, Emma.'

I hold up my wrists, neatly bandaged. I don't bother correcting her about my name. Now that the cloud-faces know who I am, it doesn't seem to matter. I'm still trembling and all I want to do is sleep.

'You have a condition,' she says. 'Specifically, I believe, a low level of a hormone called serotonin. Of course, we'll have to run a few tests. Blood samples, that kind of thing. In my experience, there's often a medical explanation.'

'So, I'm not completely mad.'

'Madness is not a medical term.' She smiles. 'Do you feel mad?'

'I cut my wrists,' I remind her.

'But not particularly badly. Of course, I'll also want to talk to you about what's happened to you over the years. That's also part of the assessment process. However, my view is that, if you'd really wanted to kill yourself, an intelligent woman like you would have made a much better job of it.' She makes it sound like a rebuke.

The Baltimore sits at the end of a long drive. It comprises a Georgian mansion, once the home of a shipping magnate, which houses the recreational and dining areas, offices, and treatment rooms, with modern living blocks built at the back. The Baltimore boasts deep carpets and pastel colours, and the long drive is fringed by tall trees. It's very quiet inside, like a library, but without books.

I have a room on the second storey of a new accommodation block. It is almost clinical: a single bed, bedside cupboard, a desk, a flat-screen TV screwed to the wall, and a walk-in wardrobe, with plastic coat-hangers. My room overlooks a manicured lawn bordered by a high wall; on the other side of the wall are residential streets. Opening the window, which doesn't open much, I can hear children playing: a trivial, everyday sound, magnified and made unusual by their sanity and the lunatics on my side of the wall.

I could simply pack my bag and walk out. There are no locks on the doors and we can wear what we want. I haven't yet heard screams from down the corridor, nobody dribbles or shouts obscenities, and the few other patients I've met seem reasonably normal. I can't stop thinking about escape. Although the fruitcakes aren't supposed to leave the grounds, there's nothing to stop us.

The driveway doesn't have closed gates at the end, there are no burly nurses to stop us wandering. We are all here voluntarily; creatures of our own terrors or addictions. We can leave at any time. Hermione has made that abundantly clear to me, although she also emphasised that it would not

318

be a good idea.

I can also just glimpse the sea. It is tantalisingly close. The Baltimore is in east Edinburgh; I could walk home in less than an hour, and perhaps should walk home because I don't know if Oz has remembered to feed Knox, or if the Dalek has gone berserk and exterminated the Greek nymphs. The thought of escape is tempting, almost overwhelming. Instead, I uncap my medicine bottle and swallow the two white capsules it contains. My afternoon dose, carefully rationed, and I close my eyes, feeling nauseous but more in control. Diazepam, I have concluded, is quite possibly *the* greatest invention of all time, and I include fire and the wheel in that assessment. I appreciate that fire offers warmth and the means to cook food. I understand that the wheel has paved the way for almost all mechanical inventions, including the wheelbarrow. From my window, when I reopen my eyes, a gardener in blue overalls is pushing one. It's full of grass cuttings. He dumps them somewhere down the side of my block. A tabby cat chases any clumps of grass that fall from the wheelbarrow. If, God forbid, I was to come back here next year, I'm sure the scene would be much the same: the same wheelbarrow, gardener, and lunatics, the same Dr Hermione Madison.

In remembering that distant confusing time when she first treated me, I am also confronted by her return to my life. I have been reconnected to a shared past in which I am once again her patient. It makes me wonder whether I can ever break free, or if hurting myself has become a habit, like cigarettes. Seeing her again reminds me of the span of years since we last met and how, for me, nothing much has changed. I am older, nothing more, although Dad is no longer in the waiting room, if he ever was, wearing his clown's mask or burka.

Hermione's hair is greyer, and she seems thinner – but

that might be a trick of memory. She hasn't changed much. I've simply grown up, still trapped in sticky mud and hiding from dark clouds. I wonder just how much of my mother's genes I have inherited. Probably all of them. I could have inherited my father's or grandfather's genetic code and become a famous actress or scientist.

She wants to see me after breakfast. Although the patients can eat in their rooms if they wish, we're encouraged to be sociable and to mix with the others. Hermione keeps repeating the word *illness*, as if I'm suffering from a bad cold.

I eat breakfast alone, a slice of toast and coffee. I sit near the windows. The dining room is in the old part of the house. It has ornate cornices picked out in gold and dark red wallpaper. Majestic oil pictures of Highland scenes line the walls, a salmon stream, with a single fisherman casting his line, a purple mountain with deer ranging along its flanks, a dark loch, with low hills on which sit menacing clouds. That is my least favourite picture.

From my table I can see down the driveway to the open gates at the entrance. One or two of the other nutters sit at tables together, chatting reasonably normally, or reading newspapers and commenting on the weather or pontificating on the state of the world, which even lunatics are allowed to do, I suppose. They don't laugh uproariously or roll on the floor. They could be anybody; mostly middle-aged and seem remarkably normal.

I look between them for signs of lunacy but can see none. Some, like me, sit by themselves; we tend to occupy the tables near the windows. We could be in the dining room of a once-grand hotel. French windows open to a lawn on which are grouped iron tables and chairs. Some of the patients sit outside to drink their morning coffee, wrapped warmly in heavy sweaters. But I don't encourage conversation, I don't want to be sociable. I spread butter on my toast with a plastic knife.

I missed Dad's funeral, of course, which didn't much matter as I was there at his death. I wasn't in a fit state to go anywhere and although I felt bad at missing his final big day, I was still shaking and crying, and didn't want everyone to think they were tears of grief, and to feel sorry for the little orphan girl. But I watched it on the Scottish TV news, remembering the church and Mum's funeral service, and recognising some of the same sombre faces. Brad Pitt was there, and Captain Ramius, who had beaten Dad to the *Red October*, and outlived him. Dad would also have been furious about that.

After the funeral, Granny and Gramps came to see me. Granny's eyes were red-rimmed and Granddad's moustache was sad. After I leave here, I'll be spending a few weeks with them, and renewing my acquaintance with the Stormtrooper, and that seems like something to look forward to.

Fran also came to visit and, to cheer me up, regaled me with tales from the Big Apple, and news of her latest failed love affair. Fran doesn't suffer fools gladly, so she says, and most of the men in her life turn out to be fools. As always, I was struck by her similarity to Mum; the same laugh, the same tilt of her head when she's listening, the same eyes. She told me that I really was my mother's daughter, but in a nice way, with a small smile. 'Your mum was off and on pills for most of her life, Emma. Mostly on.'

She still had her English accent, and sounded just like Mum, so it also seemed like maternal advice. 'I've had a breakdown and have a hormonal imbalance. But I'm not really mad,' I told her.

'I don't doubt it,' replied Fran. We were in the communal day room, with uncomfortable chairs grouped around coffee tables on which sat ancient magazines probably foretelling the start of the Second World War. It was like being in a doctor's surgery, which was why nobody ever went there. 'Your dad did try to protect her, you know.' She had leaned over the low table to say this, as if to confide a secret. 'Keeping her out of the limelight. Moving to North Berwick. Trying to give her a quiet life.'

'I never saw it like that.'

'No, because you were a child. You may not accept it, Emma, but he did what he could for her.' Abruptly she stood up. 'Just get better, OK?'

'I'll try,' I said.

Hermione doesn't seem to think that hacking at my wrists with a knife was a real suicide attempt, because Oz had been in the next room phoning for an ambulance. She says that people who commit suicide usually do it when they're alone. I can't really remember anything about being in the kitchen with Knox and a knife, so I have to take her word on it. Dr Madison thinks it was a mental breakdown, brought on by hormonal imbalance, extreme exhaustion, and triggered by Dad's death. She says that I will be on medication for some time to come, with regular check-ups, until I can prove that I can cope with a world with real cutlery.

'How do you feel?' Dr Madison asks.

'Like shit.'

'That's only to be expected.'

I've been in captivity for days now, but I don't know how many; day has melded into night, and feeling like shit hasn't helped. Mostly, I try to sleep; mostly I fail, descending into a tormented half-slumber from which I wake drenched in sweat. For the first few hours or days all I wanted to do was be sick. In between vitamin injections, or whatever they were, I was sometimes sick. Bile and nothingness, I couldn't even be sick properly. Mostly I just lay on my back, trying to quieten my shaking hands, the TV turned down low. In those early days, thunder rumbled on the horizon, so I mostly kept the curtains shut and lay on my back on the narrow bed.

'Everything hurts.' My brain feels frozen and lumpen, and I find it difficult to think. 'Actually, feeling like shit pretty much sums it up.' What makes it barely tolerable are large quantities of drugs, morning, noon and night.

Dr Madison makes a small squiggle in my file and pushes her half-moon glasses up her nose. 'This is our third session, Emma.'

'So?'

'At our first session you said that you felt like utter and complete shit.'

I have only a vague memory of that first meeting and merely shrug apologetically. At that first session I was in two minds; my feet were still glued to the ocean's floor and the journey upwards seemed hardly worth the effort.

'At our second meeting you said that you only felt like *complete* shit.'

'Only?' I can't see what point she's trying to make.

'Today,' she says, once more looking over her glasses, 'you just feel like shit. The diminishing use of adjectives suggests progress.'

I don't know if this is the good doctor attempting levity and, after a thoughtful pause, I choose only to nod warily.

'Good!' she continues brightly. 'As I said, progress is being made. It will take time, of course, but initial recovery will be reasonably rapid. After that, it's down to you.' Hermione looks at me sharply. 'We've known each other a long time, Emma,' she says suddenly. She has been tapping her pen against my file. Abruptly, she now flicks back through pages.

I don't say anything, remembering a younger Hermione in a different consulting room. I was frightened of her then. I thought she might be in league with my father.

'We last met about ten years ago,' she announces,

having flicked back to a point where the pages look old and discoloured. She lays down the pen and closes the file. 'And I still don't know how this all started. To help you, to *really* help you, I need to understand.' She says this with emphasis, leaning over her desk.

'There's nothing to understand,' I tell her. I can feel my hands begin to tremble. I want to be back in my room, or walking down the long driveway, the sun on my face, freedom beyond the open gates. I bite my lip. I don't want to be here, feeling wretched. But I concede, I don't want the alternative either.

'You wouldn't talk to me ten years ago, Emma.'

'I was a child.'

'No, you weren't,' she sighs. Hermione can sigh eloquently when she wants to. 'You were a mixed-up teenager, that's all. Look, I'm not endowed with mind-reading skills. Psychiatry is a two-way process, Emma. You help me and I help you.'

'I don't know what you want to know.'

'Yes, you do. This is all about your mum and dad. I'd like you to tell me about them.'

'In simple terms, she was nice, he wasn't. What more do you want?'

I can see Hermione swallowing irritation. She wants me to confess my most private thoughts, to be sobbing over her desk, pulling tissues from the jumbo-sized dispenser in front of me. But I can't do that. I have nothing to confess, and I don't want to cry.

'Look, if you still find it difficult to talk to me, then why not write about it,' she continues more brightly, as if the thought had just occurred to her. I suspect it hasn't.

'Write about it?' I echo.

'A kind of journal.'

'What, like a diary?'

She can see that I'm looking sceptical. 'Well, why

324

not? Your immediate mental recovery will, as I've said, be relatively quick. However, that doesn't explain the underlying causes of your illness. To tackle that, I have to know what the real problem is.'

I spread my hands wide. 'I can't write. It's a stupid idea.'

'You're a journalist, Emma! Of course, you can write.'

'Crappy stories for a newspaper. Sorry, doctor, I just don't see the point.'

She perseveres. 'The point is that you don't much like talking about yourself. Maybe you could write it instead. It might also help both of us. From your perspective, it could be cathartic. To set down your real feelings. It might get them out of your system, as it were.' She pauses, peering over her glasses. 'So, what do you think?'

'I wouldn't know what to write,' I say.

Dr Madison leans back in her chair and twirls her glasses between long fingers. 'What about the truth?'

I think about this only briefly. 'Believe me, that would be very boring.'

She smiles. 'Then write whatever you want.' She picks up my file and makes another squiggle in it. 'The brain is a complex bit of equipment, Emma, and yours has suffered a degree of trauma. To help you recover, it would be helpful for me to know as much as you're prepared to tell me.' She pauses for a moment. 'I'm simply here to help you understand what's happened to you.'

'I rather thought you were here to cure me.'

'I can only help in that process, Emma. The cure is in here.' She taps her head with one finger and regards me rather sadly. 'You see, I need to know who you really are,' she says softly, although a small smile seems trapped between her lips.

The trouble is, as Hermione understands full well, I no longer quite know who I am. 'I don't know what the truth is any more,' I tell her.

'Speaking words is easy,' she continues briskly, speaking as if from a manual. 'Writing them down takes more effort.' She leans over the desk again, and this time she is smiling. 'Who we are is whoever we invent for ourselves, isn't that right, Emma?'

For two days after that meeting with Dr Madison I sat in my room and watched the sun move over the sky. The white pills I was asked to swallow made me drowsy and I still had no real sense of time. My dreams were dark and vivid, my bedclothes damp. I again contemplated leaving but knew that this might be my last chance. At night, shaking and sweating, I felt trapped in water; above, there was sunlight playing on the surface; below was darkness and cloying mud. Several times I nearly stuffed everything into my backpack and walked out.

Hermione came to my room, eyed my laptop, but didn't seem bothered by my lack of application. 'You don't have to write anything if you don't want to,' she said, glasses perched on the end of her nose. 'There again, no reason not to get cracking, eh?'

'I don't know where to start,' I replied lamely.

Dr Madison bestowed a small smile. 'Then why not start with something important?'

Outside, fallen leaves were eddying in the breeze and the elderly man in blue overalls was trying valiantly to rake them into a pile. From my room's vantage point, I could keep watch over the old man and the ever-present tabby cat, each fruitlessly chasing leaves or darting sparrows. The tabby cat had retreated to the shade of a bush and was watching a blackbird pick seeds from the grass. Raising my eyes, the sky looked grey and ominous.

Hermione now lowered her chin and looked at me over the top of her glasses. 'You could, of course, just start at the beginning?' she suggested.

More is known about the universe now, but most of the big stuff is a complete mystery. We know that about sixty-eight per cent of the universe is dark energy and that about twenty-seven per cent is dark matter, but what they are is still guesswork. Einstein also decreed that space is actually very clever – it allows for more space to come into existence, so that the universe can expand into it.

But, like space, if I am to expand outwards from The Baltimore and rejoin the real world, I now admit that I will have to try and understand what's happened to me, and to glue together all my bits and pieces, including the bits that are too small to see and which might not exist, but which sometimes coat my airways and lungs when thunder is about.

My worry is that Hermione may have unspoken tricks up her sleeve. What if I don't write stuff down for her? Does lack of cooperation mean that she'll wash her hands of me? If I am deemed sufficiently mad, would that mean a transfer to a state hospital, with real bars on the windows and burly nurses with tasers strapped to their belts. I've seen *One Flew Over the Cuckoo's Nest*, and I have a vivid imagination for bad things.

But would Hermione do that to me? She likes me, I think, and we've known each other – sort of – for a lot of years. But despite myself, despite my anxieties, I'm no longer against her idea. Not enthusiastic, but no longer wholly opposed. Frankly, I'm bored. The Baltimore isn't exactly a palace of entertainment. Apart from walking in the grounds, trying to avoid other inmates, and eating regularly, there's nothing much to do.

Group therapy and sessions with Hermione are what occupy my day. Writing about the past would, if nothing else, pass the time. But I still don't have a story to tell. I am defined by the casual cruelties of one person, not by who I am or what I've done. How can I write about that? What sense would it make? But she's right about one thing:

it might be cathartic. Maybe I need to understand who I am and who he was.

I sit down in front of my laptop, and stare at it for a few minutes, thinking about beginnings and points of singularity. How do I write a diary that starts when I was little? I can barely remember what I did last week let alone a decade or more ago. But I remind myself, I have maybe tried to commit suicide – with an, admittedly, blunt knife – and am suffering from exhaustion and a hormonal imbalance. I have had a mental breakdown. I have to start somewhere.

I take a deep breath and start to type.

"Hurray! Mum is taking me to the cinema, and I haven't been to the cinema for a while"

That's the trouble with words: unless you're very clever, and know lots of them, words can't always describe what you feel, and I don't know what words to write and in what order. The things that Hermione wants to know are deep inside, in a dark place where words can't reach. I know what I feel but can't explain what I feel. I suppose that makes me an odd person, although I don't think it's my fault. I blame other people and can therefore absolve myself of guilt, although that's just an evasion to make me feel better about myself. I am on the point of closing my laptop when my fingers, almost unbidden, start to type.

"Yippee! Mummy is taking me to the cinema and has told me that it's a surprise."

$$\frac{33c^2}{t^2 T^4 \pi G \alpha g_{\text{hii}}} = 22$$

Time vs. Temperature in an expanding universe

The first time I was taken to the Royal Infirmary by ambulance wasn't remotely my fault, and although Mum and Dad tried to make me feel guilty afterwards, I think that was just their way of evading parental responsibility. Specifically, it was Mum's way of evading parental responsibility because Fran was visiting, and both of them had spent the day – and most of the evening before – cackling like children and drinking gin.

Fran wasn't long separated from her husband, and so the cackling was interspersed with a few tears and tantrums. We were still living in the semi-posh mansion flat and I taught Fran how to slide down the hallway and into the living room, and she was very good at it – although not as good as me – until she fell over and banged her head against a door, and then had to drink a huge gin to make herself better, while Mum lounged on a sofa and sang a Beatles song, and didn't seem to be paying any attention.

Dad unexpectedly arrived in the early afternoon. He'd been away in Birmingham, acting in a Shakespearean play, and there were still traces of gunk on his face. By then, Fran was also singing along with Mum and although she'd cleaned most of the blood from her forehead, there was still a trace on the hallway floor. Dad surveyed the scene and suggested a trip to the beach, because it was a nice day outside and Emma needed the fresh air.

I didn't think that I did need fresh air and seeing Mum and Fran like that was very entertaining, but Dad was insistent, and so we all climbed into his new – second-hand – Bentley, with only a few dents and scratches, and set off for Portobello. Mum and Fran sat in the back, looking almost identical in dark glasses, while I sat in the front with my swimsuit under a summer dress and a large towel on my lap. Mum and Fran, having drunk quite a lot of gin, hadn't noticed that it was summer and that the sun was shining. It was the first time I had ever been to a beach, and I was quite excited, even though it was only Portobello beach and half of Edinburgh's human population and all of its dog population were on it.

We found a spot near to an ice cream van and pretty soon Mum and Fran were fast asleep on beach towels. Both were wearing skimpy dresses, but neither had stripped off to a bikini, because both had said that going to Portobello beach was a waste of time and effort, that the beach wasn't a real beach, and don't even *think* that either of us is going to swim in the North Sea.

They made it sound as if polar bears would find it chilly, which was odd to me because the beach was sweltering, and the ice cream van had a lengthy queue. Dad bought me an ice cream, shaking his head at Mum and Fran, who were unconscious, and I walked to the edge of the sea and watched young children splash around and throw balls to one another, squealing and diving.

I looked back to our little group, with Mum and Fran lying flat out, and Dad, in shorts and T-shirt, sitting on a towel and reading something. I dipped my toes in the water, feeling a frisson of cold running up my legs, and then stood there for some moments until the water felt warm, so I waded in a few more feet, and then some more, until the water was up to my middle, and it was difficult to stand still against the current, and even more difficult to eat my ice cream without getting it wet.

I don't really know what happened then because I should have stayed where I was, or gone back into shallower water, but I was mesmerised by all the people around me, all diving and throwing things, and laughing, with Edinburgh's dog population also joining in, and who were also probably laughing, although it's difficult to tell with dogs, and I felt my feet slip and then was falling backwards and water was closing in over my head.

But I felt safe under the water, if only for a few moments, because it was warm and I could still hear people all around me, their thrashing feet, the barking of dogs. I didn't know which way was up and where the bottom of the sea was.

I turned underwater, and saw sparkles above me, and tried to fight towards them, but they seemed to be getting further away, and I started to feel frightened, and the water tasted salty in my throat and I couldn't breathe and, although I was gulping down air, there didn't seem to be any air underwater, and I realised that I was being stupid because I wasn't a fish.

But then I was being roughly propelled upwards, and Dad had his arms around me, and I was screaming and retching and coughing up water, and even Fran and Mum had woken up and were rushing a little erratically to the shoreline. I could also see a lifeguard running over, and he had a phone to his ear.

All four of us shared the ambulance to the hospital, although, by the time we got there, it should have been Mum and Fran being admitted rather than me. Mum was in a terrible state in the ambulance, shouting at Dad and blaming him for not keeping a better eye on me, 'because I was having a nap, you bastard!'

'I didn't know she couldn't swim!' I heard him say.

Blah, blah, blah.

'No I haven't taken her to swimming lessons!'

Blah, blah, blah.

'Because you're never fucking here, that's why!'

Blah, blah, blah.

'You're drunk!'

'Well how was I to know we'd end up at the bloody seaside!'

And so on, until I was sick and tired of their shouting, and we mercifully arrived at the peace and quiet of the hospital, where a doctor examined me, and said that the sea 'doesn't taste very nice, does it?' and a nurse checked my pulse, and looked accusingly at Mum and Dad. Fran was in the waiting area and had gone back to sleep. She'd also been asleep in the ambulance, and so had missed all the shouting.

The next week I started intensive swimming lessons, and Mum was only satisfied when I was deemed capable of swimming across the Atlantic and back again. But my abiding memory of my encounter with the North Sea is one of peace. It had felt like home under the water; a different kind of home, a home in which I wasn't an alien blob, but a place that I understood, and which would always understand me and that, in a strange way that I have yet to understand, I was a child of the sea.

Hermione puts on her glasses and flicks through pages of my manuscript, and it maybe seems to her to have been a waste of my time writing it, and a bigger waste of her time reading it. I haven't written much of it yet, so it can't have taken her long to wade through it. Has she pored over every word, I wonder? Or simply skimmed through it? All the same, I feel like I'm back in school and my English homework is about to be marked.

'It's very creative, Emma,' she begins, 'and not at all what I was expecting.'

I'm not sure whether this is criticism or praise. Probably neither. Hermione's job doesn't allow her to judge. 'I don't know how else to write it.'

She smiles. 'It's absolutely fine just as it is. So, you're writing it as a kind of novel?'

'That's the idea, doctor. But probably not a very good one.'

She flips to the first page, and stares at it for a few moments. "But, I wonder, will you be a reliable narrator?"

'I can't remember half the stuff that happened back then. Why shouldn't I make things up?'

'No reason at all, just so long as some bits are true. There is some truth in here, isn't there?' She taps my journal – or memoir, or whatever it is – with her glasses and holds my gaze.

I look away. 'I'm just not good at confessions, doctor.'

She inclines her head. 'Nobody is asking you to confess anything. Confession suggests you've done something wrong. I'm here to persuade you that you haven't.'

'That's not entirely true,' I tell her. 'I've spent time in police custody. For throwing a brick.'

'Oh?'

'On a demo.'

'And did you?' She seems merely amused.

'No. Mistaken identity.'

'Then put it in your journal. At least I'll know that bit is true.'

I hadn't planned on writing about that. Maybe I will, maybe I won't.

Hermione leans forwards and places both hands on her desk. 'OK, then let me ask you this. Do you blame your father for hurting your mother?'

'Yes,' I reply.

'Did you hate him?'

'Often.'

Hermione lets this hang for a few moments. 'However, you also saw yourself as your mother's protector, didn't you?'

'In the absence of my father, yes.' I can feel the dull stab of a headache behind one eye. I don't like talking about Mum. It feels like betrayal.

'Yet he wasn't absent, was he?' Hermione's chair wheezes as she leans back. 'At least not all the time.'

'You know what I mean, doctor.'

'So, you felt doubly guilty when she died,' she says. 'You'd failed to protect her.'

That's the paradox, I think; I can't feel gratitude to Dad for saving my life when I nearly drowned, but I absolutely blame him for Mum's death.

'You still feel that guilt, don't you?' She has taken off her glasses to make this point. She taps her glasses against my file. 'You felt guilty about her death and believed that you should be punished in some way. You've been hiding from that guilt ever since.'

'I don't know what you mean.'

'Then perhaps you should think about it.'

The headache has swelled, and I put a hand to my face.

Hermione now places her glasses on top of my journal. Each page face down. 'But try at least to accept that you have nothing to feel guilty about.' I hear her words through a spasm of pain, and don't reply.

After my session with Hermione, and after my headache has subsided, I walk down the manicured driveway to The Baltimore's main entrance. I stand at the threshold for a few minutes, trying to detect if the air tastes different on the sane side of the open gates. The gateway leads onto a small road; across the road is a high wall behind which sit detached Georgian houses. I can see a plume of smoke from a chimney, hear the rustle of branches. It is chillier now, colder than when I was admitted. I wonder how Knox is coping, or if he's missing me, and if Oz is still feeding him and, if so, whether his fingers are intact. I don't worry about the Dalek because I now accept that he's plastic, and that Daleks don't really exist. Granny and Gramps have phoned every day, and I keep reminding them that I'll be in Italy with them soon.

Although I wasn't originally keen on the idea, I'm quite glad to have started on Dr Madison's journal. It has been a little bit cathartic, I have to admit, and it's passed the time. Time hangs heavy here, unless you like daytime TV, which I don't. I suppose that's how the other loonies spend their days. The clinic is comfortable enough, but it's a place that wants you to leave, a place that wants you to *want* to leave. Hence the narrow beds and appalling food.

I'm still not sure how long I've been here or, worse, how long I'll remain. Mostly I now stay in my room writing this journal, except when I have to attend group therapy, which is the worst thing about this place. I take no interest in my fellow inmates, although I've spotted what could have been a former Spice Girl in the communal garden, but I might have been wrong, arms wrapped around herself and looking unhappy. I don't socialise with the other loonies; I don't see the point. But am I learning anything about myself? Do I feel better about myself? Probably not, but I now realise that nobody can travel under a false passport forever.

My days are mostly spent writing, swallowing medication, and sleeping. I have regular blood tests, and blood pressure tests, and they keep changing my medication, which can be nice, except when they get it wrong, and I start to behave like a tearful zombie. Luckily, that only happened once.

Generally, it's a bit like being on holiday, but with bad food and, although I know where I am, and what's happening to me, I have also lost a sense of self. I have unresolved 'issues' says Hermione, which is stating the blindingly obvious, but I'm also suffering from hyperthyroidism, which is nice to know, because it's an actual word, a real diagnosis, and therefore something with an actual treatment.

My busy little thyroid has been making too much stuff and my options are antithyroid drugs, beta blockers, radioactive iodine or surgery. I don't like the idea of any of them, particularly surgery and radioactivity – would I glow in the dark? – and have opted for more conventional drugs. They look as innocuous as the other drugs I'm taking and, now that they're working, I feel calmer, more in control, and no longer worry about Knox, because Oz has phoned several times to say that the cat is fine, and that the scratch on his hand is healing nicely.

But I feel a little lost within myself, as if I'm missing a coordinate, which Albert Einstein would have understood perfectly. His special theory of relativity treats time as a coordinate in unified space-time, because light from a distant galaxy takes a while to reach us, so we're not just looking upwards at a star, we're looking at what it looked like hundreds or thousands of millions of years ago.

Einstein then got bored one wet afternoon and decided that what was needed was a fuller theory of space-time, extending his thinking to curved space-time, where time and space make up the basic tapestry, but which is curved and stretched by matter and energy, and he called it general relativity, and it's a bit like I feel, my mind being pulled and stretched, but without having a sense of time, the fourth dimension that governs the properties of all known matter. I exist in The Baltimore, that much I know, but what's happened to my other, younger self? In what coordinates of space and time does she exist? And can I glue my two selves back together again?

Group therapy is the absolute worst part of my incarceration. My group meets in an airy room in the old part of the clinic. Incongruously, there is a grand piano in the corner, which reminds me of North Berwick, although it doesn't have any photographs on it; large oil paintings of Highland rivers and mountains adorning the walls. Some do hang in the dining room, each enclosed in gilded frames. It must once have been a grand room given over to clever conversation or important discourse: tailored men in frock coats smoking cigars, fluttering ladies in long dresses drinking tea.

Now, in the centre of the room is a semicircle of plastic chairs. Facing the semicircle is another chair, always occupied by Clara Bushell, who is either a psychologist or psychotherapist, I can't remember which. She did introduce herself to me at our first session; I wasn't paying much attention, to Clara or to anything else. She looks to be younger than me, is very tall, and wears ankle-length tents in vibrant colours. She has thick glasses and shoulder-length hair that she ties in a knot on the top of her head. She is friendly and carries a clipboard. When she's not writing on it, she presses it against her chest like a shield. During our sessions, she takes copious notes, even if nobody has said anything remotely interesting.

I suppose she reports back to Hermione after each session, sharing our confessions and her observations. I don't therefore say anything at group therapy, I don't see why a bunch of strangers should know anything about me, and I have absolutely no interest in them. Clara has tried several times to cajole me into saying something; each time I have politely declined. I don't want to bare my soul, and I don't trust the company of strangers, however therapeutic it's supposed to be.

I look around the group. Mr Dobbs is our star turn; the one lunatic who does like to talk – no, who absolutely *loves* to talk – and who hates listening. For him, there is only Mr Dobbs. He is, of course, already seated by the time the rest of us shuffle in. He's always the first to arrive, fidgeting in his seat, crossing and uncrossing his legs, a new pile of injustice just waiting to erupt. Then there's Ruth, a lawyer, whose husband left her. She is shy and doesn't say much either. Like me, she'd rather keep her secrets locked away.

Next to her is Phil, a dentist, who had become sensitised to his patients' pain, and then took to his patients' pain-killing drugs. Phil always looks sad, perhaps missing tooth decay and halitosis, I feel sorry for him.

Next to him is Rachel. She looks to be my age but is probably a few years older. She is the beauty of our group; immaculately dressed, slim and tall, with red hair and big eyes. She doesn't wear make-up. I've spoken to her a few times; once in the garden, other times in corridors. She seems nice in a selfish look-how-beautiful-I-am way. Her parents were killed in a car crash, so she explained in a matter-of-fact way at the first session. To get through the funeral, and its aftermath, she snorted cocaine and then couldn't stop. That was six years ago.

Clara sits in her seat and wishes us 'good morning'. Her clipboard has slipped from her chest and now rests on her knee; her pen is uncapped, waiting for our indiscretions. She is, as always, beaming happily. The group, like an obedient primary class, all wish her 'good morning' in return.

Clara smiles around the semicircle. 'Good! Then who'd like to start?'

She is, as always, is met with silence. Rachel is examining her nails, Phil is looking out the window, and Ruth is frowning at her toes. I look at Mr Dobbs, just waiting – as we all are – for him to sally forth.

It doesn't take long. 'Well, if nobody is going to say anything, then I will.' He looks belligerently around the small group, willing us to challenge him. I shrug and also look out the window.

'That's the trouble with you lot,' he now says. 'Nobody is prepared to say anything. Particularly you,' he adds with emphasis. I now see that he's looking at me. 'This is supposed to be group therapy. We're all supposed to contribute.'

Clara is making notes on her clipboard. She is still smiling happily.

'Well?' demands Mr Dobbs. He is still looking at me. I glance around. The others are still looking out the window or at their toes and nails.

'No, you go on,' I tell him.

'But that's just it,' he says. 'I try to participate, but you lot don't. I want to take things seriously – talk about what I feel. I try to do that. All you do is sit. It isn't fair.'

'Fair' is a word that Mr Dobbs uses a lot. Nothing, it seems, has ever been fair in his life. Not his job or his marriage. The others in the group only have first names. I don't know their surnames. Mr Dobbs is different; he doesn't want us to know his first name. He doesn't want friends or allies because he's been abused by the ones he's had. I suppose I should feel sorry for him, but I can't. He still believes that whatever happened to him was all the fault of others. I suppose I feel the same about myself.

'Nothing is ever fair,' I say, suddenly angry with him.

'I beg your pardon?' he asks. He hasn't expected me to reply. All I've ever done is nod or shrug.

'Life isn't fair,' I tell him. Clara, I notice, is scribbling like a dervish.

'And what do you know about life?' he demands scornfully. 'You're barely out of nappies.'

I contemplate walking out. Instead, I feel resentful; nobody has problems as big as his, the whole world is his enemy. 'I know enough to know that you don't like yourself very much.'

'Is that so?' he asks.

'Which is probably why nobody likes you very much,' I tell him. The rest of the group are now taking an interest. Ruth's eyes are round with surprise. 'My advice, Mr Dobbs, is to accept that life isn't fair.'

I hear the purr of a car on the drive, I catch a fleeting glimpse of a low-slung shadow. A car door slams.

Clara says, 'That's a very interesting observation. Does

anybody else want to contribute?'

'She might have a point,' ventures Phil. 'I suppose that's why we're all here, isn't it? None of us have liked ourselves very much.'

Clara's beaming smile suggests that this is group therapy at its very best; the fruitcakes all discussing their anguish and their deepest feelings. I slip into an inner place and close my eyes. I've said enough.

It's late and The Baltimore's corridors are quiet. There is a full moon that comes and goes from view, shadow-clouds churning in the night sky. The light in my bathroom is on, and I walk across and turn it off. Then I go to the sink and in the darkness scour my face with cold water. It's so cold that it almost hurts, like shards of glass. My shadow obediently follows me back to the bedroom. I stand again at the window, thinking about Mum and the person I have become: the person she helped to shape. I am who I have invented for myself, without conviction or foundation. My laptop sits open on the desk by the window. My fingers have found a new dexterity: I can hit the right keys in the right order, and I seem to have found a pattern to my memories and even now, in the middle of the night, I sit in front of the laptop and place my quietened hands on its keyboard.

Hermione is smiling over her table. 'You're still writing it like a novel,' she says brightly.

'Isn't everyone's life just a kind of novel?'

'Maybe, but not always a very good one,' she says, and I don't know whether she's talking about my journal or my life which, given where I am, could mean both. Once again, I'm transported back to school, with my English homework about to be torn to shreds.

But Hermione doesn't do that. She doesn't make judgements about how well I'm writing. She doesn't really comment on my journal at all. But I know she's reading it. I can that see sentences have been underlined. I can see squiggles in the margins, although she's careful not to let me see which sentences or which passages have been squiggled. Instead, she keeps asking questions, although they seem to be the wrong questions, so that we're always focused on different things. She wants to talk about the past, weaving meaning into the inconsequential. I want to talk about the future, weaving meaning into the present. But they're all intertwined – I can understand that – and that the threads of who we were are just the incomplete tapestry of who we will be.

In the intervening days since I last saw her, I have done little except write. My fingers have gained fluency. I no longer need to think what to write; the words mostly write themselves. I am often surprised by how much I've written. Sometimes I can write whole passages almost without realising it. I have found a mental capacity that I didn't know I possessed.

'Are you a religious person?' Hermione asks.

'No. There are no gods.'

'You sound so certain.'

'My grandfather says so. Why?'

'It's just that people with strong religious conviction often look at the world in a different way. They see things through a different prism, as it were.'

'Is that important?'

'To some people, suicide is a sin.'

'But I didn't commit suicide, did I?'

'No, but you tried. Or maybe you deliberately didn't try hard enough because, inside, you didn't want to die. Or maybe you saw it as a sin.'

I shake my head, because I believe in the Rossini Theorem, which I don't understand, but which was written by Granddad, so it must be right. 'Put it this way, doctor, if killing someone, even yourself, is so wrong, why is it only the sixth Commandment? Honouring your father and mother is a much more important edict. I find it strange that, if I had a row with Mum, it's a bigger sin than hitting her on the head with a baseball bat.'

'And did you?'

'No, of course not. We didn't own a baseball bat.'

'I mean argue with her. Say something unpleasant to her.'

No, never.

Oh God. Oh God.

Yes. Once.

$$\frac{23 t_{\text{hy}} h c^2}{10240 \pi^2 G^2 M^3} = 23$$

Lifetime of a black hole

Every morning a nurse takes my blood pressure and, sometimes, a blood sample. I'm repeatedly asked how I feel. Did I sleep well? When she leaves, the nurse takes away the newly written pages of my journal. Every time I see Hermione, they've been added to my manuscript's growing pile. She mostly keeps them face down, so that I can't see her annotations. My pile of scribbles – 12-point, Times New Roman, thank you professor – now needs a paperweight on top to make sure it doesn't topple over.

I'm gratified and a little unsettled by how much I've written. How have I written so much? Most of the time, I'm barely conscious of writing. Instead, I'm remembering how it was, and how it could have been. And what happens when I've caught up with myself, when the manuscript of my life is complete? Will I suddenly be cured? Will I understand how things went wrong? Will I be normal again if I was ever normal?

Hermione keeps asking lots of questions, flipping through pages, peering at me over her glasses, peeling back the onion skin; fathoming the tug and pull of my parents' marriage and the ebb and flow of my relationship with them, how I'd become filled with dark matter, like a balloon slowly being inflated, until it popped. 'You'll be going home soon,' she says. 'Should I be worried for you?'

Hermione isn't given to grand gestures. She doesn't flap her hands, she doesn't flick her hair or toss her head, her expressions are generally neutral. As she's said, she's not here to judge me or criticise. There are no rights and wrongs, she's said. What you did to yourself wasn't wrong. You did what you felt you had to do. Medication will give you other options, better options. She's suggested long-term counselling many times, but I've always said 'no'. Hormone malfunction; emotional overload. It won't happen again, hopefully.

Instead, Hermione is able to give expression with an imperceptible movement of her hand, a finger even. I have learned the vocabulary of her minimalism: the way she looks over her glasses, or through them, or takes them off, the way she leans forwards or backwards, the cadence in her Irish lilt, the subtle inflections she can infuse in small words. She should have been an actor; or maybe Dad could have been a psychiatrist.

She's not asked if I was worried. She's asked if *she* should be worried. It is a precisely crafted question, making her an accessory to any future crime against myself. I don't say anything, and feel guilty about saying nothing, and she seems disappointed by my silence, sighing a small but eloquent sigh, then removing her glasses and laying them on her desk. 'I'm not sure why you've put me in your journal, Emma.'

'You're part of my life, doctor. I couldn't not write about you.'

'Maybe I should feel flattered.' I'm not sure if she's asking a question. 'But I'm sorry if I frightened you. When you were young, I mean.' She touches her hair, almost self-consciously. 'But your life didn't quite happen like you've written it, did it? You mostly make everything seem like a comedy.'

'No, it wasn't quite like that,' I concede.

'You could have written other things, but you've written about the funny things. Or made them funny, when they probably weren't.' She pauses, looking thoughtful. 'Can I ask why you changed your name?'

'To hurt my father.'

'Because he'd changed his name and hurt his father?'

'Something like that.'

'But as your illness progressed, it became more than that, didn't it? Emma hadn't protected her mother. Emma deserved to be punished. But Maria was innocent.'

I feel the start of a headache and a tremble in my hands.

'You came to believe that Emma had been bad. That she deserved to be punished. That you had to hide to hide from Emma's guilt.'

'A thunderstorm killed my Mum,' I say.

She ignores me. 'You started to live your life as someone else. Someone who couldn't be blamed for your mum's death. But your two worlds kept colliding when thunder and lightning was about.'

'It seemed to be looking for me,' I stammer, and immediately feel foolish.

'It's time to stick yourself back together,' says Hermione. She's said this loudly, the first time that she's ever raised her voice.

She's right. Emma and Maria had become entangled in ways that, even now, I don't fully understand.

Let me try to explain. Two observatories in the Canary Islands have demonstrated that entangled particles can be teleported to a different location. OK, it was *just* the physical properties of one particle of light, a photon, but it did whizz between the Jacobus Kapteyn Telescope on La Palma and the European Space Agency's Optical Ground Station on adjacent Tenerife. Actually, it didn't 'whizz' because speed doesn't come into it. The particles were somehow instantaneously connected across space-time.

More recently, the Chinese have sent intertwined quantum particles over a thousand kilometres from a satellite to an Earth ground station. Gramps is a bit sceptical about this, as he is about anything Chinese, having once contracted food poisoning in a Chinese restaurant in Blackpool. Quite what Gramps was doing in Blackpool is a mystery even to him.

But it does raise the serious possibility of a space-based quantum internet, which would be very exciting if I knew what that was and why I should be excited.

But that's what happened to Emma and Maria. I thought that one no longer existed and that I could live my life as someone else but that, across time and space, we had always been inseparable.

What does a caged bird sing of? Of a freedom it's never known? To call for a mate who will never hear her? Or is it simply singing: I tweet therefore I am?

'So, it all comes down to a golf club,' says Hermione. 'The instrument of your mother's death.'

'It wasn't the golf club. That didn't kill her.'

Hermione has steepled her fingers and doesn't say anything. I gulp back tears, cold metal bars against my wings. 'The way I saw it, my father killed her. He put the gun to her head. He gave her no option but to pull the trigger.'

In the silence, Hermione sighs softly. I can't tell what the sigh is expressing. 'Do you still believe that?' she asks after some moments.

I don't reply, because I can't reply, and because I'm crying. I've never cried in front of her before, and I feel ashamed, but I can't stop. I use up most of her jumbo box of tissues before my eyes run dry. I feel numb inside.

'I'm so sorry,' says Hermione and, another first, puts a hand over mine. She stacks the most recent pages of my journal on top of the pile and places the paperweight on top of it. 'You have nothing to feel guilty about, Emma. Guilt about your mother's death. A sense that you've needed to punish yourself. That your father went unpunished.'

Outside, mist has come in from the sea, making the trees along the driveway appear sepulchral, like ghosts. Ever since Mum's death, I have felt the weight of darkness. In

346

daylight, the air can seem insubstantial; at night, I can find it hard to breathe. The air in my lungs can seem heavy. For some reason, with my eyes now dry, I'm also thinking about Oz, and how I'd like to be in North Berwick, and be walking by the sea's margins, like we used to do, with the waves warmly lit by moonlight, so that I can walk forwards again, and not look back.

I suppose that I have been an unreliable narrator, but what memoir is ever reliable? I have chosen what to write and what not to write, and – yes – to make some things funnier than they really were, and to omit things which weren't funny at all. I could have written about lying in bed crying, because Mum was in the next bedroom crying, or that Dad had again forgotten my birthday.

I could have written about the shouting matches, which Mum always won, and the things she sometimes threw at him – with remarkable accuracy – and how everything was always his fault. At the time, I believed her utterly, because I loved her. Now, despite the misgivings of a lifetime, I'm not so sure.

I could have written lots of things like that, but for what purpose? To make you feel sorry for me, doctor? Instead, I believe that life is full of the absurd, and that everything that's important is also an absurdity, and that anything that isn't just a little bit absurd can't be important. More than anything, life should be about laughter, and everything else should be banished to the naughty step until they learn to be stupid again.

Patsy's been to see me a few times, once with Carlo, although he kept expecting knife-wielding lunatics to jump out and stab him, and so didn't much like The Baltimore and didn't come again. For such a big and fearsome man, Carlo is, I realise, a bit of a softie.

Oz has also been a few times, bringing my 2CV on one visit. It's now stabled in the small car park around the back, and I hope it's making friends with the other cars, and I'm sure it is, because 2CVs are friendly by nature.

At times here I've felt closed in, looking out in soft focus, not quite able to make sense of my surroundings – getting lost in corridors, heading off somewhere then being unable to remember what or where I was heading off to. Although I haven't been hemmed in by walls or locks, it's felt like incarceration. I've missed meals because I've simply forgotten to eat or been too busy with my journal. But today is a morning of sharp clarity.

Oz and I don't talk about much, because the past is a long time ago, and we don't really share a present. But when we do talk, years dissolve. If I half close my eyes, I can hear a shorter boy with shorter hair, and then notice he has a tattoo on his left forearm.

'Why do you have "I love Carlotta-Sue" inked on your arm?'

'It's Sanskrit.'

'For "I love Carlotta-Sue"?'

'Who the hell is she?'

'Dunno, Oz. You tell me.'

'It's a lucky symbol. It means long life, or something. I had too many beers one evening and it seemed like a good idea.'

We're sitting on a bench in the garden and facing out over the manicured garden to the driveway entrance. As if reading my thoughts, Oz says, 'You'll be leaving soon.'

'Except that nobody has said exactly when. When exactly does a lunatic become sane again? How can anybody tell? Come on, Oz, you're the doctor, you tell me! Is there an exam I have to pass? Some kind of sanity test?' I stare down the drive, seeing freedom. 'Some of us inmates have set up an escape committee.' I lean in close to him. 'Don't tell anyone, but we're digging a tunnel.'

'But the gates are open. You don't need to dig a tunnel.'

'It's something to do, Oz. Something to pass the time

and keep the enemy on their toes. Our other plan is to steal nurses' uniforms, learn German, and simply walk out.'

We stare at the driveway for a while. I glimpse the tabby cat mincing about beside a bush. 'You could have been sectioned. Put away in a secure unit. I said that you'd be OK here.' I know this, because Hermione has told me, and I'm glad that Oz was there to talk them out of it. 'But don't get completely better,' he says and I turn to look at him, but he's still looking towards the sea. 'I always liked it when you were a bit mad.'

'But not completely barking bonkers.'

'You know what I mean, Maria.'

'Actually, it's back to plain old Emma.'

He doesn't say anything, but when he leaves he hands me Dad's letter, and tells me that I'll have to read it sometime.

Illness and disease can strike any part of our bodies, particularly if you're old, when age has clogged its canals and tributaries, and sparking brain cells send faulty messages. Dr Madison keeps telling me that it's not uncommon. Doctors' surgeries are full of the mentally infirm, demanding medication to regain a kind of balance. It's a new epidemic, she's said on several occasions, twirling her glasses. Today she seems in buoyant form; her smile is wider; her hair has blonde highlights.

'Well, we can't keep you here forever. Clinically, your course of treatment is nearly finished. Does the thought of leaving here worry you?'

I rub my temples. I don't know whether to feel worried or not.

'I'll take that as a maybe,' she says.

'Like you say, doctor, I can't stay here forever.'

She sighs, as she often does, and changes track. 'You should have got help before now, Emma. I can't believe you didn't.'

'I thought I could cope,' I reply lamely.

349

'I did ask you, if you remember. Well, I know you remember because it's in your journal. I asked what your axe-murderer was called. You said that he didn't have a face. That's all you ever told me.'

'I couldn't tell you, doctor. You'd have put me in a madhouse.'

'Is that what you really thought?'

'Yes, Hermione. It's where I thought I should be.'

We all have our heroes, I suppose, and mine is my Granddad. Not so much for what he wrote, or the secrets he may have unravelled, but the stoicism with which he dealt with ridicule and accepted that new thinking can come with slings and arrows. His hero, whom he lavishly praises, was Harvard University's Henrietta Swan Leavitt, who discovered that, by measuring the light from a Cepheid, generally a big yellow star, you can find out the relative distance between other Cepheids, and she termed those stars 'standard candles' – which is how astronomers still describe them.

It's a bit like having celestial signposts dotted around the universe, which tell you the distances between things and between those things and Earth. Without her discoveries, the Hubble telescope wouldn't have got off the ground. But this was 1906 and, being a woman, Henrietta wasn't even allowed to look through a telescope. I suppose Gramps likes her because she faced up to what she was and overcame her limitations. Henrietta Swan Leavitt was also deaf.

I have his book with me now and, distracted, I flick through pages: the calculations, the stellar images. Whether he's right or wrong doesn't matter; he wrote a theorem, and he dedicated it to us.

"To my family in Scotland and to my other family in Italy. We are bound, all of us, by ties of blood and dark matter."

It was then that I understood, in a moment of perfect clarity, how dark matter is the point of singularity from which everything started, and not just because my grandfather says so. The great agnostic knew precisely what he was doing, and I bet he wrote his theorem with a big smile on his face. He was putting forward a theory of universal spirituality, a quasi-religion but without the inconvenience of gods.

It is dark matter that binds us, from the humblest mouse to the greatest king. It was there when life was first created and will still be there when life, like our Sun, is finally extinguished, linking the universe and time itself. It was that which I also sensed: that everything is connected and that the strands of our being are interwoven with everything else, and to those we have loved but not completely lost. My grandfather had found God but also discovered that He didn't exist.

It was then I realised why I'd waded my way through his book. I'd been looking for answers, about myself and about my place in the world. The same reason, I now supposed, why Dad had taken that book to the hospice, the fading star looking to the stars for final peace.

My grandfather had found the missing part of the universe. I'd been looking for the missing part of me. Maybe, for my father, the missing part of both of us.

I take my father's letter from the desk drawer, and look again at his neat handwriting, the hand of a man who had written his name thousands of time, on bits of paper, autograph books, baseball caps and T-shirts. I read what he has to say.

"Dearest Emma

I just wanted you to know that I love you very much. I always have. I was probably not the best father, and probably not the best husband, but I also loved your mother, despite her bad language and twisted knickers! For much of her life she was mentally unwell. Well, I suppose you know that. I really did try to look after her, but maybe not well enough. Maybe I could have tried harder. Maybe things could have been different.

But I've always been so proud of you and am so sorry to now be leaving you. Perhaps your mother is waiting for me. I hope so.

All my love

Dad xxxx"

I read it again, and then fold it into the envelope and put it back in the drawer. It's strange, I think, how little he had to say. I'd been expecting lengthy excuses, or pleas for forgiveness. But, I decide, he has written the perfect goodbye letter. Something to memorise, something that sums everything up, something without flamboyance or evasion. Something, maybe, to remember him by.

The morning sunshine takes me outside, I feel charged with restless energy. I'm noticing things for the first time: the vase of flowers on the main reception, the texture of the carpet, the smell of floor polish. It's a bright, chill day and I stroll round the grounds. For a while I sit on a wooden bench that looks down the main driveway. Then I walk its length once more, a final dress rehearsal.

A spider has been busy on one of the iron gates; an intricate latticework of diamonds glitters on the web. I look at my watch and retrace my steps. It's my last session with Hermione. As always, I knock on her door and wait for her to open it. She ushers me in and, as always, gestures to the chair opposite.

Hermione regards me in silence for some moments. 'You really have been the strangest of patients, you know. Although you've never really talked about your problems, you've also been utterly eloquent.' She indicates my journal. 'So, after all these years, we finally get to the root cause of your problems. I just wish you'd been able to talk to me. Back then, I mean, not now.' She purses her lips, presses one hand to her hair and draws stray wisps back from her ears. I can still smell the outside air; see the handiwork of one insect. 'But it needs an ending.'

'I'm not so sure it does, doctor.'

'Everything has an ending,' she says. 'Nothing lasts forever.'

'I suppose.'

'Then send me an ending, Emma. It doesn't have to be tomorrow, or next week, or next year. Just sometime, when you think you know how it might finish.' She's looking wistful, as if she's a bit sorry to see me go. 'Have you got anyone to go back to?' she asks.

'I'm cooking dinner,' I tell her. 'Pasta and salad, for a doctor friend.'

'Oh,' she says, but doesn't say 'Doctor who?' as I'd hoped she would.

There are forms to fill in. A nurse in administration indicates where I should sign my name. I am also given repeat prescriptions and the number of The Baltimore's 24-hour helpline. I put the phone number and prescriptions in my bag.

I've said goodbye to everyone, to Phil, Ruth and the lovely Rachel. We've joked about setting up a Fruitcake Club and having regular meetings in odd places. I saw Mr Dobbs at breakfast. As always, he was sitting alone. I had to pass by his table as I left and, on impulse, I stopped and told him I was leaving.

'I know what you are,' he said, brushing his right hand down the seam of his trousers, and turning his Icarus eyes to mine – the look of someone who knows how far they have fallen and still can't quite believe it. 'You'll be back,' he then said. 'People like you always are.'

Ruth is also leaving; she offers to give me a lift into town. A friend is coming to pick her up. I decline. My bag is on the floor, and the 2CV is around the corner. I have only to walk the length of The Baltimore's reception area and I will be officially free.

The nurse calls me back. 'Oh, and Dr Madison asks if you could call by her office.'

This time I knock but don't wait for her to open the door. I'm no longer a lunatic, I hope, and can open doors by myself. She's behind her desk and my file is open in front of her. 'I just wanted to say goodbye,' she says, rising from her chair, 'and to remind you that if you ever need to talk, if you need encouragement, you must call us.'

'Mr Dobbs says I'll be back.'

She laughs. 'I wouldn't pay any attention to him. He's not really qualified to offer an opinion.'

I turn and place one hand on the doorknob, smelling floor polish and freedom. 'But could you do me a last favour?' she asks as I open the door. She indicates the shelf behind her chair. 'I wonder if you could put that picture on my desk.'

I wordlessly lift it down, her children looking at me for a moment, and then place it in front of her so that they're looking at their mother.

'You wrote about it in your journal,' she explains. 'I could see it bothered you, and I got to thinking you were probably right.'

$$\frac{3hc^3}{2\pi^2 GMk_\mathrm{E}} = 24$$

Hawking radiation temperature

Hurray! Mum is taking me to the cinema, and I haven't been to the cinema for a while, and it's Dad's new film. I'm older now, and don't actually say things like 'hurray' anymore, but it's still nice to be going to the cinema with Mum, and it's the last day of term tomorrow. My world is in equilibrium and I'm smiling broadly as we leave North Berwick in Mum's sensible little car. It only has a few dents and scratches on it, mainly from 'fucking loonies in Bentleys,' although I don't understand who she's cross at because Dad's car, which is rarely here, never has any dents or scratches on it.

We're going to see Dad's latest blockbuster which has only just been released. I would have liked to have gone to the London premiere, but Mum was adamant that school was more important, although I suspect that it was Mum who didn't want to go, and so we watched the red-carpet parade on the BBC news, with Dad looking immaculate in a dark tuxedo and Sandra Bullock clinging to his arm. She looked very pretty, but not as pretty as Mum, and I told her that, and Mum smiled, but a little sadly.

The film is called *The Space Between Time*, which is a bit silly because it doesn't have space in it. It's about a shy young woman – Sandra – who falls in love with Dad, has a number of near-death experiences – mainly caused by Dad – and grows into an alpha-female spy who eventually comes to Dad's rescue when his cover as a secret agent is exposed, and then persuades him that he should leave the CIA, marry her and live happily ever after.

In one of the early scenes, on a small dinghy, they're buffeting into quite big waves, and Sandra's T-shirt gets wet, and we can clearly see her nipples, and that's when Mum starts growling, and doesn't really stop growling until the final credits have rolled. She made louder growling noises when Sandra took her wet T-shirt off – they were back on dry land by then – because Sandra's back was to the camera, and it was only Dad who could see her nipples.

In another scene, Sandra asks Dad 'Is that a gun in your pocket or are you just pleased to see me?' and Dad says, 'Both,' and produces a revolver with a very long barrel. Everyone else in the cinema was laughing, except Mum, because Sandra Bullock was clearly taking her trousers off.

Back home and Mum puts a lasagne in the oven – cooked by Mrs Boyce, so I'm looking forward to it – and pours herself a very large gin, which she downs in a couple of mouthfuls, then picks up a piece of paper on the kitchen table. It's a note from Mrs Perkins to say that Sarah has phoned and that there is going to be a story in tomorrow's newspaper.

'Bastard!' says Mum, already pouring herself another large drink. Her hands are shaking.

'But people are always writing about Dad,' I remind her.

'But not about *us*, Emma! That's what we agreed! That's what he *absolutely* promised! Christ, this really is the last fucking straw!'

I have no idea what she's talking about, but know better than to prolong the conversation, because Mum is clearly in a foul mood – other people's nipples have that effect – and has already drunk her second very large gin. We appear to have run out of tonic, because she's not bothering to add anything to her gin except more gin.

We sit and eat the lasagne in silence, although it's only me who's eating it. Mum merely chops hers into squares, then into smaller squares, then mashes all the squares up with her fork. None of this lasagne vandalism actually involves eating, and she's also now consumed most of a bottle of wine.

'You are a good girl,' she says at one point, and puts her hand over mine for a moment. There are tears in her eyes, although I don't know why. 'You know I love you, don't you?'

'Ditto,' I say.

Afterwards, after the dishes have been put in the dishwasher, and the lasagne dish in the sink for Mrs Perkins to slave over, she suddenly bursts into tears and pulls me onto her lap. She seems to be saying something, but her voice is muffled, because she has me pressed into her woolly jumper, but I wriggle free, and she's saying, over and over, 'I don't want to leave you, I don't want to leave you.'

But suddenly I'm angry, because she's now onto her zillionth gin, and there's nothing for her to be so distressed about, and I just feel that I've had enough of her being mad.

'Let me go!' I scream.

'Emma, there's something I have to tell you.'

'You're drunk! I hate you when you're like this! Let me go!'

'Emma, please ...'

'I hate you!'

'Please, there's something I have to ...'

...but the phone is ringing and, reluctantly, Mum lets me go, and I know it's Dad on the phone because Mum's foot is tapping rhythmically on the floor. I can't actually hear her foot tapping because our carpets are thick and lush, but I see it tapping as I pass the living room door. 'Bastard!' she shrieks down the phone at him.

She was still in bed when I left for school the next morning, slightly dreading the results of my geography test, but not really caring because it's the last day of term, and although I'm vaguely worried about Mum, I know that she loves me, and I utterly love her, and that she's far prettier than Sandra Bullock, and that's all that counts.

It was the only night when she didn't kiss me goodnight, and I wish I'd let her speak to me because I could have talked her out of it. It was the last time I saw Mum alive.

But if that was my worst of times, I also remember my very best day. It was a day in which stars had lined up in perfect harmony, and I could almost hear the music of the spheres over the din of London traffic. My room was high up in a swanky hotel so that I could see the lights of the city stretching into the far distance. It seemed like London went on forever. We ate in the hotel's restaurant with another couple, a husband-and-wife production team who had worked on the film, and Dad ordered bottle and after bottle of champagne, and Mum gave me some to taste. It tasted of bubbles and happiness. Judi Dench passed our table and Mum introduced me, but she must have misheard because she called me Emily, which didn't matter as everybody was in a good mood.

The next morning Mum and I went to Harrods, not really to buy anything, but just to look around. We must have visited every department, with Mum picking things up and peering at them, and then putting them back down. We went to the toy department last, and I fell in love with a rag doll which had sleepy eyes and bright red hair and Mum bought it for me. I still have that doll, and I hope my other dolls don't feel jealous because it's always been my favourite, bought on my diamond day when the sun was shining, and virtually every London bus had Dad's face on it.

'Is Dad famous now?' I ask Mum as we leave Harrods and I see Dad's face weave in and out of traffic headed for Hyde Park Corner.

'I suppose so, yes,' she says, almost philosophically, as if not quite believing it herself, looking at the disappearing bus with a small frown on her face.

I was so happy to hear that, happy for him and Mum, but happy also that I was now the daughter of a somebody, and would be able to drink more champagne, and maybe live in Hollywood with other famous families, and lounge around our enormous swimming pool wearing oversize sunglasses.

But I know that Mum isn't quite so sure about Dad's face on the side of buses, or on the front cover of glossy magazines. She has resolutely refused to have journalists into our semi-posh flat or to have gushing articles written about 'Paul Ross's happy little family.' She positively shuddered when one magazine suggested an article on 'Sunday lunch with Paul Ross at home' – which also made Dad and I shudder, thinking about the culinary disaster that Mum might produce. How I'm still alive is anybody's guess.

But, pure and simple, Mum doesn't like the limelight, or light of any sort; she wants to remain in the shadows, unseen, and Dad accepts this. If anything, it adds to his mystique as the housewife's favourite, because nobody gets to see his wife or their young daughter. It also makes him seem protective, shielding his family from the pressures of the media, and producers and directors respect him for his courtesy and decency, and for shouldering the burden of fame on his shoulders alone.

But sometimes she has to be seen, and this evening is one of them, because it's the première of Dad's new film, the one that will cement his star onto the Hollywood pavement and for which he received his first Oscar nomination. Mum reluctantly agreed and has been swallowing pills all day. A car arrives to pick us up at the hotel and drive us to Leicester Square, and Mum is getting nervous because she'll have to walk up a red carpet and have her photograph taken, and she doesn't like doing that, but the producers and PR people insisted and, making things worse, she's fidgeting in her seat like a schoolgirl. I'm sitting pertly and not fidgeting.

'I've got my knickers in a twist,' she informs us, tugging and pulling.

'Then take them off,' suggests Dad.

'I'm not taking my knickers off in a fucking Mercedes!' says Mum loudly.

'It's a BMW,' says the driver, and Dad and I laugh, although Mum is still squirming and making faces.

We arrive at the cinema and the car door is opened by a man in a uniform with gold buttons, and Mum and Dad step out. Mum is holding onto my hand with a vice-like grip and drags me out of the car like a recalcitrant puppy.

We emerge into a wall of light. There are photographers everywhere, on both sides of the red carpet, and all shouting at Dad to turn this way or look over here. John Hurt is also on the red carpet with Judi Dench, and she gives me a little wave, and mouths, 'Hello, Emily.' A PR lady steers us along the red carpet and then motions us to stop and to look in a certain direction.

Mum has stopped fidgeting and is smiling bravely, although her knickers may still be in a twist because she's holding my hand so tightly that it's almost painful. She's also holding Dad's hand, so that she has no other available hands to tug and pull at her knickers, although she's also wearing high heels and is probably now more worried about tripping up. Her hand trembles in mine, or maybe it's my hand trembling in hers, because this is the most exciting thing I've ever done.

The PR lady tells us to turn around and face the other wall of cameras and, as we dutifully turn around, Dad winks at me. I'm grinning broadly and my eyes must be big and round, but Dad's eyes suddenly look wistful, and I see that he's looking at the cameras as if distracted by something, and I try to see what he's looking at, but all I can see are pointing cameras, and I look at Mum, and she smiles down at me, and I have never been happier in my whole life because we are a perfect little family, and I'm so proud of both my parents.

It's the film that he absolutely knows will make him a star. No more seaside fleapits, no more matinees and second-rate hotels. This is the moment he has planned; the moth finding its bright light. But, looking back, it also marks the moment when his trajectory will take him away from us, and he absolutely knows that as well, and it's not until we're inside the cinema – Mum surprisingly didn't fall over – that I understand what Dad's passing expression was all about. For a fleeting moment he'd wished that he could have been on the other side of the roped-off red carpet, standing alongside all the ordinary people, and able to see us as others must – the little girl with the big toothy grin, and the stunningly beautiful woman in the black Dior dress who is his wife – and that nothing will ever be the same again.

It's the picture he painted, the one I found after his death, and I still wonder what he was thinking about when he painted it. Why leave himself out of the painting when he was its star?

Was it regret at what might have been? Or his way of finally admitting that we were the real stars, Mum and I, and that everything should have turned out differently.

$$\frac{5(18\pi)^{2/3}h^2}{8\pi^2 R_{zg} Gm_h M_{zg}^{1/3}}\left[\left(\frac{Z}{A}\right)\frac{1}{m_K}\right]^{5/3} = 25$$

The Chandrasekhar limit

"Dear Doctor Madison

I hope you're well and still ministering to the afflicted or terminally stupid. (Not sure which category I fitted into). But you did ask me to send you a final chapter, although it's not really a final chapter, is it? I've probably got lots more chapters to come (I hope).

You once talked to me about axe-murderers and asked me what my axe-murderer looked like. He doesn't have a face, I'd stammered, but that had been a lie. Well, I suppose you knew that, didn't you? You see, when I found Mum, cares and years had been peeled from her, and it was only then, on top of the Law, that I realised how similar we both were. Gone were memories of her mad neuroses; for the first time, I was able to look under her outer layers and see what lay beneath. The same slightly furrowed eyebrows, the same stoicism around the eyes.

We were different, but very similar. With her years stripped away, I felt that I was looking at myself, only dead. In that eviscerating moment, I knew what death looked like, perhaps my own death. It wasn't exactly an axe in her hand, but it could have been.

So, in writing my story for you, I haven't exactly written a complete book. Maybe just the first few chapters. I suppose, when we're born, we have the capacity to be anybody, to write whatever story we choose to write. I am reminded of this, my grandfather's book lying closed on the table beside me as I write this. He could have chosen to become a baker, like his father, but he didn't. He could have chosen to drive trains, like his grandfather, but he didn't. Instead, the brains of the family, he chose academia and, in time, wrote a theorem on the universe.

I still go back to North Berwick whenever I can. It reminds me of childhood, when mermaids might swim ashore, or Viking ships appear on the horizon. Even now, if I walk down the High Street, I know virtually everyone. Despite the passing of the years, the same people are still there, doing much the same things.

The boat out to the Bass is still captained by the same man. Greggs still sells the same things, although healthier sandwiches have crept onto the shelves. The town's many charity shops still sell pre-loved items, the air tastes of the same salt, and the same birds patrol the skies.

I can understand how unhappy Mum must have been, and more than a little mad and how, as she'd once told me walking the coastline, she couldn't go on. I can imagine her, too frightened to contemplate suicide, standing on the hilltop with the rain pouring down, the golf club held high above her head, daring God to strike her down, if He existed, making it His decision, not hers.

I went down to North Berwick last week and climbed the Law. I was thinking about Mum, and how much I still miss her, and about Dad, and how I can't really hate him anymore and how, in the strange shadow-worlds of quantum mechanics and probability theory, even the seemingly impossible can sometimes happen. Like my father beating Tiger Woods at golf. Or sharing my birthday with someone else in class. Or that the universe is possibly made up from different dimensions through which, one day, we might travel to distant galaxies millions and millions of light years away.

Energy, my grandfather says, can be changed from one form to another, but it cannot be created or destroyed. It remains a universal constant. It means that, somewhere, Mum is still around, still worrying about flower arranging or fretting that she's become president of the Intergalactic Paedophile Society, and that Dad, in a different quadrant of the galaxy, with his slicked-back hair and booming baritone, is treading the celestial boards to rapturous applause.

I had a knife in my hand, an ordinary knife pillaged from the cutlery drawer, a knife without significance, but I had a decision to make; a decision not borne of failure or success, or of who I could be, a simple decision about who I was. That's what it comes down to; that illusion can seem real, that reality can be ephemeral and that, somewhere in the middle, between who I was and who I had chosen to become, was the more fundamental question of what to do next. We are who we invent for ourselves, isn't that so, doctor?

I reminded myself that I have always been a child of the sea and I threw the knife far down the hillside, the same hillside down which I had thrown a golf club many years before. I felt a coming together, a shift in my pulse: a profound sense of connection with those who I had once loved, and always will. I had made my decision: a symbol thrown away. It was time to put aside childish things and false recriminations. It doesn't mean I'm cured, but it might mean that I can now look at myself with fresh eyes. Maybe it was time to grow up. Over the years, I've hurt myself enough.

Then I lay on my back in the grass and watched the clouds, devoid of faces. I could smell the scent of flowers and suddenly found small connections between my past and future, my eyes following the flight of a small flock of birds high above, turning gently on the thermals.

Perhaps my grandfather's name will someday be bracketed with John Lennon and Einstein. Maybe I'll live to see it. Maybe one day I'll be able to travel to Jupiter or Mars. Until then, I am simply content to have found a new beginning, and I walked thoughtfully down from the Law.

Oz was still where I had left him, leaning against a fence post, looking bored and slightly irritated, but he didn't ask questions, which is another reason why we're still together, as well as little Caitlin, our baby.

She's an adorable thing, just learning to crawl, which she does in an erratic bumbling way, with a worried expression on her face. In other words, she looks exactly like Mum must have looked as a baby. I bet her first word is 'fuck.'

It's tempting to look back, a new baby in my arms, and see my childhood as a sequence of logical events: a linear string of cause and effect stretching back to the cradle and beyond. I often think this, invisible hands from long ago creating personal stories that we are then expected to live, one stitch at a time, as if conjoined by distant stars, each with our scripts and entrances, and final exit. Perhaps that does mean that I have inherited some of my mother's fatalism, and all of Granddad's atheism.

But sometimes, unwittingly and unwillingly, I can see patterns: that one thing leads to another, and then another. Maybe that's the story of everyone's life, the random connections that we make, the coincidental meetings, and the inconsequential events that only later gain purpose or significance.

But, you're thinking, am I better now? Or a little less mad? Well, let me put it like this. When I came to you, I was scared stiff of big open spaces, which is understandable because space has about twenty million million billion star systems. All those stars, all that space, and each one of us no more than the smallest bit of nothingness I sometimes still feel against my skin. But I no longer worry about open spaces, or hide from thunderstorms, which must make me a little bit less mad, which is OK, although I keep medication close at hand, just in case.

I do also still wonder if there's another Emma out there. According to NASA and Gramps, one in six star-systems has an Earth-sized planet. In our own paltry galaxy alone, that means there may be thirty-three billion Earth-like planets right on our doorstep. Maybe she's living on one of them, looking at the stars, wondering if I exist. If so, I hope she's happy, as I suppose I am now.

Since changing my name back to Emma I have felt a sense of liberation. It seems to offer a new beginning, free from the baggage that Maria brought with her. Maria was born out of sadness and desperation; a cloak of invisibility to hide me from my demons and a tool to hit my father with. It made me Italian, made me exotic, put distance between us. Disposing of Maria was part of the healing process; ditching an old friend who had turned out to be a hindrance.

I'm now *The Scotsman's* showbiz editor, by the way, although I don't do very much. Maria does most of the hard work, like going to film premières. She's a little bit star-struck by celebrities and writes gushing nonsense that I have to rewrite into English. She doesn't mind, and I think she's forgiven me for eating her chocolate. I only work part-time and mostly from home. Oz is working as a GP and sometimes cycles to work, which I think is completely mad, although 'madness' isn't a word we much use. We've discussed marriage but haven't decided anything.

We're also in the process of moving from my ridiculous Edinburgh flat to North Berwick, and I insisted that the Dalek came with us, although Oz didn't put up much of a fight. I think that Oz quite likes it now, although it's hard to tell whether the Dalek likes him. I've put it at the foot of the stairs, and it scares Mrs Perkins every morning. Between leaving in the evening and arriving the next morning, she keeps forgetting about it. We haven't decided on the Greek nymphs yet, and the Dalek hasn't offered an opinion.

If nothing else, moving to North Berwick will give Mr and Mrs Perkins an extension on their employment, although the weeds won't be happy. Knox is already in North Berwick and tries hard to ignore Mrs Perkins, who is generally quite hard to ignore. We've installed a cat-flap into the French windows in the kitchen, so that he can taste freedom once more. Do you know how hard it is to install cat-flaps in bullet-proof glass?

A highly trained glass and cat-flap expert called Denis, presumably an SAS veteran, had to come up from Devizes with specialist equipment. Knox now brings Mrs Perkins little presents, which means he must like her a little bit, despite his presents mostly being dead birds. Mrs Perkins either eats the dead birds or throws them out, I don't know which, and I don't ask.

Patsy is still with Carlo and has managed further renovations to their flat without him noticing. He's also in regular correspondence with Gramps about Einstein-Rosen bridges and seems quite excited about it.

I've also been prowling in the basement. A cinema room we don't need, and who wants a cavernous wine cellar? I've had builders in to quote for an indoor swimming pool, although I haven't yet told Oz. I might try to keep it a secret until it's finished, but I don't know if that'll be possible.

I suppose that I have a lot to thank Dad for, and the photograph of the three of us on the London red carpet is in pride of place on the baby grand piano. The alien blob photograph is no longer on the mantelpiece.

The picture Dad painted of Mum and me, the observer looking from the other side of the roped off red carpet, is above Caitlin's crib. It's a painting filled with sadness and regret, painted by someone who wished things could have been different, but which also reminds me of the best day of my life. I suppose I'll now have to forgive him, although I don't suppose he ever did much wrong. In forgiving him, I'll also be forgiving myself. One day, I'll try to explain it to Caitlin.

So that's my ending, Hermione: walking back to North

Berwick, the sun low over the sea, the same sea I remember so well, with evening light conjuring red streamers in the water. We're going to the beach, where Mum's ashes are scattered, and Dad's, although a little way up the beach, just in case Mum doesn't want eternal intimacy. My new baby is asleep in her buggy, and I hold tight to Oz's hand as we walk slowly towards the sunset, towards the sea.

Thank you for everything.

Kindest regards

Emma Rossini

Acknowledgements

Although it's my name on the front cover, the publication of any book is a collaborative effort. Among the talented team at Ringwood Publishing, I would particularly like to thank my Editor, Mridula Sharma, Chief Editor Isobel Freeman, cover designer Skye Galloway, with unstinting support from Jade McKeogh.

About the Author

Charlie Laidlaw teaches creative writing, and lives in East Lothian. He is a graduate of the University of Edinburgh and was previously a national newspaper journalist and defence intelligence analyst.

He has lived in London and Edinburgh, and is married with two children. His other novels are *Everyday Magic, Being Alert! The Things We Learn When We're Dead* and *The Herbal Detective*.

W: www.charlielaidlawauthor.com

T: @claidlawauthor

F: @charlielaidlawauthor

Printed in Great Britain
by Amazon